1/06

DISCARD

Sometimes,

just when you

least expect it,

love gives you a

dream come true.

SOLOMON'S
Song *of* Love

Let the SONG OF SONGS *Inspire*
Your Own Romantic Story

DR. CRAIG GLICKMAN
FOREWORD BY DR. HENRY CLOUD

HOWARD
PUBLISHING CO.

Our purpose at Howard Publishing is to:

• *Increase faith* in the hearts of growing Christians

• *Inspire holiness* in the lives of believers

• *Instill hope* in the hearts of struggling people everywhere

Because He's coming again!

Solomon's Song of Love © 2004 by Dr. Craig Glickman
All rights reserved. Printed in the United States of America
Published by Howard Publishing Co., Inc.
3117 North 7th Street, West Monroe, Louisiana 71291-2227
In association with the literary agency of Alive Communications, Inc.
7680 Goddard Street, Suite 200, Colorado Springs, CO 80920

04 05 06 07 08 09 10 11 12 13   10 9 8 7 6 5 4 3 2 1

Edited by Between the Lines
Interior design by John Mark Luke Designs

Library of Congress Cataloging-in-Publication Data

Glickman, Craig, 1947-
     Solomon's song of love : let a Song of Songs inspire your own romantic story / Craig
Glickman ; foreword by Henry Cloud.
       p. cm
   Includes bibliographical references.
   ISBN 1-58229-376-7
   1. Love–Religious aspects–Christianity. 2. Bible. O.T. Song of Solomon–Criticism,
interpretation, etc. I. Title.

BV4639.G57 2004
223'.906–dc22

                                                                          2003056995

I dedicate this book to my mother and father;

with thanks to God for their love for each other,

for my brothers, my sister, and me,

and for their twelve grandchildren.

Contents

CONTENTS

Foreword

BY DR. HENRY CLOUD

When Sandy expressed her dilemma to me, I could not help but think how many times I had heard it over the years. "There is just no passion in our relationship. Tom is a good man and a great father to our kids, so I feel sort of bad for even saying this. But I just don't feel anything. I appreciate him, but I don't feel anything." My heart hurt for her as I saw her longing for their relationship to be more.

Then I was reminded of the exact opposite problem that I had heard just as often, as Tiffany had expressed it: "We had such a romantic, sexual connection. I had never felt that kind of attraction and energy. It was intoxicating. But after we really got into a real 'relationship,' there were so many things missing. It seemed like our bodies were in sync, but the rest of us was not. Is there such a thing as 'romance without relationship?'" she asked. "As strange as it seems, we really don't have much of what I would call a real relationship."

There they were, two of the most common problems I hear in clinical practice, in hosting a radio call-in program, and in speaking to groups across the country. On the one side, there is platonic love without passion; and on the other side, passion without deep relationship. A woman once called our radio show and actually said, "The guys who are attractive are all shallow and the guys who are spiritual and deep are never attractive. There are two types of men out there and I can't find one who has it all."

Her assessment of the entire male population aside, chances are that single or married, male or female, you might have encountered the problem she described and that Sandy and Tiffany experienced. And it naturally poses questions. Is it possible for sexual and romantic love, friendship, respect and admiration, values and spiritual depth, and just plain enjoyment of another person to all exist in the same relationship? And if it is, how does a couple sustain such love over time? And even more basic, how do you create romance and passion in the first place? Many people can identify with these questions.

As a psychologist, I can attest that the individual dynamics behind those quandaries differ from person to person and from relationship to relationship. And although there are answers, they are sometimes neither simple nor easy. But at the same time, common to all the different answers is a need: the need for a vision of a love that "has it all." We all need to see that kind of relationship—what it looks like, sounds like, feels like, and does—before we can actually create it. And today, with so many people feeling like their own parents did not provide that kind of vision and with a culture that often promotes lust without love, we especially need a clear picture of what that love is like.

Solomon's Song of Love provides that vision. A vision of love and friendship, passion and respect, sexual and emotional intimacy—in one fulfilling relationship. It is a vision of beauty to inspire us and insight to guide us. From the timeless Song of Songs comes a vision for our times.

Acknowledgments

The origin of a book is a story of those who inspired it. The love of my parents first inspired me. In *The Wizard of Oz,* Dorothy went on a perilous journey to learn that "there's no place like home." Because of my parents, I never doubted that was true.

The people who were my teachers and professors inspired me too. They taught me skills in understanding literature, even that which was written long ago. That training helped me realize that in the short span of written history, people have remained remarkably the same. Still, understanding some of their languages was certainly more of a challenge than reading English. So I thank especially my professors of ancient languages and literature. Thank you, Dr. Waltke, Dr. Merrill, Dr. Barker, Professor Glenn, Dr. Hoehner, Professor Hodges, Dr. Johnson, and Dr. Blum. And thank you, Professor Jenni, and especially my "Doktorvater," Professor Reicke—you were always in the forefront of scholarly studies and have now graduated to the celestial courts, ahead of the rest of us as usual.

The origin of a book is sometimes also the story of a gifted coach— a person who brings out far better than the best the author might otherwise achieve. This book owes its creation to that person. I owe an immeasurable store of gratitude to Lee Hough, who worked countless hours to make this book the best it could be.

Lee, you are the most excellent agent I can imagine. But more than that, you were the book's driving force. If I believed in former lives, I would think you had been a trainer and I had been a plow horse you thought could be Seabiscuit! You were reviewer, editor, and critic; drill sergeant, counselor, and coach; in short, the perfect friend. Without your encouragement, your hours of painstaking labor, day in and day out, from early planning to the months of work on the manuscript, there would be no book. I remain in awe of the rare combination of skills you have to inspire the highest standards for academic integrity, artistic beauty, and personal relevance. You did everything in your considerable power to help me try to reach those standards. You were truly "the wind beneath the wings" of these pages. Thank you.

Tim, certainly without your unflagging support, I could never have written this book. Catherine, you were the first to read it, and your approval, not only as a friend but as a former professor of English literature, was not only a relief but a delight.

To Howard Publishing, thanks for believing in the project and doing so much to improve it. Denny, thanks especially for taking the time to first talk to me in Dallas about the book. Philis, thanks for letting me be the beneficiary of your literary sensitivity and insight. To John and Chrys and all of you at Howard, thanks for letting me be part of your incomparable publishing family. Your competence is exceeded only by your warmth, integrity, and love.

Thank you again, Ed, Frank, and Kevin at the HCSB translation center, who gave generously of your time so we could discuss some of the more technical problems of the Song. And to Dawn and Tammy at Between the Lines, thank you for applying your skills so expertly in vastly improving the book. You both are truly gifted editors and writers. To Greg and Julie Meredith, thanks for your assistance with the book and letting me glimpse true soul mates living and working together.

Thanks also to my friends who encouraged me to begin. Warren, your words were a turning point, and thank you for the fine suggestions that improved the work. Paul, your enthusiasm for the book and your unselfish giving of time to read it, I will never forget. Ken, I know you didn't have the hours you gave to review it, but you did it generously and with excellence. And Bob and Mike at GES, thanks for your help too.

Henry, thank you, too, for your help. Guy, Ted, and Jack, thanks for your kind support. John, I thank you and Claire not just for suggestions but especially for the examples of love you have always displayed in your care for each other and your children. How could I not believe in saints after knowing you both for so long.

Alan, thanks for your painstaking review! Tony, thanks for your friendship and encouragement. Weston, thanks for your review and suggestions. I'm sure you'll sing this song in your life.

To my sons, Taylor, McClain, and Dawson—I'm counting on you to join in the singing as well. Thanks for letting me hear your first notes. Anton Chekhov told his friend, "Quit writing page after page about the moonlight. Tell me what you feel. Show me the reflection of the moon in a piece of broken bottle!" Boys, no matter what the journey of life has brought us, you have always been that reflection of the moon for me.

Joe and Jody, thanks for the living example of the romance of the Song. Randy and Ellen, thanks for letting me see how much Mom and Dad instilled their love in your hearts for others.

To my niece Daphne Khoury, thanks for your special insights and memories of living with your grandparents, my mother and father, during difficult times for us all. And to my nephew, Joe, thank you for your encouraging support.

I know the reader must be thinking I'm spreading around the credit so if the book isn't very good, I can also spread around the blame.

Actually, that's not a bad idea! But I'm afraid I have to admit that I didn't always take everyone's advice, and it's probably precisely in those places where the book could be better. So, as with many authors, I should admit in advance that any credit should be shared, but I am the likely culprit where quality wanes.

Poets once explained love as the work of Cupid's arrow or the effect of magic stardust cast upon the earth. By such myth they honored the mystery of love. They knew the heart had reasons which reason did not know.

And the heart of love revealed love not in science but in song. The best songs let them see love, and the great songs let them feel love. One song, it was rumored, had even the power to instill love. The ancient poets spoke in awe its name. The Song of Songs, they whispered.

Some believe its power still remains. And for those of us who brush time's dust from its enchanted pages, the Song still sprinkles stardust on our dreams.

I dwell on your love through day and night,

the hours I am lying down,

and at dawn when I have awakened…

We will be together even when the peaceful

days of old age come.

—FROM "The Crossing," A TWELFTH CENTURY B.C.
EGYPTIAN LOVE SONG

When Love Breaks Through

Sometimes love breaks through, and an artist captures it.

Like in the film *Jerry Maguire* when Tom Cruise breaks through his fear of commitment. He's hurriedly explaining his feelings to Renee Zellweger until he pauses to catch his breath, and she says, "You had me at hello."

Or in *As Good as It Gets* when Jack Nicholson breaks through his awkward neuroses and tells Helen Hunt, "You make me want to be a better man."

It's the first kiss in *Titanic* between Leonardo DiCaprio and Kate Winslet, with the sound of "My Heart Will Go On" in the background.

It's Romeo's first kiss of Juliet.

It's all those wonderful moments in film and novel, poem and song, when love breaks through the clouds of ordinary life.

The songwriter composes music to sing about love in a new way. Poets create new images to describe love in an original way. Or a talented group of scriptwriter, director, cast, and crew captures aspects of love in a romantic scene which is like—and yet quite unlike—any before it.

The best of these moments have a timeless quality about them: the scenes of love in the drama of *Casablanca, The English Patient,* or *Sense and Sensibility;* the realization of love in the romantic comedies of *Notting Hill, You've Got Mail,* or *Sleepless in Seattle;* the poetry of love in Shakespeare, Shelley, or Donne.

We feel these timeless moments especially in song, that mysterious and moving marriage of melody and poetry.

I saw and felt the power of romantic song unforgettably once in Stockholm, Sweden. At a festival in the city, several thousand people mingled from one tent to the next, sampling the foods, listening to the various bands, enjoying a perfect summer day.

One of the bands started a new song. A man with a wonderful tenor voice began to sing, softly at first. Then his voice rose slightly above the din of the crowd. The people nearest him were the first to quiet their conversation. Gradually a hush spread out like ripples in a pond, and even those far away stopped, turned, and listened. The entire crowd became like an amphitheater, with the vocalist on his small stage in the center. He sang with passion and warmth, from the depths of his heart. I could see the pain and joy, disappointment and hope, in the expressions of the listeners as he sang "The Rose."

Some say love, it is a river,
that drowns the tender reed.
Some say love, it is a razor,
that leaves your soul to bleed.
Some say love, it is a hunger,
an endless aching need.
I say love, it is a flower,
and you its only seed.

It's the heart, afraid of breaking,
that never learns to dance.
It's the dream, afraid of waking,

4

that never takes a chance.
It's the one who won't be taken,
    who cannot seem to give.
And the soul, afraid of dyin',
    that never learns to live.

When the night has been too lonely,
    and the road has been too long,
And you think that love is only,
    for the lucky and the strong,
Just remember in the winter,
    far beneath the bitter snows,
Lies the seed, that with the sun's love,
    in the spring becomes the rose.

As the last words lingered in the summer air, no one moved. Then a few began to speak softly. Others began shuffling off to the various tents of the festival, many with meditative expressions. The song had touched our hearts, and we silently acknowledged the insight of its lyrics. Because for some of us, love had been harsh. What we thought would be a refreshing source of water became a river drowning us. Romance had felt like a razor leaving our hearts to bleed. And for many of us, the nights had indeed been lonely. All that remained was a yearning hunger, "an endless, aching need." And some had no doubt concluded that love was only for "the lucky and the strong."

But the song reminded us that the seeds of love are within us still, like the seed of the rose beneath the bitter winter snows, and we can't be afraid to let the warmth of the sun give it life.

The song encourages openness to love. And it freshly expresses a timeless paradox: In giving love, we receive it; but in withholding it, we lose what we are trying to protect.

Why do love songs from various times and places speak to all of us? Because they arise from the heart, and since the hearts of lovers remain the same, the songs from their hearts speak to ours.

The songs are not only a treasury of lyrics to delight us but a reservoir of wisdom to guide us—a collection of insights from lovers everywhere.

They show, for example, love's unusual timing—its frustrating elusiveness, but also its delightful unpredictability. No one knows when Cupid's arrow will strike. Love comes unexpectedly and often after painful longing.

It's true that love is only for the young, the middle-aged, and the aged! People at every stage of life long for love and find its arrival a wonderful surprise.

English scholar and author C.S. Lewis married Joy Gresham when he was fifty-seven. It was Lewis's first marriage and an experience he'd come to assume he would never have. His romance was as surprising as a summer snowfall.

Even when love does come early in life, it seems like we've waited forever. I was reminded why when I was tucking my eleven-year-old son into bed. He usually saved his serious comments for this time. After I turned out the lights and started to walk out, he spoke.

"Dad."

"Yes," I replied.

"I'm president of the Hot Girls Club," he said neutrally.

In the dark my eyebrows pinched, and I proceeded cautiously. "Really? Who's in the club, Son?"

The members were the usual suspects—his three closest friends.

"What do you do in the club?" I asked curiously.

"At recess we go sit under the tree on the playground, and we talk about hot girls."

"I see. Anything else?"

"No. I just wanted to tell you."

"OK, Son." I kissed him goodnight, reminded of conversations I'd had years ago as one of the earlier members of the "club"—whose still earlier members, no doubt, included my father and grandfathers. I'm sure when my son first falls in love, it will seem like an endless wait has gone before.

Romantic songs also speak of love's transforming power. Black-and-white blushes with color. Winter blossoms into spring. The dormant life under the surface rises in all its flowery beauty.

Love songs describe a heightened awareness of the world around us and feelings of joy and wholeness. "Till There Was You," you didn't hear the birds in the sky singing or the bells on the hill ringing.

Even the love songs from Egypt three thousand years ago described the changes love can bring. The hearts of lovers remain wonderfully the same no matter what the century. So I felt no surprise when a somewhat cynical, twentieth-century Meg Ryan, as Kate, fell in love with nineteenth-century Leopold in *Kate and Leopold*.

The songs speak of the oneness love brings too.

The Greeks claimed this as evidence that one preexistent soul had been split in two to make a man and woman on earth. When those two people found each other, they immediately recognized their other half, and they so perfectly completed each other that each knew they had found their soul mate. It's a picture in myth of the completion love songs describe.

Their lyrics say love meets our deepest needs, involves every aspect of our personalities, and can bring caring support in all of life. As Celine Dion sings, she found strength "Because You Loved Me."

Lovers have always said, "You complete me."

It's no wonder then, with the experience of love described in these lyrics, that perhaps the most common theme of the songs is the promise that love will last a lifetime. It was clear in *Titanic* that Kate Winslet would never forget Leonardo DiCaprio, even as he drifted off to the icy grave of the Atlantic. Decades after the tragedy, he still lived in her heart, and so she could sing, "My Heart Will Go On."

Another common theme of love songs, unfortunately, is the depth of pain when love is lost. It could not be otherwise, of course. If love brings so much pleasure, then its loss must bring great pain.

Celine Dion expresses the pain of loss poignantly in, "It's All Coming Back to Me Now."

She captures the escalation of hurt: "There were those empty threats and hollow lies, and whenever you tried to hurt me, I just hurt you even worse and so much deeper"; the anger from rejection: "You were history with the slamming of the door…and I banished every memory you and I had ever made"; and the emptiness of loss: "There were nights when the wind was so cold that my body froze in bed, if I just listened to it right outside the window."

Equally emotional is the rebirth of their relationship, beginning with the vivid recollection of memories from the past: "But when you touch me like this, and you hold me like that, I just have to admit that it's all coming back to me…it was gone with the wind but it's all coming back to me"; and based on forgiveness and acceptance: "If you forgive me all this, if I forgive you all that, we forgive and forget, and it's all coming back to me now."

This song touched my heart deeply when I first heard it. I was in a relationship that was ending, and I felt isolated and rejected. It was an impossible mixture of anger and love; of disappointment and hope; and finally, of hopelessness and despair.

The song was like an empathetic friend. It expressed the feelings deep inside that I couldn't reach. And in doing so, it put me in touch with those feelings so I could understand and accept my loss.

I was surprised that the lyrics and melody of the song so accurately expressed my emotional struggle. I had naively thought I was one of the few who had been through so heart wrenching and disorienting an experience.

When "It's All Coming Back to Me Now" achieved worldwide popularity, I realized that a great many others understood the journey as well. The song and its wide acceptance made me feel like I belonged in the human race after all.

Sometimes, of course, the love is lost forever.

Who cannot empathize with the pain of Fantine in the stage musical *Les Misérables*? Her song comes from the heart, but it is a broken heart.

Almost to the end, Fantine clings to the hope that her lover will return, and they will "live the years together." But in sorrow she realizes also that "there are dreams that cannot be, and there are storms we cannot weather."

Many of us pass through the dark disappointment of relationships that end. We journey through anger and pain, cynicism and doubt. I cannot pretend to have experienced the depth of Fantine's sorrow. But I know something about loss. My own marriage ended painfully some years ago. We had hoped to live the years together too. And it was devastating to accept that there were dreams that could not be. The landscape of life never looked so barren and empty as then.

When I needed help to begin new dreams, I found it in the same places as the old dreams had begun—talking with friends, reading about relationships, contemplating the insights of artists who created pictures of love I could grasp and songs of love I could feel.

It's hard to compare the benefit of, say, reading a self-help book on relationships and of listening to a song like "The Rose." Both are helpful in different ways. The book instructs me, and I learn from its insights. But the song inspires me, and I long to feel deeply again.

Some of us hesitate to begin the journey because we fear we cannot reach the ideals. But they are guides to help us, not rules to discourage us. I love the expression of this in a poem I memorized years ago:

> Ideals are like stars;
>> we never reach them,
> but like mariners of the sea,
>> we chart our course by them.

To end with "we never reach them" would promote cynicism. But to say, "we chart our course by them," provides encouragement. It tells us the ideals should be guides to the best we can achieve.

The ideals of song and film have lifted my heart many times. They have expressed the way I'd like to feel and the love I would like to experience.

One song I haven't yet mentioned has helped me most of all.

The influence of this song upon me is, perhaps, surprising. It's from another time and culture, composed nearly three thousand years ago. The original melody has been lost, leaving only the images and story of its lyrics. And the poetry of its verse is often filled with figures of speech difficult for the modern reader to understand.

Yet many regard it as the greatest love song ever written. In fact, that's why they call it the Song of Songs.

Perhaps the absence of an original melody contributes to its timelessness. Musical arrangements often have short life spans, and what seems delightful in one decade will seem outdated in the next. But it shouldn't surprise us that its lyrics can still speak to us today. Since they arose from the heart, they will always speak to the heart.

The Song isn't lengthy, but it is long enough to develop characters and a storyline more comprehensively than any other song I know, ancient or modern. It also captures almost all the themes love songs through the centuries have expressed: that love is unpredictable and often comes only after painful waiting; that it has magical, transforming power and promises to last a lifetime; that the loss of its intensity brings terrible pain, and the regaining of it is life itself.

In portraying these themes, the Song provides ideals for various aspects of romantic love: growing in intimacy, resolving conflicts, passionate lovemaking.

Yes, even lovemaking.

In comparison with contemporary songs, its lyrics of sexual love are quite lengthy, beautiful, and explicit. I was once surprised, in fact, to discover that several world religions include this song in their sacred literature. I hadn't realized that any of them had identified a romantic, passionate work of art as coming in such a special way from God.

I knew, of course, that many people believe God is, in some way, mysteriously behind every great work of art—inspiring all artists to be reflections of his own creative activity.

But sacred literature goes a step beyond this. Those of us who believe in such a thing believe that at rare times an artist captures beauty so flawlessly that it reflects God's own creative work. Or that God so guides the creation of the art that it echoes his own message to humankind.

You or I may recognize a Renoir painting or the voice of our favorite vocalist singing a new song. The original listeners to the Song believed they recognized the same Artist who had given them Creation and the same Voice that had given them their other sacred writings.

I assume they thought this for the simple reason that they believed this Song captured the ideals of romantic love as its Creator intended.

The love in the Song seems qualitatively different. It's the difference between a lovely painting of a sunset and a brilliant sunset itself. The canvas offers a glimpse, a likeness, but the sunset is the original. The original listeners had caught glimpses of love in their lives, but they saw the breathtaking original in the Song.

Just as importantly, the Song touched their hearts deeply—and can touch ours as well. "It's All Coming Back to Me Now" reaches inside us to find feelings buried in winter snow. It shows us we're not alone in our pain. The enduring presence of the Song of Songs tells us we are not alone in our dreams.

The origin of the Song is almost a miracle in itself. Although Solomon was both the writer and a main character, he was an unlikely candidate to be either. His father had committed adultery with his mother and murdered her husband to take her as his wife. Not exactly role models for courtship. Afterward, his father maintained other wives, whom he often had married for political reasons. He also kept his harem for sexual pleasure. So their marriage likely provided little more inspiration than their courtship.

Neither did Solomon's schooling in the use of power prepare him to understand love. In a scene that could have come straight from *The Godfather*, his father, on his deathbed, transfers the authority of kingship to him with instructions to kill the rivals that could challenge Solomon's rule. The aged patriarch whispers their names with his last breath.

In the first days of his regime, Solomon directed the killings. He learned how control could be taken but not how love must be given.

Naturally then, Solomon used marriage and pleasure to serve power. He forged political alliances through marriages to foreign women, beginning strategically with Pharaoh's daughter. He gathered hundreds of young women for pleasure, some to be wives and others just for his harem. And he built a lavish palace to enjoy all his wealth. Solomon grew up seeing men use marriage to increase power, and power to acquire pleasure. Now it was his turn.

He plunged forward like a thoroughbred at the Kentucky Derby, opening bell clanging, metal gates clashing, hooves thundering, crowd roaring—urging him on as he surged ahead, exuberant, vigorous, intoxicated by his strength, galloping faster than any gone before. But then he slowed, his competitors long since left behind. The excitement subsided, his enthusiasm waned; his body grew tired, his mind numb, the victories empty.

He felt the futility of his conquests. And he knew what it was like to have people all around but still feel alone. Like the contemporary songwriter, he could have written "All by Myself."

Solomon's despair was, in fact, the result of real insight. He was disillusioned because the happiness from his selfish life was an illusion. He was ready to see something else, and fortunately he did. He caught a glimpse of something beautiful, like a dying man given the vision of paradise. Perhaps he remembered a moment of true love between his parents. Or perhaps some distant memory of adolescent love came back to him, or a special woman showed him real love.

However it happened for Solomon, love broke through with a splendor that changed his world. It made power seem shallow and pleasure incomplete, because power could not coerce love, and pleasure could not replace it. Power was in fact powerless, and empty pleasure was painful. His world was upside down. And he would have traded his kingdom and his harem for genuine love.

It's an interesting question, whether Solomon ever experienced love or only glimpsed the ideals he expressed in his Song. I would like to believe he found it. I hate to think of him like Beethoven, who, deaf at the end of his life, wrote symphonies he would never hear. But one thing is certain: Solomon's song portrays a fascinating, captivating love. And if the vision of it could break through his lust for power and pleasure, it can break through to almost any of us.

The lovers of the Song help us see not just what our partners should *be* like, but what our relationships should *feel* like: the role of emotion, longing, and sexual attraction; the foundation of friendship, respect, and commitment; the experience of intimacy, certainty, and forgiveness. The lovers put flesh and blood on these words in their unforgettable romance. Love broke through, and the artist captured it!

Whether viewed simply as great art or great art that rises to the level of sacred art, the Song of Solomon is a love song for all time. It can touch our hearts, awaken our deepest longings, and provide ideals to guide us.

Ideals like the stars in the sky, by which we, like mariners of the sea, may set our course.

She walks in beauty, like the night

Of cloudless climes and starry skies,

And all that's best of dark and bright

Meet in her aspect and her eyes.

—LORD BYRON (1788–1824)
"She Walks in Beauty"

A Night to Remember

I had romantic aspirations from an early age, but I got off to a rocky start when I fell in love with a girl who didn't exist.

It happened at the Inwood Theatre, located appropriately on Lovers Lane. Sometime during the hour-and-fifteen-minute animated version of Peter Pan, I fell in love with Wendy. She was pretty and kind and not afraid of adventure. Also, she had learned to fly, so maybe she could teach me too. At five years old, I was ready for some romantic adventure!

I smiled dreamily for the next few days, thinking about Wendy. But it was hard to keep so much happiness to myself. So I decided to send her a letter.

The problem was, I didn't know how to write. Mother agreed to help me, and we sat on the front porch and composed my first love letter. As we discussed how best to send it, I saw the solution right in front of me. The trees. Since Wendy liked to fly, the best place to put the letter was at the top of one of them. I wanted to put it in the elm tree on the far side of the yard, since it was tallest, but the branches began so high on the trunk that I couldn't climb it. So I settled on the mimosa tree in the middle of the yard.

I put the letter in one of the empty Mason jars my grandmother used for her homemade blackberry jelly. The jar was waterproof and clear, so my letter would be protected from the weather, and Wendy could see it. I placed the jar on the highest branch I could reach. It was a little scary, but I managed it and made my way down the tree.

I was relieved that Wendy would finally know how I felt about her. When I climbed back up the tree a few days later, my heart beat fast when I saw that the cap was still on the jar, but the letter was gone.

As time went on, I was disappointed that Wendy didn't come to see me or at least write back. But it wasn't really such a rocky start after all. Although Wendy wasn't real, her attractive qualities were. And I learned what I'd like to find in someone who would someday write back. I realized how important it was to find someone who made me feel happy just to think about, to be with, and even learn to fly with.

Solomon and his bride, whose name in their language is Shulamith, found all of that in each other. The dreams hinted at in childhood and only glimpsed in adolescence became reality in their life together. The Song of Solomon tells their story.

It is like a map to hidden treasure. Some of that treasure is buried deep within you, and the Song will help you find it. Some is hidden in someone else, and the Song will help you find that too. I want to brush the dust from this Song, translate its language, and let it take you to the riches of romantic love.

Solomon and Shulamith's wedding night is a wonderful place to begin the journey—but not simply because it describes a beautiful sexual experience. In fact, the most erotic sexual love occurs later in the Song. But the lyrics of this night present figures of speech we must grasp in order to comprehend the rest of the Song. More importantly, these lyrics conclude a delightful courtship and lay the foundation for a remarkable marriage.

It is the night their courtship will end and their marriage begins. Years of anticipation and preparation have led them to this moment.

Now the wedding guests have gone. Evening has come. The festive chatter has echoed softly to silence. At last these two lovers are alone in each other's presence.

And they are spellbound.

As Solomon gazes at his bride, he breaks the silence with praise.

Solomon

4.1 Behold! You are beautiful,
    my darling companion.
Behold! You are beautiful.

Your eyes are doves
    behind your veil.
Your hair is like a flock of goats
    moving briskly down Mount Gilead.
2 Your teeth are like a flock of newly shorn sheep
    which have come up from the washing,
each one bearing twins
    and bereaved of not one of them.
3 Like a scarlet ribbon are your lips,
    and your mouth is lovely.
Like the sliced opening of a pomegranate are your
    parted lips behind your veil.

4 Like the tower of David is your neck,
    made for strength;
a thousand shields hang upon it,
    all the shields of the mighty men.
5 Your two breasts are like two fawns,
    twins of a gazelle,
    which graze among the lotus flowers.

6 Until the day breathes

and the shadows flee,

I will go my way

to the mountain of myrrh

and to the hill of frankincense.

7 You are completely beautiful,

my darling companion,

and there is no blemish in you.

You probably aren't surprised by what Solomon compliments, but you may be puzzled by his figures of speech. To unlock their meaning, the first step is to realize that the images often have several points of comparison.

One point may be something the two things have in common objectively, such as color: "Like a scarlet ribbon are your lips." Another point may be a common association of the image, like the association of doves with love, as in "your eyes are doves."

But another point of comparison, often overlooked, is the feeling Solomon would have toward the image. For example, when he likens Shulamith's breasts to "fawns, twins of a gazelle," it's not simply the softness in common with the fawns that captures his meaning but the emotional response evoked by them.

Baby animals prompt feelings of tenderness and affection and a desire to hold and caress them. That, I believe, is the heart of the comparison. Shulamith's breasts elicited a longing in Solomon to tenderly caress them.

So we need to consider not only objective comparisons with the images, but also the powerful feelings they would bring. Certainly it is unclear on a casual reading what Solomon means to say to Shulamith. But let me show you what the images would have meant to her, because they reveal an appreciation for every aspect of her beauty.

Solomon begins and ends with praise of her total beauty: "Behold! You are beautiful, my darling companion. Behold! You are beautiful," he exclaims. He concludes with "You are completely beautiful, my darling companion, and there is no blemish in you." The repetition of both compliments captures the excitement flowing through him. And for many women, these heartfelt words alone would make them aware of how special they are to their husbands.

But Solomon goes far beyond these two compliments, and between them extols seven aspects of his princess with poetry of appreciation. Everything about her is so beautiful, however, that he hardly knows where to begin. With her smile? Her eyes? Her hair?

As he glances at the contours of her body against her gown, the light from the oil lamps sensually outlines her breasts and hips like gifts wrapped in silk.

He takes a deep breath to steady himself and looks again at her face. Their eyes meet openly, deeply, connecting their hearts. And suddenly Solomon knows where to begin. "Your eyes are doves behind your veil."

Doves are the ultimate lovebirds, first courting one another, then raising families as newlywed couples. They represent cooing affection and innocence in almost every culture in which they appear. Since many artists of that time rendered lovely eyes in the uniquely oval shape of a dove, Shulamith's eyes are pictured here as beautiful as art could make them. But they're most beautiful because they are windows to her heart of love for Solomon.

Perhaps the artists who pictured doves as "messengers of love" capture best what Solomon means. In one of many such drawings from their day, a goddess sends two doves fluttering to her lover while fervently expressing her longing for him. Shulamith's eyes are like this: dovelike messengers of love, arising from her heart, flying radiantly to her beloved.

When she later describes Solomon, the only identical praise she returns is about his eyes. They, too, are like doves, tenderly communicating his deep love for her. Solomon and Shulamith are embarking on one of life's most intimate experiences, and it begins with one of life's most intimate encounters—gazing unashamedly, lovingly, openly into each other's eyes.

Solomon then gently strokes her hair. He loves the feel of it against his face and the vibrancy of it when she moves. "Your hair is like a flock of goats moving briskly down Mount Gilead." Her long, flowing tresses are like a flock descending the mountain, blending together as one but with scampering individual members giving movement.

Since a shepherd guides his flock back to safety at the end of the day, the glow of sunset surrounds their descent. The enchanting scene mesmerizes those who view it from the valley below; just as Shulamith's hair, her flock of femininity, captivates Solomon with its beauty.

Surely Shulamith cannot help but smile at such sensitive praise. And Solomon cannot help but note how happy a smile it is. He compliments the evenness and completeness of her teeth when he says they are like sheep, "each one bearing twins, and bereaved of not one of them"—a phrase which in the Song's original language is cheerful with melodic alliteration. And Solomon appreciates their glistening whiteness, so lovely when she smiles, when he adds, "which have come up from the washing."

But the feelings evoked by this image tell the real story. The shearing of sheep was a festive occasion; neighbors gathered from miles around for the celebration. The newly shorn sheep scurrying out of the water was a happy sight, bringing smiles to the adults and laughter from the children. Shulamith's bright, playful smile is like this—a picture of joy that makes Solomon smile like he's at a festival and laugh with the delight of a child.

When he looks at his bride's sensual lips, his heart beats faster. He longs to touch his lips to hers. "Like a scarlet ribbon are your lips," he gently whispers, "and your mouth is lovely." The delicate curves of her lips and their blushing fullness express a message without words, beckoning him to kiss her.

Solomon is fascinated by Shulamith's color and energy.

Her hair is like a flock of *black* goats cascading *down* a mountain.

Her teeth are like a flock of *white* ewes scampering *up* from a washing.

Her eyes are like doves flying *from* her with love.

Her lips are like a *scarlet* ribbon inviting him *to kiss* her.

What a beautiful allusion Solomon makes in the praise of her lips like a "scarlet ribbon." The phrase is used elsewhere in their literature only once, in a dramatic story about a woman named Rahab, who became legendary for words of insight and courage. Shulamith's words are like this, too, revealing a person Solomon deeply respects. He longs to kiss her lips, not simply because they're sensual but to express affection to the person those lips reveal.

The single scarlet ribbon implies that her lips are closed and suggests a wish for her to open them. Scarcely does Solomon express this, however, before she opens her lips in longing to kiss him. "Like the sliced opening of a pomegranate are your parted lips behind your veil," he whispers in response.

Myth in Solomon's day attributed aphrodisiacal powers to this fruit. Shulamith's lips, bright and alive with the pomegranate's color, and her open mouth, moist and sweet as its fruit, arouse him as if by mythical power. At this moment Solomon is keenly aware that he desires to taste her moist lips, not talk more about them.

He brushes her lips with his own, like touching and smelling a fragrant, exotic fruit. And when he tastes the interior of her mouth, it's like savoring the juicy taste of the fruit through a sliced opening to its soft and flavorful center.

I hear playful innocence in Solomon's praise of his beloved. In some ways he has returned to his happiest moments of childhood—to a time when he, too, could have dreamed of flying with Wendy. I can picture him as a boy, somewhat restricted by his privileged position and taking great delight in the freedom of birds to fly whenever and wherever they want.

And I can imagine his longing admiration of a flock of goats on a mountaintop, with no palace restrictions—seeming like dozens of friends, bouncing, scuffling, teeming down the mountainside at day's end.

He must have laughed with childlike joy at the festivals when the sheep, once proud bearers of woolen coats, embarrassingly scampered out naked and wet from their shearing and baths.

Perhaps he remembers a hot festival day when his mother handed him a piece of fruit she had sliced open for him, which he eagerly grasped—placing his tongue inside, tasting the sweetness, swirling his tongue slowly around to gather every drop.

That childhood had seemed lost long ago, obscured by a life too complex. But now it's all coming back in ways he never anticipated. He sees the graceful freedom of the birds in her dovelike eyes of love. In her hair is the playful beauty of flocks descending a mountain. He finds in her smile the same delight he once had at festivals. And the sweet refreshment he once tasted in the fruit, he now savors in her wet, flavorful kisses.

⁂

Just as Solomon begins to lose himself in the dazzling details of her beauty, he draws back to regain his perspective.

He has implied appreciation of Shulamith's character in all his compliments. But now he is explicit. "Like the tower of David is your neck," he says almost reverently, "made for strength; a thousand shields hang upon it, all the shields of the mighty men." Her graceful neck, encircled with a bridal necklace, is like a fortress tower boasting the shields of great warriors.

In Solomon's day figures of speech about the neck described aspects of one's character: A stiff-necked person was stubborn; a neck bent down was humbled; a neck held high showed pride. What does Solomon's comparison of her neck to the tower of David tell her?

The tower was a military fortress. A country's safety depended on the integrity of its towers and the bravery of its soldiers. So the tower was reassuring to look upon, its mightiest warriors standing with shields ready at a moment's notice to resist the violation of its boundaries. No one could view the tower without a profound respect for all it represented.

So Shulamith realizes that her stately demeanor reflects a character Solomon deeply respects, seeing in her a strength to resist anyone who would attempt to cross her personal boundaries. He loves her commanding integrity.

But if approaching someone so awe-inspiring tempts him to draw back, the graceful form of her body beckons him forward. As he is drawn to the sensual curves of her breasts, he poetically expresses his desire.

"Your two breasts are like two fawns, twins of a gazelle, which graze among the lotus flowers." Her breasts are as soft and youthful as fawns. When Solomon was a child, he undoubtedly loved to play with such fawns and pet them affectionately. Now he longs to caress Shulamith's breasts just as tenderly.

But the lotus flowers tell her more. They were believed to have mythical power to give life and awaken love. Artists of that day frequently portrayed goddesses offering lotus flowers to arouse their lovers. Doves were messengers sent ahead, but these flowers were held before them, extended to the face of the lover.

Often the lotus blossoms surrounded displays of fruit or were designs on the outer rims of plates on which food was served. Now Solomon imagines these fragrant flowers of love around her breasts, offering them as tender gifts of erotic delight that he is eager to taste.

Solomon fervently promises to make love to her all night, delighting in her breasts until dawn: "Until the day breathes and the shadows flee, I will go my way to the mountain of myrrh and to the hill of frankincense."

This is an answer to a request made by the princess before their wedding. In a lovely lyric during courtship, she asked, "When the day breathes and the shadows flee, turn, be like, my beloved, a gazelle or a young stag on the divided mountains."

The new day "breathes" and the shadows of darkness "flee" at daybreak. The phrase "divided mountains" was her poetic reference to her breasts. So she asked him to make love on their wedding day and all through the night.

Solomon has made a slight but significant alteration to her words. She had referred to her breasts merely as divided mountains. Yet, to Solomon they are not as ordinary as that. They're hills of myrrh and frankincense—fragrant, refreshing, and as intoxicating as perfume.

Now that the wedding night has come, it is perfume he will enjoy. He will fulfill her request, and he promises that "until the day breathes," they will give their love to each other. With the lightness and grace of a gazelle bounding on the mountains, Solomon will delight in the spice-laden hills of her breasts.

 Solomon concludes his praise as he began it, by telling Shulamith that, to him, she is perfect. "You are completely beautiful, my darling companion, and there is no blemish in you." He carefully chooses a word for *blemish* that can describe both the inner and outer person. In saying she has no blemish, he marvels at both her beauty and her character, emphasizing how thoroughly flawless she is to him in every way.

Even in the number of qualities he praises, Solomon communicates how perfect his bride is to him: The number seven indicated perfection. Cosmopolitan travelers would one day regard the seven wonders of the ancient world as representing the most marvelous achievements of that time. But the seven wonders of Shulamith were all Solomon wanted.

❖

Solomon's passionate praise gives way to praise of their passion.

4.8 With me from Lebanon,

O bride,

with me from Lebanon come.

Descend from the peak of Amana,

from the peak of Senir and Hermon,

from the dens of lions

and the mountains of leopards.

9 You have made my heart beat fast,

my sister, my bride.

You have made my heart beat fast

with one glance of your eyes,

with one strand of your necklace.

10 How beautiful is your lovemaking,

my sister, my bride.

How much better is your lovemaking than wine

and the fragrance of your perfumes than any spice.

11 Honey from the comb your lips drip,

my bride,

Honey and milk are under your tongue.

And the fragrance of your garments

is like the fragrance of Lebanon.

It's normal that a bride might have fears on her wedding night. Shulamith is no exception. Solomon tenderly asks her to take an emotional journey from fear to trust. Perhaps she fears leaving the security of the home she has always known. Or perhaps she fears her new husband will not find her as sexually attractive as he anticipates.

Solomon's initial praise has helped calm those fears. And as their lovemaking begins, he addresses her fears more directly. He asks her to journey with him from the high peaks of Lebanon, from the snowy heights of Amana, Senir, and Hermon. It's unlikely, of course, that she ever lived in these dangerous mountains. The journey from the "dens of lions" and "mountains of leopards" is more likely symbolic of movement from the anxious places in her heart to safety with him.

Solomon may be alluding to drawings of the day that featured unapproachable goddesses on the mountains, surrounded by the lions and leopards that guard against intruders. He assures Shulamith she has no need to keep up her guard with him.

In addressing these fears, Solomon implies a simple but important purpose for his caresses. He wants the foreplay of touch not only to prepare her body for loving but to prepare her heart for giving—to melt away any thoughts or feelings that might distract.

He calls her "my sister" because in their culture this was an affectionate term for one's wife. This figure of speech arose from the confidence that marriage creates a family relationship as real as that between brother and sister. In fact, Solomon calls Shulamith "my sister, my bride" four times, tenderly reminding her of their intimate bond at each stage of increasing intimacy.

He says it first as he describes his arousal from her presence. His heart beats faster with just one glance of her eyes, one glimpse of her necklace. In an earlier part of the Song, Solomon described her necklaces as like those on a mare among the stallions of war chariots. If you've ever seen the powerful emotions surging through a stallion at the sight of a beautiful mare, you'll sense the arousal surging through Solomon as he looks upon his beautiful princess on their wedding night.

Solomon calls her "my sister, my bride" a second time as they begin to kiss and caress. This intimacy is reflected in his whisper that her lovemaking is better than wine. A first glass of wine relaxes and brings heightened awareness, like her caresses comfort and arouse him. They kiss passionately, tongues tasting, exploring, intoxicating each other with the wine from their lips.

Shulamith's kisses are also as fresh and sweet as honey dripping from a newly discovered comb: "Honey from the comb your lips drip, my bride, honey and milk are under your tongue." His description of her kisses is wonderfully melodic in the original language—as beautiful as the kisses he describes.

Even more beautiful is what else Solomon means by his compliment. The people in their nation believed that God had promised and given them a land "flowing with milk and honey." Shulamith realizes that all the happiness their people have found in the land, Solomon finds in her kisses. And he believes that she, like the land, is a wonderful gift from God.

The nation had come into that land after years of nomadic wandering, never having a place to call home. But when they entered the land, they began to build permanent residences, cities, fortresses to protect them, cultivated fields to sustain them.

Shulamith is now the place Solomon calls home. With her, he will build a new life. With her, he will find new direction. He will build fortresses to protect their life together and cultivate fields to sustain them. *She* is the "land" of their new life together. And as she fully comprehends all that Solomon's words convey, she kisses him even more passionately, perhaps as tears of happiness wet her cheeks.

After tasting the sweetness of her kisses, Solomon tells his bride that the fragrance of her garment is like that of a forest in the mountain air of Lebanon. He has moved from her lips to the top of her clothing. Having praised her perfume just before kissing her, he now compliments the fragrance of her garment just before consummation.

Solomon intends, I believe, that we imagine him lifting her gown to his face to breathe in its aroma, then removing it from her body in preparation for more intimate love.

❦

Solomon describes their lovemaking with images of a garden, a stream, the winds, and a feast. By speaking so poetically, he achieves a delicate beauty in the description of the sexual love they experience.

After Solomon likens Shulamith to a garden and stream, she asks the winds to stream the fragrances of her garden before him, beckoning him to enjoy its fruits. Then he celebrates his enjoyment of this banquet of delights.

Solomon

4.12 You are a garden locked,
    my sister, my bride.
You are a garden locked,
    a fountain sealed.

13 Your tender shoots are
    a paradise of pomegranates,
      with delicious fruits;
    henna blossoms with nard plants,

14   nard and saffron;
    fragrant reed and cinnamon,
      with all trees of frankincense,
    myrrh, and aloes—
      with all the best spices.

15 A fountain of gardens you are,
    a well of fresh water
      and streams flowing from Lebanon.

Shulamith

4.16 Awaken, O north wind,

and come, wind of the south.

Blow upon my garden

and cause its spices to flow like a stream.

May my beloved come to his garden

And eat its delicious fruits.

Solomon

5.1 I have come into my garden,

my sister, my bride;

I have gathered my myrrh with my spice.

I have eaten my honeycomb with my honey.

I have drunk my wine with my milk.

Songwriter

Eat, O darling companions.

Drink and be drunk, O beloved ones.

As the couple prepares for the deepest level of sexual intimacy, Solomon tenderly calls Shulamith "my sister, my bride" a third time. He also tells her, "You are a garden locked, a fountain sealed." The locked garden and sealed fountain symbolize virginity before marriage, a romantic ideal they shared. Shulamith has kept the fruits of her garden and refreshment of its fountains just for him.

He marvels at the garden of her body. "Your tender shoots are a paradise of pomegranates, with delicious fruits; henna blossoms with nard plants, nard and saffron; fragrant reed and cinnamon, with all trees of frankincense, myrrh, and aloes—with all the best spices."

The plants and trees of her garden seduce his senses. He adores her beauty, inhales her fragrance, and longs to taste her exotic fruits. Everything about her entices him.

Solomon calls her a "paradise," speaking specifically of a royal garden, but perhaps hinting at the innocent world of God's first couple, believed to have lived in paradise—a vast and beautiful garden. Perhaps he's telling his bride that she is as lovely as that original garden, and their love as perfect as the Creator intended.

But more than a mere paradise, she is a paradise of pomegranates. Since this fruit was a common symbol of lovemaking, Solomon is telling his bride that her effect on him is like a garden filled with aphrodisiacs. Her sensual body and aromatic fragrances are these fruits with mythical power. So when Solomon describes additional details of her garden paradise, he sensitively crafts poetic compliments of her intimate sexuality.

She is as delicate and beautiful as the henna's red and white blossoms, famous for the wonderful dyes made from them. And she is as fragrant as the costly, aromatic ointment from the nard plant. She is the garden's incense, her body the source of perfume.

Perhaps he likens her to saffron because of its shape and texture. The flower's stigmata, which contain its aromatic ingredients, are about one to two inches in length—slender threads of spice. But when they're gathered and placed in clusters, they resemble a handful of short strands of yarn.

Solomon links the musky, moist ointment of nard with a cluster of fiber-like strands of saffron in his compliment. He is perhaps making a very poetic reference to the intimate sexuality of his beloved. And he seems to fashion a similar image in praising her garden as "fragrant reed and cinnamon." The fragrant reed is likely the calamus plant with its scores of slender green ribbons rising softly out of the marsh and alongside streams, the base of its leaves reddish or pink. The fragrance of calamus and cinnamon sprinkle this image with perfume.

Solomon has expressed an increasingly overwhelming experience of his beloved. Gazing upon her garden, he appreciated first the delicate henna blossoms with nard; next, the saffron threads moist with perfume; then, the scores of green-ribboned calamus leaves with cinnamon. Each image is more descriptive and more captivating than the one before.

Solomon's next words describe the most captivating experience of all. Shulamith's garden is filled with the trees that produce the exotic perfumes of frankincense, myrrh, and aloes. The delicate plants of henna, saffron, and calamus symbolize the treasures set before him. But these aromatic trees form a canopy surrounding him. Like a man in an enchanted forest, he marvels at her lush, fragrant beauty.

The delicate references to the sexuality of his princess give way to more vivid compliments. Solomon expands upon the imagery of a spring and fountain, describing Shulamith as "a fountain of gardens…a well of fresh water, and streams flowing from Lebanon." The waters are a poetic reference to the moist arousal that prepares his bride to consummate their marriage.

Solomon treasures those waters and their source. The fountain gives life to an exotic garden. The well of fresh water ascribes incomparable value—life-giving sustenance in an arid land. The streams from Lebanon describe their abundance and natural beauty, flowing like streams down a mountain valley. What wonderful compliments to affirm the goodness of her sexuality, washing away any sense of shame or embarrassment.

As their desire for each other intensifies, so the amount of water increases with each image: The fountain provides water for several gardens; a well for a city; streams from Lebanon for an entire region.

When Shulamith reaches the pinnacle of arousal, she voices her first recorded words of the night. Perhaps too shy to speak much before now, her desire breaks through her reticence. She expresses her longing in the same imagery of garden and spring that her beloved has introduced, creating a duet of romantic passion.

Shulamith

4.16 Awaken, O north wind,

and come, wind of the south.

Blow upon my garden

and cause its spices to flow like a stream.

May my beloved come to his garden

And eat its delicious fruits.

The princess asks the winds to blow upon her garden, to cause her fragrances to flow like a stream to Solomon, drawing him irresistibly to her paradise of pleasures. Earlier in the Song, she had asked for patience in awakening love. But she has no need to restrain herself now. So she asks the winds to awaken and carry her invitation to him. And the winds fulfill her request.

The curtains of the bedroom close as Solomon and Shulamith enjoy a time that is so personal not even the poetry of the Song will presume to observe it. But when the curtains of the bedroom open, Solomon can scarcely restrain himself.

Solomon

5.1 I have come into my garden,

my sister, my bride;

I have gathered my myrrh with my spice.

I have eaten my honeycomb with my honey.

I have drunk my wine with my milk.

They have enjoyed a beautiful night of uninhibited love. It has all the grace of elegant dancers, pausing and increasing speed as the music of love plays, yet enjoying the full release of energies in the experience of the dance.

But Solomon's expressions of love do not stop with the end of their lovemaking. He sensitively calls his princess "my sister, my bride" a fourth and final time. More fully than ever before, those words describe their relationship. When the union of their bodies completed the oneness of their hearts, they created one new family. His precious names for her tenderly assure her that he embraces this new reality. I'm sure she smiled warmly in response.

Then her smile broadens, and she raises her eyebrows in mock surprise when she hears his unrestrained celebration of their lovemaking. Solomon lavishly describes it as a sexual feast celebrated with fragrant aromas, food, and drink. Her love is as wholesome as pure milk, as fragrant as spice, as sweet as honey, as intoxicating as wine. He completely delights in the banquet of her body.

I imagine she then pulls his face to her neck to press his lips against her and stop this outpouring of excitement. As he breathes the fragrance of her skin and she holds him close, their world feels perfect and complete.

Could this much happiness be too much? More than they have a right to expect? Of course not. Their happiness is not about a right to expect but a gift to enjoy. The last voice to speak makes this clear.

Songwriter
>   5.1 Eat, O darling companions.
>
>   Drink and be drunk, O beloved ones.

The moment is dramatic. Immediately after the lovemaking, it is the only time in the Song that someone speaks to both lovers, and it falls at the exact midpoint of all the Song's lyrics.

The speaker's identity is mysterious. He is, of course, the same person who first invited all the guests to enjoy the procession of the wedding day. In artistic symmetry he now encourages the couple to enjoy the pleasures of the wedding night.

But who could be apart from all the participants and yet the most intimate participant of all, orchestrating the celebration at beginning and end? Who could be present on the wedding night? And who could know a king and queen so well that he calls them both by their favorite names for each other? Who could have so intimate a relationship with them that he can encourage euphoric pleasure in their sexual love? And whose voice would be given the most prominent position in the Song, at the center of a design that peaks precisely at this point?

It must be the voice of the ultimate Songwriter, who has enjoyed the celebration from beginning to end. Like a joyful parent taking pleasure in a gift he has given his children, the Songwriter delights in their happiness.

What a transforming view of love and sexuality—to believe the Creator would enter the world he created to celebrate this beautiful moment of lovemaking. It's something like Shakespeare appearing at a production of *Romeo and Juliet* to praise their passionate embrace. But this entry of the Great Songwriter into his Song is even more meaningful. His joyful encouragement gives the healthiest possible freedom to enjoy sexual love. "Enjoy the feast!" he tells them. "Be intoxicated with your love for each other!"

When my youngest son was five years old, he fell in love with a girl named Emily. Children must be wiser today than when I grew up, because Emily was a real person in his kindergarten class. But it didn't protect him from heartbreak. She moved away, and all he had were memories, which he often shared with me.

On a day in spring after she moved, he and I were sitting on a park bench on a bridge that spanned a wide creek, beautifully landscaped with myriad flowers, tall trees, and overarching mimosa trees like the one I had climbed long ago. From the bench, looking down the length of the creek, it was a vision of pastels against shades of green that was too beautiful to describe.

My son was the first to speak. "Dad, I want to draw this and send it to Emily."

Then he added, "Will you write something for me at the bottom of the picture?" I remembered a similar obstacle.

"Sure. What do you want me to write?"

"This is real," he said. "Write, 'This is real.'"

He wanted her to know that this world of beauty really existed, even if drawn imperfectly, and he wanted her to experience it. In a very real way, he reflected the wishes of the Creator who made such beauty. Hasn't the Songwriter just said to Solomon and Shulamith, and to those of us who try to draw their story,

This love is real. I want you to enter this world of beauty. I want you to fly!

The sense of the world is short,

Long and various the report,—

To love and be beloved;

Men and gods have not outlearned it;

And, how oft soe'er they've turned it,

'Tis not to be improved.

—RALPH WALDO EMERSON (1803–1882)
"Eros"

The Birth of Love

I love the breathtaking beauty of the Song's wedding night. Naturally, I want to know more about the lovers and how their love began. What was it like when they met? How did they know they were meant for each other? And how did they feel when they first were together? Where is the picture album of their first months of courtship?

I was in my parents' living room recently when I noticed a weathered album of photographs on the coffee table. It looked out of place on the highly polished surface. Curious, I picked it up to take a closer look.

The photographs within were black and white, and for a brief moment I didn't recognize what I was seeing. But then it became clear. I smiled to see my parents like this, so young and carefree. They had always been a handsome couple, but here they were stunningly attractive, radiantly in love, undimmed by age and time.

Before I realized it, the pictures had transported me into a romantic world from the past. I saw my parents walking hand in hand by a lake. Smiling. Laughing. Holding each other. Scenes that would have embarrassed me when I was growing up. But as an adult, I couldn't take my eyes off them.

"Craig," my father said.

But I didn't hear him.

"Craig!" he said, a little louder.

Startled, I looked up.

"Haven't I ever shown you those photographs before?" he asked with a smile.

"No, Dad," I said, smiling back. "Not of you and Mom when you first met."

"Scoot over," he said, "and I'll tell you about them."

He started at the beginning of the album, telling me the story of how she, a beautiful southerner from Georgia, and he, a native Texan, fell in love at an army base in Kansas during the uncertain years of World War II. They saw each other secretly, he said, because as an officer he was prohibited from dating enlisted personnel. And his imminent transfer to serve in a B-29 bomber squadron in the South Pacific threatened to cut short their budding romance. But these circumstances created a sense of urgency that heightened their excitement. Under the storm clouds of a world at war, they found a private world of love and hope. The album of photographs captured that magical time and place.

The beginning of the Song presents a similar album of Solomon and his princess—pictures that capture the progress of their courtship, allowing us to see the qualities of love that led to the beauty of the wedding night.

The style, simplicity, and insight of the first picture is a work of art. Not simply because it presents inner thoughts of a young princess, but because in doing so, it captures feelings that are universal at the birth of love and the suddenness with which they appear.

Shulamith

1.2 How I wish he would kiss me with the kisses of his mouth!
    because your lovemaking is better than wine.

3   For fragrance your perfumes are wonderful,
    and perfume poured fragrantly is your name.
    Therefore young maidens love you.

40

4   Draw me after you! Let us run together!

    How I wish the king would bring me to his chambers!

Young maidens

    We will rejoice and delight in you.

      We will celebrate your love more than wine.

Shulamith

    How right they are to love you.

The Song begins like the burst of a Roman candle on the Fourth of July: "How I wish he would kiss me with the kisses of his mouth!"

If we weren't ready for the ride, we'd be jerked back in our seats as the Song takes off in a flash. C. S. Lewis, in his book *The Four Loves*, describes this kind of experience: "In one high bound It [love] has over-leaped the massive wall of our selfhood. It has made appetite itself altruistic, tossed personal happiness aside as a triviality, and planted the interests of another in the center of our being." In this passage of the Song, the love of the princess appears in "one high bound": The opening of the Song is like the beginning of love!

Even if preceded by long friendship, love happens like this—as though new sight has been given, and for the first time, lovers truly see each other. It may not be love at a literal first sight, but it is the sudden burst of love at the first insight of who that other person really is to you.

The experience is based on more than outward appearance, of course. Love cherishes the whole person. So after pouring out her desire to kiss Solomon, Shulamith proclaims admiration for everything about him. "For fragrance your perfumes are wonderful, and perfume poured fragrantly is your name."

In Shulamith's day a person's name expressed the person's essence. So when she says that Solomon's name is "perfume poured fragrantly," she means that everything about him is as fragrant as cologne and draws her to him.

Her delight is also reflected in playful language. In her native tongue, *name* and *fragrant perfume* sound alike; *fragrance* and *perfume poured fragrantly* sound similar and poetic together too. No wonder this kind of language is called word play—it creates a playful, Shakespearean mood of sound and sense. And the lovers cleverly create this mood throughout the Song.

Naturally, Shulamith longs for this man she finds completely attractive: "Draw me after you! Let us run together!" She is like a young girl surrounded by friends, wishing Solomon to come and take her by the hand to run and play outside like children. With the same childlike joy, she hopes someday to be alone with him in the palace: "How I wish the king would bring me to his chambers!"

Shulamith is certain her feelings are not just adolescent infatuation: She is not the only one who knows what a wonderful person Solomon is. Others love him as well. "We will rejoice and delight in you," they say. "We will celebrate your love more than wine." The princess wholeheartedly agrees: "How right they are to love you." And how right it is for her to love him!

It is no wonder that this person has completely transformed her world.

I had not seen my youngest son's face for a couple of years, it seemed, even though we lived in the same house. He always wore a baseball cap pulled low over his eyes, and he combed his long hair straight and forward. Although the two barriers made it difficult to get a clear view of who was underneath, I could tell from his approximate size and body language that he was still my son.

He astonished me one day when he asked me to take him to the barbershop. I explained that he would have to remove his baseball cap to get a haircut, but he was undeterred.

Not only did he take off his cap but he also asked the barber to cut his hair to a quarter inch in length.

I was delighted to see his face again and thought he had matured nicely in the time I hadn't seen him. But I wanted to find out what led to this unveiling at the age of eleven. He wouldn't say, but his older brother was happy to volunteer an explanation.

"New girlfriend," he said casually.

One day hidden by his cap and shaggy hair, the next day shorn like a sheep and grinning for all to see. I smiled at the sudden transformation romance can bring. It didn't last forever, and he has periodically lowered his hat and grown his hair longer.

But the event foreshadowed more lasting transformations—the same magical beginning the princess portrays: when the world has been changed in a moment and lovers long to kiss, love to admire, and anxiously wait to meet again.

Romantic love brings not only endearing thoughts of another person but also thoughtful reflection about ourselves. The second picture in the Song's album shows the princess doing just this—looking at herself and the past in light of her romance.

She is in the palace, where many disapprove of her appearance. Because her skin is darkened from working in the fields, she looks like a common laborer. Reminiscent of Cinderella, Shulamith has worked long hours with no opportunity to care for herself. After explaining this she expresses her desire to see Solomon—not in his authoritative role of king but in his gentle role of shepherd. What a breath of fresh air that would be after the stuffy snobbery of aristocratic women.

Shulamith
> 1.5 Dark am I,
>> but lovely,
>>> O young women of Jerusalem,
>> like tents darkened,
>>> but like curtains of Solomon.

6 Do not stare at me
  because I am dark,
    because the sun has gazed upon me.
The sons of my mother
  burned in anger toward me.
They appointed me caretaker of the vineyards,
  but of my own vineyard,
which belongs to me,
  I have not taken care.
7 Tell me,
  you whom my soul loves,
where you graze your flock,
  where you rest them at noon;
for why should I be like a veiled woman
  by the flocks of your close friends?

Young maidens
  1.8 If you do not know,
    O fairest among women,
  go forth on the trail of the flock
    and graze your flock of female kids
      by the dwellings of the shepherds.

Wherever Shulamith turns she encounters the heat and burning gaze of the sun. She felt its literal heat when she worked in the fields. She felt its burning in the anger of her brothers. Now she feels its inescapable gaze in the glaring stares of the women. By cleverly using a word that could describe the sun in reference to her brothers, and the action of a person to describe the effect of the sun, Shulamith artistically creates a picture of suffering from labor and at the hands of other people that is like the relentless heat of the sun.

Shulamith's father evidently has died, since her brothers have authority over her. They have mistreated her, making her care for the vineyards. Then, just when she anticipates some relief in the palace, glaring gazes replace the glaring heat. Deeply tanned from her labor, she receives harsh, condescending stares from the women in the palace. It would be hard to say which was worse: the physical pain from working long hours or the emotional pain of rejection by the only men and women she knew.

Such hardship and rejection could tempt Shulamith to self-conscious doubt, but her self-esteem is grounded in more than the opinions of others. Shulamith responds to the women that she is dark, it is true, like the cloth of weathered tents. Nevertheless, she is lovely, like the curtains of Solomon.

The comparison of her darkened skin with tents and curtains shows the basis of her self-worth. A person lives inside a tent or within the curtains of a home and is not changed by the color of the cloth. Whether the cloth is a Bedouin's poor tent or the king's rich fabric, the real person is more than the exterior. And the real Shulamith is as beautiful as Solomon's luxurious tapestry.

In Shulamith's brief account of her circumstances, she alludes to a famous person who suffered hardship similar to her own. Angry brothers had mistreated their young brother Joseph, but he also refused to allow their rejection to undermine his self-worth, and he triumphed over his misfortune.

Since Shulamith knows that outward appearance alone does not define someone, her regard for others is based on the total person. She loves Solomon not for all his wealth as a king but for his kindness as a shepherd. Her request to meet him in this role suggests this. "Tell me, you whom my soul loves, where you graze your flock, where you rest them at noon."

The character of shepherds was legendary. A shepherd worked long hours for little pay and gave sympathetic care to his flock. He gently inspected each for injuries. And at the risk of his own life, he would defend his flock against predators. He would certainly protect them from the dangers of the afternoon heat, and he sensitively rested them during the hottest time of the day.

Shulamith wants to know where Solomon pastures his flock in order to see him, of course. But her request to know where he rests them at noon alludes to her recent suffering. The suffocating noon heat in her life seemed never to end, with the sun's intensity felt literally and figuratively in the fields and in the palace. Now she longs to find rest with Solomon, like a flock finds rest in the care of a shepherd.

❦

Shulamith explains further why she wishes to know Solomon's location: "Why should I be like a veiled woman by the flocks of your close friends?" She doesn't intend to leave the meeting to chance. As a single, veiled woman wandering directionless in the fields, she might appear to be a prostitute.

Her determination to avoid this may have called to her mind another famous person in her nation's literature whose outward appearance did not reveal her true identity. Her name was Tamar. And it's a strange story!

Tamar's husband had died, leaving her childless. According to the laws of that time, a brother, near relative, or—as a last resort—the father-in-law had the responsibility of impregnating her in order to carry on the family name. In this instance one brother shirked his duty; another was prevented by his father from fulfilling his obligation. So out of loyalty to her husband, Tamar veiled herself as a prostitute and enticed the father-in-law, Judah, as he was on his way to the shearing of the flocks.

Judah offered to send the veiled Tamar a young goat as payment for her services, and she asked for his seal as collateral. The seal was quite valuable, since by its signature imprint a person identified himself and his possessions. When he sent the goat in exchange for his seal,

Tamar had gone back to her home. A few months later her pregnancy scandalized the family and brought Judah's outrage. But the truth came out when she showed him the seal that identified the baby's father. It was his own seal.

Judah probably turned eight shades of red, but he admitted that Tamar had been the virtuous one—taking desperate measures to entice him to fulfill his responsibility. Tamar had first appeared to be a prostitute, then immoral. But she was neither.

Shulamith's allusion to Tamar tells the original listeners a couple of things. It illustrates how misleading outward appearance can be. (Shulamith was not a common laborer any more than Tamar was a prostitute.) And Tamar's strategies contrast with the dynamics of Shulamith and Solomon's relationship.

Unlike Tamar, Shulamith has no need to pretend to be someone she's not. She has no need to manipulate Solomon into pursuing her. "Why should I be like a veiled woman?" she asks. Tamar veiled herself because Judah had been dishonest and reluctant. But Solomon is not reluctant in any way, and Shulamith's playful question suggests she knows this already.

The lightheartedness of the question comes through in the clever play on the word *why* that appears only like this in their nation's literature. It is a form that looks precisely like the name of Solomon. On a quick hearing, Solomon might think she has said, "Solomon, I will be like a veiled woman by the flocks"; then he would realize from the word's pronunciation that it must be, "Why should I be like a veiled woman?" I smile every time I read that, because it seems so much like the flirtatious, playful language of a young woman in love.

The young maidens answer Shulamith's request by telling her to graze her flock of young female goats by the flocks of Solomon's companions. This is a strange response for two reasons. First, they don't give the definite directions she wants. Perhaps they're waiting to see

Solomon's response to her before they give her their full help.

Second, the maidens tell Shulamith to graze her flock of young female goats. This could not be a literal flock, since no shepherd's flock consisted of only female goats, so it appears to represent something about her feminine charms. But at this point in the Song, we don't know what it is. Not until the wedding night do we see what the young maidens meant.

Shulamith's hair, remember, is like a "flock of goats moving briskly down Mount Gilead." This is the flock of femininity the young maidens ask her to "graze" by Solomon's companions. When she goes to see Solomon, her dark, flowing hair bouncing on her shoulders, Shulamith likely stirs up quite a response among the men. But she has the confidence to walk right by them on the journey to her beloved.

No wonder Solomon's next compliment compares Shulamith with a mare among chariots. She disorients Solomon's friends as much as a mare's long, flowing mane and magnetism would distract chariot stallions.

How supremely confident she appears, prancing right by all these men—not the least bit intimidated or embarrassed to have such an effect. Solomon must be so proud of her that he beams with admiration.

If he could, perhaps Solomon would grab a camera for this picture and put an end to any speculation that the princess is less than stunningly beautiful, despite the disapproving looks from some in the palace.

Solomon

1.9 To my mare among the chariots of Pharaoh

    I liken you,

        my darling companion.

10 Lovely are your cheeks with ornaments

    and your neck with strings of jewels.

Young maidens

1.11 Ornaments of gold we will make for you

with beads of silver.

Shulamith no doubt elicits a stirring response when she confidently strides by Solomon's friends to her meeting with him. Surely she has a charismatic presence in the palace as well.

I live in a sort of fraternity house, comprised of myself and my three teenage sons. We frequently play touch football after school, gathering some of the neighbors for the game. The boys' school is just down our street, so other students walk past our yard while we're playing.

It's easy to tell when a girl walks by whom the boys find attractive. The first sign may be a football bouncing off a chest or even hitting someone in the face—incidents they seem not to notice, so transfixed are they on the vision of beauty.

Then a surge of energy flows through the players, and they make unusual effort and dramatic moves to gain her attention. I don't think the boys could tell you much about the history of Egypt, but they could show you what it's like when a "mare [is] among the chariots of Pharaoh."

It is the transforming effect eligible females have upon eligible males: disorienting at first and humanizing at last. Solomon's princess is like a mare supremely confident in this process. The sparkling jewels of her necklace are like the jewels on the bridle of a mare, increasing the stunning effect of her beauty.

Solomon expresses his admiration: "Lovely are your cheeks with ornaments, and your neck, with strings of jewels." Even the women of the palace have changed their attitudes in response to Solomon's obvious love for the princess, and they promise to make gifts of jewelry for Shulamith: "Ornaments of gold we will make for you, with beads of silver."

Even in this description of gifts, Solomon and the young maidens praise Shulamith's character. Shulamith's brothers had promised to reward good choices with an "embankment of silver" and bad choices with "planks of cedar" to restrict her. The presence of silver in the necklaces and later lyrics describing unrestricted movement among the cedar trees praise her excellent character, for which she is rewarded.

Solomon also cleverly describes the jewelry with rare words that sound like *embankment* to affirm her character and a phrase that sounds like *planks of cedar* to contrast the threat of restriction with the adornment of necklaces. His gifts were designed not merely to impress Shulamith but also to show deep respect for her.

Deep respect. It is, perhaps, the most overlooked ingredient in the recipe for healthy romance. So I'm glad my youngest son ranks it high on his list of values for a relationship. I asked him when he was ten years old if he had a girlfriend. "Yes," he replied.

He was embarrassed when I asked her name, but finally he told me. Of course, I had learned that the next question to ask a boy his age is, "Does she *know* she's your girlfriend?"

He shrugged. "I don't know. I haven't told her yet."

"I see." I nodded. "Why did you select her to be your girlfriend?"

"She's different from the other girls."

"Uh huh," I said, and paused. "How is she different?"

He shrugged again. "I don't know."

"Think about it," I encouraged. "What is it about her that makes her different from the other girls?"

He thought a minute, then his face brightened. "Well," he said, "If we tease the other girls in class, they all just go tell the teacher and get us into trouble."

I nodded again, thinking I knew where this was going.

"But if one of the boys teases *her*," he said, bursting with pride, "she hits him right in the face!"

I tried not to register my surprise.

"I see," I mumbled distantly as he walked away, happy to have concluded the discussion. Well, I thought, at least he wants to find someone he respects for a partner. He wants her to be strong and self-reliant. And maybe, I hoped, the particular form of those traits will become a bit more civilized as time goes on!

When Solomon gives Shulamith gifts showing respect, he also gives her one of his favorite names for her: "my darling companion." It is, perhaps, the most important gift he bestows. This name underscores the companionship he highly values. He not only loves her; he *likes* her. He desires her to be his friend, not just his lover.

When Shulamith wants to know where she could find Solomon during the day, she's told to look for him where his close friends, the shepherds, might be. In Solomon's language the special word for *darling companion* sounds very much like *shepherd*. Solomon's play on the word suggests that not they, but rather, she will be his closest friend.

His desire for this is based on his complete admiration of Shulamith. Even though she has suffered somewhat, she is supremely confident. And even though she is attractive, she values the total person more than appearance. Yet she is not too solemn. Shulamith fills her speech with clever word plays, delightful allusions, and amusing flirtations.

Solomon's gifts show concretely how much he admires her, and his new name for her expresses his wish for her to be his dearest companion. As his evident love transforms the attitudes of those around Shulamith, prompting their gifts as well, it was like the spirit of Christmas had come to the palace.

I loved Christmas as a child. It was the happiest time of the year for me. And, of course, I loved all the presents. I lay awake the night before, waiting for the crack of dawn that signaled the race to the gifts under the tree. My two brothers, my sister, and I would excitedly rip open the packages, yelling out thanks as we put aside one present and looked for the next.

At last the pace slowed as we gathered up our gifts and checked under torn wrapping paper just in case we had missed one. But the big event was saved for last: Dad's gift for Mother. He always waited till we were finished before he gave it. Then the entire focus was on her.

She was always delighted and appreciative, although then I couldn't understand how someone could like glittering stones more than a basketball. Only as I grew older did I realize that the gift he gave her cost much more than all the gifts for us kids combined.

My father's expression of love for Mother motivated me to do the same. When I was ten years old, I had saved up a sizeable amount of money by my standards, and I gave simple instructions to the manager of the gift store: "I want the biggest thing I can buy with this." He tried to talk me into other parameters for my choice, but I wouldn't budge. I was going to make a statement with this year's gift!

I ended up with a gigantic salad bowl that could hold enough salad for about fifty people. The store clerk wrapped it for me, and I carried it out with great difficulty. When Mother saw me coming home with it, she said I looked like a walking present—the package obscured my upper body and rose above my head. But it was indisputably the largest gift under the tree. I was extremely proud of myself.

I was still feeling proud on Christmas Day, even when the bowl covered half the dining-room table, and sitting down before it, I had to look up to see the top. Although I could barely see my brother on the other side, I had no difficulty hearing his complaints. But I could tell Mother was pleased with the bowl, even if in a different way than she was pleased with Dad's gift.

The expression of love in Dad's gifts to Mother shaped the attitude of my heart, just as Solomon's gifts to Shulamith influenced the hearts of those around her, prompting their gifts.

And like Solomon's love for Shulamith, Dad's love for Mother had taken off in a flash. He can still vividly recount the first moment he saw her on that army base in Kansas. Yet the foundation of the love that blossomed, as with the lovers in the Song, was built on deep respect and friendship.

My bounty is as boundless as the sea,

My love as deep; the more I give to thee,

The more I have, for both are infinite.

—WILLIAM SHAKESPEARE (1564–1616)
  Romeo and Juliet

Hearts with Wings

The five-year-plan guy. That's what we called Randall, a friend of mine in college. It had nothing to do with his education plans. It was all about his strategy to ask the girl of his dreams for a date.

Not that the girl remained the same. Most of his competitors had adopted plans of a few days, or even a few minutes, before asking a girl out, so Randall's dream girl always ended up with someone else.

But you couldn't talk any sense into him.

I saw a cartoon once, showing two caterpillars about six feet apart and crawling toward each other. "We've got to stop now," one said. "We're on a collision course!" That was Randall.

But one time it seemed he had finally found another caterpillar who would give him time to execute his plan. She was French and worked as a waitress at a restaurant near the campus. Her name was Marie, and she was one of the most beautiful young women he had ever seen.

Randall should have bought stock in that restaurant. He ate there so often, I think he had his own table. I ate there with him on occasion. But it was truly painful to see him try to act nonchalantly, claiming to be establishing a friendship that would guarantee that this girl said yes when he eventually asked her out.

The end of the spring semester suspended his plans for the summer. When we went back to the restaurant the first week of the new school year, Marie was still there. Only, she was wearing an engagement ring. The five-year plan had failed, and Randall was crestfallen.

"She probably already had a boyfriend last year," he said.

"Yeah," I lied.

"I don't know if I could really understand someone from a different culture anyway."

"They say that makes relationships harder," I agreed.

Randall sighed. "She was too pretty to like someone like me anyway—never had a chance."

"That's ridiculous!" I sighed.

But Randall was almost relieved. And it was apparent he felt he could speak more freely to her now. When she came back to our table, he was more relaxed and talkative than he had been the entire previous year. He smiled warmly at her. "I was just telling my friend that I need to go to France and find someone as pretty as you."

Marie smiled wistfully back. "Well, maybe if you had asked me out last year, you wouldn't have to go all the way to France."

Randall was stunned.

"What did you say? I mean, I wanted to. I tried to call you this summer, but the restaurant wouldn't give me your home number." Speaking this honestly to her was so new that Randall seemed to stumble over the words like a child learning how to walk.

But that didn't prevent Marie from grasping what he said. And she looked sad.

"I should have asked for *your* number last year," she said.

"Really?" By now Randall was standing, facing her. Their gazes were like rays of sunlight to and from each other. They were speechless.

Then Randall started talking—and couldn't stop.

"Is it too late? I mean, of course, it's too late," he gushed. "What am

I asking? I'm sorry. Anyway, I hope you'll be very happy in your marriage, and yes, I'm sorry we didn't have a chance to go out, but I'm glad we got to know each other, and—"

"It's not too late," Marie interrupted.

"Excuse me…what?"

"It's not too late," she repeated.

"It's not?"

"No."

"So it's not too late," Randall said again, evidently too shocked to absorb what she was saying.

"No," Marie assured him. "It's not too late."

As it turned out, she had been having second thoughts about her engagement and was about to break it off. So she and my five-year-plan friend finally went out.

No one ever said it was easy to share your feelings with someone you really care about. Would Shulamith have difficulty sharing her feelings with Solomon? The next picture captures the intensity of those feelings while Solomon is away. She hugs her pillow as if it were filled with the myrrh of fragrant thoughts about him. And in his absence, she imagines him to be like flowers in a desert oasis.

Shulamith

1.12 While the king was in his realm,
      my nard gave its fragrance.

13 A pouch of myrrh is my beloved to me,
      which lies all night between my breasts.

14 A cluster of henna blossoms is my beloved to me
      in the vineyards of En Gedi.

The princess here describes a necklace with a perfume-filled locket that rests between her breasts. This pouch is normally the purse which held one's most valuable possessions. Shulamith's most valuable possession

Vgil

is her beloved and her thoughts about him. Her contemplation arises from "between [her] breasts"; her thoughts come from her heart and near the symbols of her sexual affection. Her thoughts about him are like a pillow she wraps her arms around, pretending it is the one she loves.

Among her pleasant reflections is the image of Solomon as "a cluster of henna blossoms…in the vineyards of En Gedi." En Gedi was an oasis in the desert wilderness—its name means *spring of a young goat*. Hot, dry sands extend monotonously for miles; then, suddenly, it appears. Green and lush and fresh, it is a welcome sight to weary desert travelers. They see palm trees and vineyards beckoning them with the promise of water and rest. Solomon is like that refreshing sight to Shulamith. After the suffocating noon heat in her life, he is her oasis!

When I was growing up, I wondered why my father would drive all the way home for lunch every day when many of his business associates went to nearby restaurants. And as busy as he was overseeing a growing business, he focused only on his wife and his children when at home. Home—more specifically, his wife in that home—was always an oasis for him in the desert of business stress.

The art of giving praise is a lost one for some and a difficult one for many. But giving and receiving thoughtful compliments nurtures a relationship, and it's a skill that one can learn. My father became better at it later in life, but frankly, he wasn't very good at it when I was growing up.

Dad was a little shy about his feelings, and watching movies featuring Gary Cooper, John Wayne, or Humphrey Bogart, whose emotional ranges were rather narrow, didn't help matters. But while he had difficulty complimenting us kids directly, he could tell my brother something nice about me or tell me something nice about my brothers or sister.

We figured out this dynamic and had an unspoken pact to pass along these compliments. So I found out from my brother that Dad thought I was a good football player or bright or funny. And my brother found out from me that Dad thought he was brilliant, hard working, or confident.

Once, in my twenties, I had a rare discussion with Dad about my dating life. As I talked about a girl I liked, he remarked—out of the blue, before he could catch himself—"You know, your mother has beautiful legs."

I was speechless. Partly for the customary reason that many of us cannot believe our parents are sexually attracted to each other, and partly because I had never heard him utter a compliment like that about her. It presented me with a dilemma. My siblings and I had always passed on compliments like this to each other. Should I pass this on to Mother?

My mother was not as shy as my father, and our talks had always been open. So when we spoke the next day, I decided to tell her.

"I was talking to Dad yesterday," I started, then paused.

"Yes," she said.

"Yeah—well—I was talking to Dad, you know, about Mary and things…"

"Yes," she encouraged patiently.

"Well, when we were talking, it was kind of funny, you know, just out of the blue, he said, 'You know, your mother has beautiful legs.'"

She responded without missing a beat. "Yes, he has always told me that!" But she clearly liked hearing it again. I realized from the way her face lighted up how much she cherished his praise—just as Shulamith enjoyed praise from Solomon. And I've never forgotten the romantic ideal of sharing our feelings of appreciation with those we love.

Solomon and Shulamith delight to share their appreciation too. And no strategic five-year wait preceded the disclosure of their feelings.

The next snapshot in their album of courtship glimpses this opening of their hearts to each other.

Solomon

1.15 Behold, you are beautiful,
    my darling companion.
Behold, you are beautiful.
    Your eyes are doves.

Shulamith

1.16 Behold, you are beautiful,
    my beloved.
Indeed, you are delightful,
    and our resting place is in the flourishing branches.

17 The beams of our houses are cedars,
    our rafters cypresses.

2.1 I am a flower of the Sharon plain,
    a lotus flower of the valleys.

Solomon

2.2 As a lotus flower among thorns,
    so is my darling companion among the young women.

Shulamith

2.3 As an apple tree among the trees of the forest,
    so is my beloved among the young men.
In his shade I longed to stay,
    and his fruit was sweet to my taste.

This dialogue in the Song is an elegant dance of mutual praise. Solomon leads with the first step, twice praising Shulamith's beauty and then saying her eyes are like doves. She follows, twice praising his attractiveness, and then expands the imagery of the dove by describing herself and her lover as doves among the trees.

Solomon likens her eyes to doves because he can see the love in her eyes. Her sparkling eyes are messengers of love winging from her heart like doves. So Shulamith is not surprised when later "my dove" becomes one of Solomon's favorite names for her. But if she is a dove, then nature is their home. In fact, they have many "houses," she says, among the cedars and cypresses. They flit from tree to tree, their resting place in the flourishing branches.

She cannot resist playful flirtation here, since the word for *resting place* in other contexts is best translated *bed.* It is true that in describing the branches of the trees, the word takes on the nuance of *nest* or *resting place;* but it also hints at a time when they will not be like birds in the trees but lovers in bed.

Shulamith creates a beautiful image of new love dancing, skipping, and chasing on a spring day—like birds flying, flitting, flirting away a timeless afternoon. Peter Pan and Wendy could not have been more like birds in flight than the lovers of the Song.

In the second movement of the dance, she experiences such a harmony with nature that she feels a part of it: "I am a flower of the Sharon plain, a lotus flower of the valleys." This is again the flower with mythical power to impart life and vitality.

Shulamith compares herself with that flower in contrast to Solomon's earlier compliment likening her to a mare among the chariots of Pharaoh. The words for *lotus flower* and *mare* sound almost alike and invite a comparison. She wants Solomon to know she is not merely someone who delights to be found attractive, like a mare among stallions. She also possesses the life-giving qualities of the lotus flower. She enjoys not only receiving attention but giving it as well.

Solomon escalates the tempo by embellishing her imagery. She is not merely a lotus flower in the field but a "lotus flower among thorns." She is not one of many lovely women but a woman whose loveliness, to him, renders any other woman as thorns by comparison.

She also isn't defensive, like a bramble bush protecting its flowers and fruit. She's gentle and trusting, open and vulnerable with him. So Solomon feels safe in his openness with her. Perhaps Shulamith is indeed a lotus flower with life-giving power: The new life and freedom he feels is proof!

The princess begins the third movement of this dance by saying she also feels safe and enlivened with Solomon. The forest in their land is a place of danger, with wild animals and treacherous terrain. But he brings security and life to her. She lovingly describes him as "an apple tree among the trees of the forest," adding, "In his shade I longed to stay, and his fruit was sweet to my taste."

He is not an imposing king, as tall and intimidating as the trees of the forest. He's like the apple tree that provides protective shade from danger, and he sustains her in the midst of a frightful place. Shulamith already told us her beloved is like an oasis in the glaring desert. He's also like a home in a dangerous forest.

She began the Song telling of her experience in the heat of the sun. Solomon met her in that place. Like a shepherd, he gave her care and rest. Like an oasis, he gave her water and safety. Like an apple tree, he provides shade and food. She feels completely safe with him.

Actually, *both* lovers feel safe in their own way. Solomon fears no thorns from Shulamith. She fears no forest with him. In their delight and safety with each other, they have the freedom to grow. More importantly, they have the freedom to love. The couple feels safe to be their true selves, to be loved for who they really are, and to give voice to their innermost thoughts.

Shulamith describes the "fruit" that nourished their love as "sweet." In the literature of their day, fruit is a common metaphor for speech, as in "fruit of the lips." And the word for *sweet* often describes speech, just as elsewhere in the Song it describes Solomon's speech. The princess longs to stay in his protective shade and savor every word from his lips.

Soon each lover will also savor the erotic fruits of the other's body. But that desire is awakened by deepening communication. Solomon often shows this by artistically transforming an early compliment of character or beauty into a new compliment about more intimate sexuality. It's a poetic way of showing how appreciation of the whole person grows into healthy sexual desire.

In the beginning, for example, *fragrance* describes Solomon's name and character; but later, *fragrant* will describe the lovers' bodies. Early in the Song, a lotus flower represents Shulamith's uniqueness among women; but during lovemaking it will describe the softness of her skin around her breasts and hips and the life-giving energy her sexuality gives to her beloved. Again, Solomon is first portrayed as a shepherd grazing his flock. But later he will take himself, not his flock, to "graze among the lotus flowers." The gentle tenderness Shulamith sees in him as a shepherd foreshadows his gentleness in making love among the lotus flowers surrounding her body.

So it is not surprising that *fruit* is used here to praise his speech, but later, erotic delights. This poetic artistry shows that the couple's physical intimacy grows out of their love, and the tenderness of it out of the traits each sees in the other in the beginning. Their growth in intimacy is as natural as the images of nature describing them. Both are like doves, but she is a princess like a flower, and he is a king like a tree. The distinctive image of Shulamith is drawn from the feminine side of nature and of Solomon from the masculine side. Together they reflect the genders of nature. The natural pattern that guides the doves in flight, the growth of trees, and the blossoming of flowers is also causing their love to grow.

The praises in the dance express increasing admiration and gradually build as each lover encourages the other to reveal feelings more completely. One ventures a slight compliment. The other reciprocates and embellishes.

The excitement from that prompts greater praise, which discloses a greater depth of appreciation. Finally the praises reach a crescendo, and it's clear to both that they are in love.

◈

Praise begins with the first compliment, of course. Like the five-year-plan guy, I couldn't get one out at my first opportunity. I think I should be excused, however, since this girl was so perfect, I felt like an angel was in my presence, and I shouldn't say a word.

We were sixteen, sophomores in high school, and it was my first picnic date. I had found the perfect place for such an outing when I was trying unsuccessfully to teach my English setter the difference between a quail and a squirrel. Chasing him into the trees, I came upon a natural gazebo of soft green grass and flowers under a canopy of weeping willows by a small stream. When I beheld the princess of the sophomore class a few months later, I pictured her there by the stream, flowers and trees around her, as in a romantic Renoir painting.

I'll never forget how she looked that late fall afternoon when I took her to that spot. It's my first clear memory of the parallel between the beauty of nature and the beauty of a person. In retrospect it's clear that the same Artist must have made them both. Her blonde hair was like the sunlight. Her eyes were blue as the sky. Her voice was soft as the breeze. And her skin was the color of wheat, with the glow of a Texas sunset.

If beauty could be worshiped, I would have placed her on its altar. Not too concerned at the time about being theologically correct, I mostly worshiped during the picnic and was too absorbed in adoration to find the courage to tell her how beautiful she was. So I just sat there most of the time, reverently and silently, and the dance of praise had no chance to begin. Still, I was happy. And as we packed our things to leave, I looked forward to a next time with her, when I hoped my courage would return. I couldn't have known it then, but I was hoping we would someday be more like Solomon and his princess.

If I had never known your face at all,

Had only heard you speak, beyond thick screen

Of leaves, in an old garden, when the sheen

Of morning dwelt on dial and ivied wall,

I think your voice had been enough to call

Yourself before me, in living vision seen…

At least I know, that when upon the night

With chanted word your voice

  lets loose your soul,

I am pierced…with Delight.

—WILLIAM WATSON (1858–1935)
  "If I had never known your face at all"

A Spring of Romance

My father was enjoying reminiscing through the album of treasured photographs. His eyes brightened to see them again and to remember the stories behind them.

"Dad," I interrupted, "since you knew Mother only a few months before asking her to marry you, did you ever wonder if you were making the right decision?"

"I never doubted my decision," he said. "And I never thought I made it too quickly. Some of the soldiers rushed into marriage, no doubt because of the war. Your mother and I went at a snail's pace compared with my commanding officer." He pointed to an impressive officer in a photo. "That man there."

"What happened with him?" I asked, looking at the picture more closely, as if that might reveal the answer.

"Well," he paused. "He got on an elevator one day, and the most attractive woman he'd ever seen was on board. He looked her over from head to toe and asked, 'What would you say if I asked you to marry me?' She looked him up and down, hesitated for a few seconds, and then without blinking an eye replied, 'What would you say if I said yes?' They married a few hours later!"

"You're kidding," I said. "Nobody does that."

"Nobody but the colonel," he said, "who later became a general and the father of seven children with that woman. Don't you remember meeting her when you were in high school?" Dad reminded me of a visitor who came to dinner at our home when she was passing through Dallas.

"I do remember her," I said, "because I remember talking about her seven children." *So that was the colonel's wife,* I thought.

"You asked her about the Vietnam War, where her husband had been," Dad continued, "and we talked about her and the colonel's record for the fastest courtship on the base."

"Dad," I said, "I remember getting the impression that their relationship developed quickly. I had no idea it was that quick!"

"Well," he said a little sheepishly, "we didn't want to give you any ideas about jumping into something too quickly."

"I see how it is," I chided with a smile. "OK for you guys, but not for me." I laughed.

Dad was right in his concern, though. Studies confirm the common sense that marriages entered too quickly are less likely to last. The same is true for marriages entered too young. Admittedly, culture and circumstance determine a lot about best ages to marry and about the ideal length of courtship. But the colonel's good fortune was no doubt an exception in any era.

The founding fathers of Israel provide an amusing example of the range of time for courtship. Isaac accepted Rebekah as his bride the day she was chosen for him. But Jacob worked for seven years in order to marry Rachel, and then seven more years when his father-in-law renegotiated the arrangement after tricking him into marrying Rachel's sister first.

Somewhere between the one-day courtship of Isaac and the fourteen-year labor of Jacob is the ideal time. But it differs for every couple.

Certainly most of us need reasonable time to confirm that someone is the partner we want for a lasting relationship. We must go through phases of growth, like the vineyards mentioned in the Song.

A vineyard in winter is like a dull black-and-white photograph: thousands of dark twigs and branches against a background of white snow. But in the spring the vineyard becomes a lush, green garden. The grapes appear like small buds at first but eventually become clusters of reddish purple or light green fruit hanging succulently from the vines, filled with the promise of wine.

The vineyard owner celebrates his harvest in late summer or early fall. By late autumn the vineyard is like a tired laborer of the harvest who packs away his tools and rests for the winter, awaiting the beginning of a new spring.

Like cycles of the vineyard, love passes through seasons of growth. Rarely do relationships progress as rapidly as the colonel's or Isaac's appear to have done. Even the sudden romance of Romeo and Juliet required some time to blossom. As they once parted, they agreed that "this bud of love, by summer's ripening breath, may prove a beauteous flower when next we meet." Love needs time to grow.

The remaining pictures in the Song's album of courtship demonstrate this truth. The princess longs for her beloved, counsels patience for herself, then sees their love flourish. This romantic cycle briefly repeats as wedding plans are made, but with greater longing, more counsel for patience, and the greatest reward—a relationship mature for marriage, like a vineyard overflowing with grapes ready for harvest.

⚜

The palace of Solomon is like a fairy tale. His court is lavish and its grandeur legendary. The banquet hall is filled with the most exquisite furnishings money can buy. But in that place of incomparable riches and elegant feasts, we see an intriguing picture of the princess.

2.4 He has brought me to the house of wine,

and his banner over me is love.

5 Sustain me with raisin cakes

and refresh me with apples,

because I am faint from love.

6 Oh, may his left hand be under my head

and his right hand embrace me.

7 I want you to promise me,

O young women of Jerusalem,

by the gazelles and by the does of the field,

not to arouse, not to awaken love

until love pleases to awaken.

Shulamith is surrounded by a banquet of strengthening nourishment, but Solomon's love has left her weak. You might remember that in the privacy of nature in the previous snapshot, he was caring and attentive. Now in public view in the "house of wine" (the banquet hall), his love is just as evident. Among the trees of the forest, he was like an apple tree, protecting and delighting her. Now among many guests, his "banner" over her is love.

In those days a banner was a tall, wide display of color used to give direction in public gatherings or to identify a group. It functioned like a portable billboard. Solomon's soft gaze, gentle manner, and loving attention said "I love you" as clearly as a public banner with those words emblazoned on it.

I remember in middle school going to the theatre each weekend with my friends to meet our favorite girls. Sometimes one of us would separate from the others to sit with a girl during the movie, but he quickly rejoined the group when the movie ended. We *never* walked out in public with a girl. What can I say? We were thirteen.

Solomon is immeasurably more consistent in his display of affection for Shulamith. He is not warm and considerate when they're alone but cold and distant when they're with others. He's delighted to have such love for her and glad for all to see its banner.

The contemporary man's banner of love is often like one of the small versions waved meekly by an unexcited fan at a football game, then put away until the next season or forgotten. Consequently, the contemporary beloved's response is equally half-hearted.

But under Solomon's banner, the princess becomes lovesick—weak with happiness she can't contain. "Sustain me with raisin cakes and refresh me with apples," she says, "because I am faint from love." Feelings of romantic love can be delightfully intense. Juliet expressed this intensity to Romeo when she faced being apart from him for just a brief time: "I must hear from thee every day in the hour, for in a minute there are many days: O! by this count I shall be much in years ere I again behold my Romeo." The voice of love has spoken these words in a thousand languages.

The only sustenance that will satisfy Shulamith is the passionate love of Solomon. So she continues: "Oh, that his left hand were under my head and his right hand embraced me." This expression occurs in other poetry of that era, depicting sexual affection. Shulamith longs for Solomon to lie beside her, propped up on his side with one hand under her head as he kisses and caresses her.

True romantic love brings healthy sexual longing. Such desires can also spring from simple lust, so they don't prove romantic love. But the lack of such desire may prove love's absence. Solomon and Shulamith, however, both passionately longed to give themselves sexually to each other.

Since they desired to wait until marriage for the fulfillment of their longings, it's not surprising that the princess counsels patience: "I want you to promise me,...by the gazelles and by the does of the field, not to arouse, not to awaken love until love pleases to awaken."

She makes her request in an interesting way. Others in her culture customarily requested a promise "by God" or "by heaven" to make the pledge more solemn. This stems from the belief that a promise brings moral duty. The request at the marriage ceremony for fidelity, for example, might invoke a promise "by God." Shulamith's request, however, is not for the fulfillment of some universal moral obligation but for the romantic ideal of patience. So she requests the promise by something that embodies romantic love: the gazelles and does of the field.

Lions are aggressive, elephants intimidating; but gazelles are graceful, attentive, and sensitive to the movements of others. The princess asks for behavior in accordance with these creatures, whose light and gentle manner is a model of the sensitivity and patience she wishes to have. She wants not so much to direct the course of love but for love to direct her course.

In drawings of that day, gazelles often appear with mythical gods and goddesses. The gazelles are counterparts in the animal kingdom to lotus flowers—symbolic of life and life-giving power. This mythical belief arises from the gazelles' ability to thrive even in the bleakness of a desert. The romantic ideals Shulamith desires may not be moral obligations, but they are a life-giving energy that enable lovers to triumph in any surroundings.

After her stay at the palace, the princess returns to her home. Time passes, the snows melt away, and winter gives way to spring. Shulamith has gone about her life and waited patiently for her beloved.

Then one afternoon she looks outside and catches a glimpse of an athletic young man walking briskly, almost running, to her residence. He is peeking through the fence to catch sight of her. Solomon! At last he had come!

2.8 The voice of my beloved!
Behold!

He comes,

    leaping over the mountains,

       bounding over the hills.

9 My beloved is like a gazelle or a young stag.

   Behold!

He is standing behind our wall,

    gazing through the windows,

       peering through the lattice.

Shulamith's excitement is evident, and Solomon's exhilaration matches hers perfectly. Falling in love has given him the grace and energy of the gazelle, and he also exhibits its light and nimble manner. The quick, darting movement of the deer looking curiously through the lattice is just like the happy, hurried movement of Solomon seeking his beloved.

Next, Solomon takes Shulamith's hand, shows her the colorful springtime, and urges her to come enjoy it with him. This is a photograph taken with a wide-angle lens, capturing the beauty of the season and the lovers' excitement. Each of them has the spirit of a gazelle: she its patience in waiting for this day to finally arrive, and he its boundless energy in coming to her. And in this most colorful portrait of their courtship, the life bursting forth in the spring parallels the bountiful love in their hearts.

10 My beloved responded and said to me,

   "Arise, my darling companion,

      my beautiful one; come away.

11 For behold, the winter has passed.

   The rain is over and gone.

12 The blossoms have appeared in the land.

   The time of singing has come,

      and the voice of the turtledove is heard in our land.

13   The fig tree ripens its figs,

      and the vines in blossom give off fragrance.

   Arise, my darling companion,

      my beautiful one; come away."

New love and spring go naturally together, and the reasons are readily apparent. In spring everything is fresh. New life flows through the world, and myriad colors triumph over winter's boring grays. Falling in love is the same. What was black and white is now full color, and happiness triumphs over the melancholy chill.

Romantic literature of every age has echoed these thoughts. Coleridge wrote that when love comes, "the trees whisper, the roses exhale their perfumes, the nightingales sing, nay the very skies smile in unison with the feeling of true and pure love."

Perhaps you've seen love transform appearance. Gentle smile, light step, cheerful eyes, fresh energy—a magical transformation. It is the transition from winter to spring.

I've mentioned the foreshadowing of such a change when I saw my youngest son shed his baseball cap for a new haircut. But I saw an even more profound example of this when a friend of mine in college went from heartbreak to newfound love. I remember the moment it began.

He had been gloomy a long time, and I could feel his disappointment. When I tried to encourage him, he just stared at the floor, certain he would never be happy with anyone else. It was a little awkward talking to the top of his head. And no amount of sound reason I offered gave him hope. In those days I thought sound reason always helped, but this was a good lesson in its shortcomings. So I tried a different approach.

"John," I said, "do you remember Melissa?"

"Who?" he asked, still staring at the floor.

"Melissa," I repeated. "The girl I introduced to you four months ago when we were signing up for spring classes. You told me you thought she was really attractive."

"I did?" he asked, not quite remembering, still unmoved.

"Yes, you did," I affirmed.

A moment passed. "Hmm," he said, still immobile.

"Hmm, what?"

"Hmm…nothing," he said.

"She's a waitress about two miles from here," I continued.

"Really," he mumbled in monotone.

"I'll tell you something else, John, she liked you. She told me so after I introduced you."

He lifted his head part way for the first time in an hour.

"Really?" he said, this time with curiosity.

"Yes, *really.*" I saw a ray of hope.

John looked directly at me. His usual, cheerful voice had almost returned. And he suddenly seemed aware of his surroundings, his focus shifting from inward to outward.

I seized the moment. "Would you like to go to that restaurant and see her again now?"

"Yeah," he said cautiously, as if to himself, then, *"Yeah,"* more definitely. "Let's go see her." He headed for the door, almost leaving me behind.

Melissa was at the restaurant that night, and they went out the following weekend. The transformation that started when he raised his eyes from the floor continued as their relationship grew. I've seldom seen a more remarkable change. They fell in love and couldn't spend enough time learning about each other. It was a new spring in their lives.

Yet it was merely a shadow of the spring Solomon and his princess experienced in the Song. After the lengthy description of season and its sounds, Solomon reveals to Shulamith the real reason for their journey into nature. He wants to reach the destination of her heart.

> 14 "O my dove,
> > in the clefts of the rock,
> > > in the hiding places of the cliff,
> > let me see your form;
> > > let me hear your voice;
> > for your voice is pleasing,
> > > and your form is lovely."

Although the cooing of the dove has been heard, the dove herself is still somewhat hidden—"in the clefts of the rock, in the hiding places of the cliff." I love this image of the elusiveness of the young princess. Solomon wants to find out all the mysterious and unknown things about her. He seeks to know the whole person—the form of her body, the voice of her heart. He loves all of who she is—her outer and inner beauty, her face and her soul. He doesn't long just for her body or pretend interest only in character. He loves her completely.

Ideal love will have this balance.

⋇⟨⟨⟨⊛⟩⟩⟩⋇

Balance, of course, is hard to find. And it's easy to understand why.

When one of my sons was eleven years old, he stood looking up at me while I was shaving, half awake, in the foggy vision of my steam-covered bathroom mirror.

"I know why people kiss," he announced.

"Tell me why," I said absently.

"No," he said. "But I know why."

"Why won't you tell me?"

"Just because."

"Come on," I pressed, "tell me why." I was more curious now, and slightly more awake.

My son held out. "No. But I know why."

Finally, I pretended frustration. "Hey, if you're not going to tell me, let's quit talking about it."

"They want to kiss," he blurted out, "so the guy can kiss the girl's breasts."

I nicked my chin with the razor. "How did you—Why do you think—" Flustered, I dabbed the cut with a tissue and started again, this time with deliberate calmness. "Now, why do you think that?"

"I saw it in *Dances with Wolves*," he replied confidently.

"*Dances with Wolves*," I thought out loud, already breathing a sigh of relief. I quickly reviewed the movie in my mind. "You didn't see that in the movie."

"No, you don't *see* it," he explained, "because the camera goes away right when he's about to. But that's the direction he's going when the camera moves!"

Dances with Wolves is a wonderful movie—it features beautiful scenery and exciting adventure and won an Oscar for best picture. But the most memorable scene for my eleven-year-old son was the one suggested by his vivid imagination about the sexual expression of love.

The mystery of sexual intimacy captured his imagination more than anything else in the film. If an eleven-year-old boy can let that one scene weigh heavier in the balance than all the other scenes in the movie, it's easy to see how the rest of us might also give too much weight to sexual attraction.

Fortunately, in the early stages of falling in love, preoccupation with the total person can overshadow the desire to express love physically. Sexual attraction takes a backseat to the delight in each other's every word.

Most romantic literature speaks of the desire of lovers to know each other in detail, to understand each mood and shade of feeling. And this takes time: lingering time for leisurely and free expression, unmeasured time for reflection and response.

Solomon and the princess enjoy this wonderful time of discovery in their celebration of spring. She had longed to be with him, and she has urged herself to be patient in waiting to see him again. At last, time rewards her when her beloved comes like a gazelle, taking her to enjoy the new season. Like the vineyard's rebirth from winter to spring, their love blossoms in its season.

Solomon and Shulamith's season did not arrive as quickly as the colonel's, which blew in like a whirlwind. Nor did it come as slowly as their forefather Jacob's, which dragged on for years. It progressed at just the right pace for them, allowing every petal of love to unfold.

My true-love hath my heart, and I have his,

    By just exchange one to the other given:

I hold his dear, and mine he cannot miss,

    There never was a better bargain driven:

My true-love hath my heart, and I have his.

—SIR PHILIP SYDNEY (1554–1586)
  "My True-Love Hath My Heart"

A Time to Marry

My college friends and I sat talking, catching our breath after playing touch football. Out of the blue, one guy asked, "Craig, what's your number one sexual fantasy?"

The other guys stopped talking. I tensed a little from the sudden pressure. I was a little shy about discussing something that personal in front of my fraternity brothers.

But I thought over the question.

"Well," I finally said, "I'll tell you my main sexual fantasy. I'll bet it's the most difficult fantasy to realize too—and that a lot of people imagine it but seldom admit it."

"Tell us," my friend said enthusiastically. The other guys nudged closer to hear, with smiles of anticipation.

"Well…" I took a breath. "My main fantasy is…to make love to the woman I deeply love."

Silence.

Some of the guys looked puzzled, as if they had walked into the wrong movie. I felt like I had placed a target on my chest at a shooting range and was waiting for shots to be fired.

But surprisingly, I saw in my friend's expression that I was not alone.

He paused and seemed almost sad. "You're right," he said. "I've never thought of it that way, but you're really right."

Loving from the heart is a dream many share. And it's a dream that became reality for Solomon with Shulamith.

As they approach this time in their lives, they're like pilgrims in search of a mythical paradise who glimpse it on the horizon in each other. Since this beautiful future has now been placed in their hands, they resolve to protect it—to guard this wonderful closeness they've discovered that longs for sexual completion.

Solomon and Shulamith

2.15 Let us catch the foxes,

the little foxes who ruin vineyards,

because our vineyards are in blossom.

Just as they would protect vineyards from foxes, Solomon and Shulamith resolve to protect their love: "Let us catch the foxes—the little foxes who ruin vineyards—because our vineyards are in blossom."

The vineyards, of course, are the lives of Solomon and Shulamith. Twice elsewhere, Shulamith uses this image to refer to herself alone. Now, however, Solomon's vineyard rests in the meadow beside hers. Although vineyards blossom in late spring, the fruit is not ready for harvest until late summer. By then the grapes have matured and sweetened and are ready to produce the best wine. So since the vineyards of Solomon are in blossom, it is that special time in the lovers' lives when their relationship is developing but not yet ready for marriage. While their love matures, they mutually resolve not to let "foxes" destroy the lovely fruit developing in the vineyards of their life together.

Foxes are furtive and stealthy, often portrayed as sneaking in to steal—eggs in a henhouse or, in the Song, the ripening grapes of the vineyard. Though a fox is small in comparison with the acres of a vineyard, given time and unfettered access, it can destroy the crop and ruin the harvest.

In the Song, foxes represent what always threatens love: dishonesty, selfishness, impatience, or even reluctance to adjust, apologize, or forgive. Like the fox darting furtively into a field, these dangers often appear small. But they can destroy a beautiful relationship. Solomon and his princess are aware of the perils love faces.

Their love is even more vulnerable because their hearts are vulnerable. Just as someone is more susceptible to injury when his heart is open for surgery, Solomon and Shulamith are at risk because their hearts are so exposed to each other.

The frequent requests for patience naturally imply that impatience is a destructive force. No matter how fertile the soil, how perfect the climate, or how productive the vines, the fruit of the vineyard will not be ready until several months after small clusters of grapes first appear. Harvested too early, the grapes are not yet sweet enough for good wine. So an early harvest wrought by impatience will be a bitter one.

Physical union born of impatience can be bitter too. Solomon and the princess are convinced their sexual love must be an expression of mature love—one that has grown from first blossom to ripened fruit, to the point each person is ready to promise a lifetime together.

Shulamith and Solomon resolve not to express with their bodies what they are not yet ready to say from their hearts. The fox of impatience will not be allowed to diminish the fruit of their vineyards with a premature harvest. They will enjoy the ripened fruits of a pristine garden when the grapes are full and sweet.

In the excitement of finding a paradise of love, the princess expresses her feeling of unity with Solomon. Each belongs equally to the other.

Shulamith

2.16 My beloved is mine,

and I am his,

he who grazes among the lotus flowers.

Had Shulamith said only, "I am his," she might have imagined her-self like one of his possessions—implying he could have others and still have control over her. Had she said only, "He is mine," she might have imagined him to be one of her possessions—implying she could have others and still have control over him.

But in saying each is the other's possession, the power of control cancels out, and the right to others is precluded. When each belongs to the other, only the influence of love remains. Neither controls; each loves; both belong.

The mysterious Songwriter who speaks at the conclusion of the wedding night underscores this equality. He calls Solomon and Shulamith both "darling companions" and "beloved ones," ruling out any misunderstanding. In the Song, Solomon uses "darling companion" and Shulamith uses "my beloved" in order for us to be sure who is speaking—not because of any one-sidedness in their relationship. They were equally "darling" and equally "beloved."

The couple's sense of belonging *to* each other comes from belonging *with* each other. Solomon and Shulamith aren't looking for a perfect part-ner, but rather for someone with whom each feels complete. They want to say not simply "he is mine" or "she is mine," but "we belong together."

Shulamith's affirmation that they belong to each other is beautiful: She identifies Solomon as "he who grazes among the lotus flowers." The life they feel with each other is like the mythical renewal found in those flowers. And she experiences this feeling of oneness with him not in his role as a powerful king but in his character as the tender shepherd graz-ing among the lotus flowers.

Why is this? Because intimate bonding is a connection between two people at their deepest level. And each of us at that level is aware of personal vulnerability, past mistakes, the brevity of life, and a need for others—aware of things, in other words, that elicit in us a shepherd's gentleness, more than feelings of a king's power. When a couple can relate with that kind of vulnerability, they lay the foundation for a lasting relationship.

Solomon and his princess are experiencing their relationship at that intimate level, and it is so precious to them that they promise to protect it from anything that might threaten it.

But Shulamith sees Solomon not only as a shepherd. She also perceives him as a gazelle among lotus flowers. In this poetic description, she joins two mythical images of life overcoming a deathlike environment: lotus flowers rising in their beauty from water and gazelles thriving even in the desert.

Solomon is to his princess like a gazelle in the desert and a lotus flower in waters unlikely to sustain life. Against all expectations of finding romance in her surroundings, she has found the love of her life.

Shulamith's deep feelings of love and unity with Solomon prompt longing for sexual expression of her affection. The princess longs to make love on their wedding night.

> 2.17 When the day breathes
> and the shadows flee,
> turn;
> be like,
> my beloved,
> a gazelle or a young stag
> on the divided mountains.

Like the other four occurrences of *day* in the Song, it likely refers here to their wedding day. Shulamith is poetic in her request: The day would breathe at dawn, when the shadows of darkness flee. She wishes her beloved would be like the gazelle, sensitive and attentive; like a young stag, virile and strong; on the divided mountains, a poetic reference to her breasts. When they marry, Solomon recounts this request and fulfills it: "Until the day breaks and the shadows flee, I will go my way to the mountain of myrrh and the hill of frankincense," he says.

When the Song begins, Shulamith longs for the kisses of her lover's mouth. Now she desires his caressing of her body. The closer she becomes to him emotionally, the closer she longs to be physically, as well.

As wedding plans are made, the young princess feels anxious excitement. We've all experienced something similar—like on the night before an early plane flight to an exotic vacation—waking every hour, hoping for the morning light so the adventure can begin. Like many young lovers, Shulamith can't sleep, and she rises to find her beloved.

Shulamith

> 3.1 Upon my bed in the nights,
>> I sought him whom my soul loves;
>> I sought him but did not find him.
> 2   I will arise now and go about in the city,
>> in the streets and in the squares.
>> I will seek him whom my soul loves.
>> I sought him but did not find him.
> 3 They found me—
>> the watchmen who go about in the city.
>> "Have you seen him whom my soul loves?"
> 4 Scarcely had I passed from them
>> when I found him whom my soul loves.
>> I held on to him

and would not let him go

until I had brought him to the house of my mother,

to the place of the one who conceived me.

5 I want you to promise me,

O young women of Jerusalem,

by the gazelles and by the does of the field,

not to arouse, not to awaken love

until love pleases to awaken.

You can hear the intensity of her longing in describing Solomon as "him whom my soul loves"—not once or twice but four times, reflecting the unceasing thoughts about him as she lies in bed during the night. Many of us have tossed and turned like this. Morning seems days away, and we give up our efforts at sleep to call, write, or travel to be with the person we love.

Time together is timeless, but time apart is an eternity. As the joy of Solomon's presence had become greater, so the sorrow from his absence had become deeper. So Shulamith throws off her covers and heads out the door.

When she finds her lover, she clings to him: "I held on to him and would not let him go." Her heartfelt desire for Solomon is at a pinnacle of intensity. When choosing a marriage partner, it's sound advice to select not just someone you can live with but someone you cannot live without. Shulamith has found that person.

The princess takes Solomon to the room of her mother because it remains a place of security. Not until the wedding day will she leave father and mother and begin a new home with her husband.

Even as Shulamith senses her deepest need for Solomon, she remembers the necessity for patience: "I want you to promise me, O young women of Jerusalem,...not to arouse, not to awaken love until love pleases to awaken." The same longing and patience that nurtured their love earlier in their relationship is perhaps even more important now as their wedding approaches.

❧

At last the day comes. The Song captures a beautiful picture of the wedding parade: soldiers marching, swords gleaming, young women straining to see, sparkling jewels, colorful clothes, then a rush of excitement when the royal carriage comes into view. Carried on the shoulders of athletic bearers, it is made of gold and silver without and purple tapestry within.

Now the focus is on Solomon and Shulamith. Their radiance is like that of a god and goddess of myth.

Songwriter

3.6 Who is this

coming from the wilderness

like columns of smoke,

filled with fragrance of myrrh and frankincense,

from every scented powder of the merchant?

7 Behold!

It is the carriage of Solomon,

sixty mighty men around it

from the mighty of Israel;

8 all of them holders of the sword,

trained for battle;

each, his sword at his side

for the terror of the nights;

9 A royal carriage King Solomon made for himself

from the timber of Lebanon.

10 Its posts he made of silver,

its back of gold,

> its seat of purple,
>> its interior inlaid with love
>>> by the young women of Jerusalem.
>
> 11 Go forth, O young women of Zion,
>> and look upon King Solomon,
>>> with the crown with which his mother has crowned
>>> him
>> on the day of his wedding,
>>> on the day of his heart's rejoicing.

The princess can scarcely grasp the king's splendor. Not long ago she had labored for hours in the fields. Overworked and exhausted, she'd had no time to care for herself, let alone contemplate the wealth of a king. Even when Solomon brought her to the palace, he had displayed little of his power. He had courted her with the gentleness of a shepherd, and most often in the simplicity of nature, not the luxury of the court.

Can you imagine how Shulamith must feel when she sees his power and wealth on their wedding day? She would realize again how important her heart is to him. He has not tried to coerce her with his strength, but rather has won her with his love.

Yet now the display of his power serves a purpose: It can calm her fears as she leaves the security of her family. Solomon's wealth shows that he can provide for her, and the elite group of soldiers proves that he can protect her. In the anxious night before the wedding, Shulamith had found security in the home of her mother. Now Solomon brings her into security with him.

Love seeks to meet the needs of the beloved. The princess needs to know she is safe to cast her fate with the king. He gives her assurance that she has placed her trust in the right person.

Love brings out the best in lovers. A Prince Charming awakens beauty sleeping, and a Sleeping Beauty inspires charm in a prince. So love also brings forth the best we have to offer. Even the wedding carriage was the best the king could make it: timber from Lebanon, posts of silver, back of gold, and seat of purple cloth. His love for Shulamith prompted his best.

Such love also brings out the best in others. The royal carriage is inlaid with expressions of love from the daughters of Jerusalem. And everyone shares in the couple's happiness: The guests delight to "look upon King Solomon" on the day of the gladness of his heart.

The image of this procession from the wilderness, led by columns of smoke, alludes to a dramatic event in the history of their people. Led by a pillar of cloud by day and fire by night, the nation of Israel emerged from the wilderness to receive the gift of the Promised Land. Now Solomon comes from the wilderness to receive the gift of his princess. On the wedding night, he will liken her kisses to "milk and honey," a description again referring to the land given long ago. Like that long-awaited promise, Shulamith is the fulfillment of his dreams.

I remember the first time I served as best man in a wedding. After the couple said their vows, they knelt in prayer while a soloist sang a tribute to love. Suddenly I noticed wet streaks on my friend's face, and I was thankful to witness the moment when he clearly saw his bride as a gift; his tears were the giving of thanks. I've often reflected upon the words being sung at that moment from "The Wedding Song":

> A man shall leave his mother,
>> and a woman leave her home,
> And they shall travel on,
>> to where the two shall be as one,
> As it was in the beginning,
>> is now and till the end.

You can hear the spirit of this song at the marriage of Solomon. He leaves his mother on the day of his wedding, and the princess leaves her home to travel together to where the two will be as one. Their destiny is an ideal that had been in the beginning, is true now, and will remain until the end. I picture them both giving thanks with their tears.

And later that night, each fulfilled the dream of loving passionately from the heart.

Love during World War II had given a little hope to everyone, when hope was clearly needed. As my dad thumbed through the photographs of his album, he saw friends who had celebrated his marriage at that army base in Kansas. He remembered the smiles and congratulations, the happiness and the humor after the wedding and before he transferred to the South Pacific.

No one could know then what the fruit of his new marriage might be. Would he return from the war? Some of his friends from Texas had already died in combat. Would his bride wait what might be years for him to return? Some wives didn't. Would they ever have children? How could they know? The future lay before them like the blank, white canvas of an artist. What the years would paint upon it, only time could reveal.

The same white canvas was presented to Solomon and his bride. Would they continue to grow in their love for each other? Would their ideal romance become more erotic and companionable, or had courtship exhausted all the excitement? When the honeymoon was over, would they experience conflict and disappointment?

A character in *Gone with the Wind* explained why newlyweds often meet difficulties: The bride seldom looks past the wedding, and the groom seldom looks past the wedding night; so both are equally unprepared for marriage. Are Solomon and Shulamith prepared for what awaits them?

How do I love thee? Let me count the ways.

I love thee to the depth and breadth and height

My soul can reach, when feeling out of sight

For the ends of Being and ideal Grace.

I love thee to the level of everyday's

Most quiet need, by sun and candle-light.

I love thee freely, as men strive for Right;

I love thee purely, as they turn from Praise.

I love thee with the passion put to use

In my old griefs, and with my childhood's faith.

I love thee with a love I seemed to lose

With my lost saints,—I love thee with the breath,

Smiles, tears, of all my life!—and, if God choose,

I shall but love thee better after death.

—ELIZABETH BARRETT BROWNING (1806–1861)
    Sonnet XLIII

The Pain of Loss

"What happened?" I asked a close friend.

"She was unhappy with everything I tried to do for her," he said. "Mother's Day, a year ago, is a good example. At breakfast I gave her not one but two presents—ones I knew she wanted. At lunch the kids and I each read a list of the things we appreciated about her. Later, we were going to surprise her with one of those giant, heart-shaped chocolate-chip cookies.

"But before we could give her the cookie," he continued, "she pulled me aside and told me how disappointed she was with her Mother's Day. I was shocked. I had done everything I could think of, from picking out the right gifts to expressing our love to planning surprises throughout the day—and she's not happy.

"No matter what I did, it wasn't enough. Not only was it not enough, but I was criticized and shamed for not having done better. Yet *better* was always unobtainable. She never seemed able to receive or appreciate the love I gave. And it killed us. It killed our friendship, intimacy, everything. The divorce was final last week." Like a cancer, ingratitude had destroyed their relationship.

Love begins with heartfelt respect and thankfulness for your companion. But ingratitude erodes love, especially when mingled with sarcasm and criticism. It opens the door to problems that eventually destroy the relationship, like opening the gate of a vineyard to foxes.

Open argument often gives way to bitter silence. The partners say it's over—perhaps not once and for all but subject by subject, feeling by feeling, until little remains. The couple may be legally married but spiritually divorced. Finally they seek the legal status they've already reached in their hearts.

Of course, it's easier to put out a match than a forest fire. So it's better to spot the match of ingratitude when it first appears than to bring in professionals after the fire is blazing out of control.

Solomon and his princess know this. At the first sign appreciation by one for the other might be diminishing, they address the problem. The lengthy account of this next experience is rather surprising. After all, the Song isn't very long, so Solomon must be selective, highlighting the most significant aspects of their ideal romance. He has thus far described what one might expect: the birth of love; time alone in nature; awakening of sexual desire; patience in waiting; anxiety when apart; wedding day and night.

I would have guessed the next important snapshot would be of their new home or the birth of a child. Instead, the Song recounts the problem of the princess taking Solomon for granted. The songwriter knows that apathy will wither this love that had begun in thankful tears. So he shows us the critical need for appreciation to make love grow.

The princess appears tired and anxious, and she's still in her morning robe. Several of her peers gather around with sympathetic concern. Like good friends, they mostly listen as the princess explains what has happened.

Shulamith

    5.2 I was asleep, but my heart was awake.

       A voice!

My beloved knocking,

"Open to me,

    my sister,

    my darling companion,

    my dove,

    my perfect one,

  for my head is filled with dew,

    my hair with damp of the night."

3 I had taken off my cloak;

    must I put it back on?

  I had washed my feet;

    must I get them dirty?

4 My beloved extended his hand through the latch opening,

    and my heart deeply longed for him.

5 I arose to open to my beloved,

    and my hands dripped with myrrh,

  and my fingers with liquid myrrh,

    upon the handles of the bolt.

6 I opened to my beloved,

    but my beloved had turned and gone.

  My soul went out when he spoke.

    I sought him but did not find him.

  I called out to him, but he did not answer me.

7 They found me—

    the watchmen who go about in the city.

  They struck me;

    they bruised me;

  they took my shawl from upon me—

    those watchmen of the walls.

8 I want you to promise me,

O young women of Jerusalem,

if you find my beloved,

that you will tell him

that I am faint from love.

It's an almost symbolic conflict and resolution. The injury that occurs in relationships can be painful and complex. Yet Solomon perceptively identifies the root cause and remedy. He uses poetic contrasts to make sure we see that taking your beloved for granted is a problem even ideal love must confront.

He is restless to see her.

She is comfortable in bed.

Solomon addresses Shulamith with more terms of endearment here than in any other part of the Song: "Open to me, my sister, my darling companion, my dove, my perfect one." *Sister* was an affectionate term for one's wife; *darling companion* was his favorite name for her during their courtship; he has used *dove* previously to describe her gentle femininity; and *perfect one* newly expresses his adoration of her.

Yet the princess gives only a lukewarm response: "I had taken off my cloak; must I put it back on? I had washed my feet; must I get them dirty?"

The king says, essentially, "I love you more than ever and want to make love to you."

The princess basically responds, "Look, I've taken off my makeup and washed my face, and I'm too tired. And could you get me an aspirin for my headache since you're still up?"

In courtship she had been "faint from love."

Now she is apathetic from indifference.

To make doubly sure that we see this change, Solomon artistically contrasts the night before the wedding with these first lyrics after the wedding night. Then, Shulamith hadn't been able to sleep, so anxious was she to see him; now, she considers it an inconvenience to get up after preparing for sleep. Then, she had risen to find him; now, he arises to seek her. Then, the night watchmen had helped her find Solomon; now, they mistake her for a criminal in the night.

Perhaps the most valuable lesson from these lyrics is simply that they are included. Even in the ideal romantic love the Song portrays, lovers encounter disappointment in the inevitable ebb and flow of emotional intensity. Realistic expectations require every couple to anticipate the same rhythms of life, to respond maturely to them, and to not allow appreciation for each other to wane.

Solomon's kind response reflects understanding love. He doesn't become angry, make demands like a tyrant, withdraw into a shell, or desire someone else. He responds in loving maturity.

The princess describes it: "My beloved extended his hand through the latch opening, and my heart deeply longed for him. I arose to open to my beloved, and my hands dripped with myrrh, and my fingers with liquid myrrh, upon the handles of the bolt. I opened to my beloved, but my beloved had turned and gone."

Solomon leaves her a "love note" of myrrh, an affectionate reminder that he had come to be with her. He knows anger cannot force love. So he heeds the wise advice not to arouse or awaken love until it wants to be awakened. He realizes this principle is just as true in marriage as in courtship.

His anger might only deepen her apathy toward him. *He isn't understanding at all,* she might think. *I was wrong about him. He's as insensitive as anyone else.*

But his patience shows that he truly loves her, and it awakens her love as well. When she discovers the myrrh, she says, "My heart deeply longed for him....My soul went out [to him] when he spoke." What a transforming effect Solomon's patient love has on her heart! His tender response accomplishes more than any demands or complaints could have done. His anger might have achieved some changes in outward behavior, but only his love can create love in return.

Unfortunately, the consequences of Shulamith's brief indifference continue even after her attitude changes—and they seem harsh for what appears to be such a small break in the relationship. Mistaken for a criminal by the night watchmen? Struck and bruised? I think the intention is to show symbolically how dangerous apathy can be. Like a car angling only slightly off a mountain road, if its path is not corrected, it will plunge to the rocks below. Wedding vows that promise always to cherish show remarkable insight into the necessity of appreciation for love to flourish. Though Shulamith happens to be the partner chosen for the Song's illustration of apathy, no doubt Solomon confronted it too.

Shulamith's mention of her shawl being taken seems to continue earlier allusions to the story of Joseph, who was mistreated by his brothers and also treated unfairly later in his life. Both times, the injustice involved the taking of his cloak. First his brothers took it, sprinkled blood on it, then presented it to their father as evidence Joseph was dead. Later, when the wife of his superior falsely accused him of attempting to sleep with her, he left his cloak in her hand when she tried to prevent his escape. The woman then presented Joseph's cloak as evidence of her claim.

Joseph was later vindicated, and all his misfortune turned out for good in the end. So perhaps Shulamith intends to show that her punishment is grossly unfair—too severe for what happened.

On the other hand, since she earlier had removed the cloak herself, perhaps the recounting of that act shows symbolically that she accepts some of the responsibility for her misfortune. On the night she got ready for bed without waiting for Solomon, she had taken off her cloak and was reluctant to put it back on to greet him.

Whatever her responsibility, the princess now needs the help of her friends. "I want you to promise me, O young women of Jerusalem," she commissions them, "if you find my beloved, that you will tell him that I am faint from love"—an echo of a feeling she first expressed in the emotional fervor of courtship. Indifference had begun the night; anxious longing concludes it.

⊙⊱✦⊰⊙

When you're upset and anxious, you don't need criticism about what you've done or a lecture about what to do next. Condemnation just makes you feel worse, and you're too worried to listen to speeches. But you do need the support of your friends. And a perceptive question at the right moment can help you. The wise friends of the princess wait for just such a moment. When the princess pauses her story and looks pleadingly at those gathered round, the discerning friends gently inquire.

> *Young maidens*
> 5.9 How is your beloved better than another beloved,
>> O fairest among women?
>> How is your beloved better than another beloved,
>>> that you so earnestly ask us to promise this?

Perhaps, as the princess contemplates this, a smile replaces her furrowed brow. The wise counselor has directed Shulamith's attention away from her fear of loss and toward what will prevent it—a fresh appreciation of Solomon. Anxiety gives way to a fountain of praise:

> *Shulamith*
> 5.10 My beloved is radiant and lustrous,
>> distinguished among ten thousand.
> 11 His hair is like palm leaves,
>> but black as a raven.
> 12 His eyes are like doves
>> beside streams of water,

bathed in milk,
    perched over a pool.

13 His cheeks are like a bed of spice,
    towers of perfumes.

His lips are lotus flowers
    dripping liquid myrrh.

14 His hands are cylinders of gold
    set with golden topaz.

His abdomen is a plate of ivory
    covered with sapphires.

15 His legs are marble pillars
    set upon pedestals of purest gold.

His appearance is like Lebanon,
    distinguished as its cedars.

16 His mouth is sweetness itself.

Everything about him is desirable to me!
This is my lover and companion,
    O young women of Jerusalem.

As Shulamith thinks about the man she loves, her excitement and energy replace the anxiety and fatigue she felt through the night. The radiance from her smile brightens the melancholy room as she happily tells her friends why she cherishes Solomon.

He is "radiant and lustrous, distinguished among ten thousand," she begins; "everything about him is intensely desirable to me!" she concludes. And in between, she compliments ten aspects of her beloved. This number underscores his worth in her eyes, since *ten*, like *seven*, is a number used to signify perfection.

The princess remembers special things she loves about Solomon.

She adores his handsome, regal face and healthy, dark hair: "His head is purest gold. His hair is like palm leaves, but black as a raven." When she says, "His appearance is like Lebanon, distinguished as its cedars," we see that he is tall, dark, and handsome. Yet the king's eyes are tender and beautiful, "like doves beside streams of water, bathed in milk, perched over a pool."

The two doves once perched by streams are now above a pool after bathing in milk. The white doves portray the healthy whiteness of his eyes. But the movement from the rushing streams to the tranquil pool is a love story. Before Solomon met Shulamith, his eyes looked into a stream and saw only rushing water. Now, perched above the glassy pool, the doves see doves looking back. In all the lengthy praise in the Song, only the eyes of the lovers are alike. The mirror image of the doves in the water's reflection show this—Solomon and Shulamith with the same eyes of love for each other.

Perhaps the king wears a fragrant cologne that she associates with him: "His cheeks are like a bed of spice, towers of perfumes." She knows how sweet his kisses are: "His lips are lotus flowers, dripping liquid myrrh." Solomon's lips impart the life-giving power of the lotus flower to her, just as hers do to him. And she values his touch more than gold. Always at the right moment, his hand touches her to comfort or caress. So she describes his hands as "cylinders of gold set with golden topaz."

Although Solomon is gentle, he is also physically and mentally strong: "His abdomen is a plate of ivory covered with sapphires," the princess tells us. He has rippling stomach muscles. And his legs, she says, "are marble pillars set upon pedestals of purest gold." He can't be shaken when the winds of adversity blow against him.

The king has royal dignity, like a tall, impressive tree standing on a mountain, unbowed by the wind. His appearance is "like Lebanon, distinguished as its cedars." He is a powerful young man.

He speaks to her tenderly and kindly: "His mouth is sweetness" refers to his speech, since "lips…dripping liquid myrrh" describes his kisses. Solomon is everything Shulamith has ever wanted—"This is my lover and companion." He is not only her lover but also her dearest friend.

Is it possible that after so long in the vineyards, the wealth of the palace had distracted Shulamith from her relationship with Solomon? Had the gold and jewels, marble and ivory, palaces and perfumes mesmerized her, capturing her attention at the expense of what—or rather, who—was most valuable to her?

Whatever the answer to that question, she now sees more clearly than ever the limited value of luxuries. They are nothing in comparison with the gold in her beloved's touch, the ivory of his abdomen, his stature like cedars, the scent of his cheeks, and the myrrh of his lips when he kisses her. She knows what is most important to her, and she longs to regain it.

What should the princess do to make sure Solomon knows she really loves him? Should she patiently wait for him to return, or take the initiative to see him? The friends of the princess ask a second simple question to guide her.

> *Young maidens to Shulamith*
> 6.1 Where has your beloved gone, O fairest among women?
> Where has your beloved turned,
> that we may seek him with you?

As Shulamith contemplates the answer, she realizes she must go to Solomon. But she is in a vulnerable position: She knows she was wrong to lapse into indifference toward her companion, but she can't control the outcome when she sees him. Is it possible he has changed and become angry? Will he turn away from her? Is he tempted to find some-one else? The mere thought of this pierces her heart.

Sometimes it's hard to admit that you're wrong, and the conse-quences can be severe if you don't. I learned that the hard way.

"I need to tell you some things about my past," my girlfriend said. "I know you've said it doesn't matter, but I want to tell you."

"OK." I knew it wouldn't change my feelings for her. I had thought only of her for the month since we met.

"When I was in high school, I sort of lost direction for a while."

"Yes," I said. But it was hard to imagine what she could mean. She was the sweetest girl I had ever known.

"I dated an older guy my senior year."

"Really? How old?"

"He was thirty-three."

"Wow." I tried to smile, but I felt threatened. I had only just graduated from college.

Trying to lighten the conversation, I asked, "What kind of work did he do?"

"He was a movie producer."

"Oh, really?" The threat level went up another notch.

"Yes, it was all very exciting at first."

"Quite understandable." I tried to wrap this up. "But those things happen. Can't live in the past."

"But that's not all I need to tell you."

"Oh, sorry, of course—tell me."

I could see the tears in her eyes. I didn't want to hear what was next.

"I got pregnant."

"Oh."

"Twice," she said.

"Oh," I barely managed to say.

"And I had two abortions."

"I see," I mumbled.

But inside I froze. When she needed me most, I froze.

"What happened to the guy?" I asked.

"He died last year from leukemia," she said.

"I'm glad!" I snapped.

I still can't believe I said it, and I feel shame to recall it even now. She knew my anger was toward her as well. I knew I should apologize immediately, but my anger and pride kept me from doing it. I didn't apologize the next day, either. And it would be a long time before I did.

Our relationship began to wilt like a flower plucked out of the ground. I made excuses to myself about why I shouldn't ask her to forgive me. But the truth is, I didn't have the humility to admit I was wrong—or the love to completely accept her. Soon the relationship became like dry, lifeless petals. And when I tried to grasp them, they crumbled and scattered in the wind.

Would Shulamith's relationship with Solomon crumble too?

And yet how easily things go right,

If the sigh and a kiss of a summer's night

Come deep from the soul in the stronger ray

That is born in the light of the winter's day.

And things can never go badly wrong

If the heart be true and the love be strong,

For the mist, if it comes, and the weeping rain

Will be changed by the love into sunshine again.

—GEORGE MACDONALD (1824–1905)
  "Sweet Peril"

A Dance of Joy

"You may not even remember this, it was so long ago," I said to her. "So indulge me if you don't recall it too clearly. But I need to apologize for the way I once responded to you when we dated after college."

"OK," she said with a smile.

"You opened up to me about some painful things in your past," I continued.

"I remember."

"You do?"

"Yes, I do."

"And I became angry with you. Do you remember that?"

"Yes. But it's OK. It was a long time ago," she responded kindly.

"But it's not OK, really. I should never have treated you that way. And I'm sorry. I'm really, really sorry about how unkind I was. When you needed me, I hurt you."

"I knew you were disappointed in me," she explained. "It's OK."

"I had no right to be disappointed in you or to make you feel that way," I insisted. "You're one of the most wonderful persons I've ever met, and the only thing you should ever have felt from me was admiration."

"It did hurt," she admitted. "I do remember that. I don't want to make you feel bad now, but I couldn't believe you would be so angry."

"I know it must have hurt," I said.

"Yes, it did. And I felt ashamed."

"The only shameful thing about our talk was my response to you," I said sadly.

She took a deep breath and let it out slowly.

"I'm so glad you brought this up, Craig," she said. "Even after all this time, I feel like a load is off my heart to hear you say this."

"I'm sorry you had to wait so long to hear it," I said. A load was off my heart too. I was immensely relieved to feel her forgiveness. I had waited far too long to apologize.

Unlike me, Shulamith refused to let her pride and fear control her. When her friends gently suggest she go to Solomon, she immediately takes steps to do so.

"Do you know where he is?" her friends ask. Shulamith answers:

Shulamith

6.2 My beloved has gone to his garden,

to beds of spice,

to graze in the gardens

and to gather lotus flowers.

3 I am my beloved's,

and my beloved is mine—

he grazes among the lotus flowers.

Her security in their relationship provides the context in which they work through problems, and the princess expresses confidence in their love for each other. She knows they belong to each other and belong together, even when they have to work through problems. And she knows that like a gazelle grazing among lotus flowers, he finds renewal of life from her as she does from him.

Neither Solomon nor Shulamith need be afraid to admit when conflicts arise, as if to do so might threaten their relationship. They can confidently resolve any issues within the security of the marital relationship they've established.

Shulamith's description of Solomon's location is likely figurative. A literal shepherd takes his flock to the fields; but the shepherd king has gone to "beds of spice...in the gardens...to gather lotus flowers." This picture is certainly of someone who is approachable, not angry. But what is meant by his gathering lotus blossoms?

In the musical *Camelot*, King Arthur sings "How to Handle a Woman," a song in which the lyrics move amusingly from the chauvinistic attitude reflected in the title to the happy answer, that the way to handle a woman is "to love her."

Solomon comes to the same conclusion. A gift of flowers may appear to work magic at times, but it's not as transforming as tender words. In drawings of the day, a lover often presented lotus flowers to the beloved, expecting these mystical flowers to evoke love from the beloved. But the life-giving lotus flowers Solomon gathers are carefully chosen words of affirmation, forgiveness, and love.

When Shulamith approaches, he gives her a bouquet of praise.

Solomon

6.4 You are as fair,

> my darling companion,
>> as Tirzah,
> as lovely as Jerusalem,
>> as awe-inspiring as bannered hosts.

5 Turn your eyes from me,

> because they arouse me.

Your hair is like a flock of goats
   descending from Mount Gilead.

6 Your teeth are like a flock of ewes
   which have come up from the washing,

each one bearing twins
   and bereaved of not one of them.

7 Like the sliced opening of a pomegranate are your parted lips
   behind your veil.

8 Sixty queens there are,
   and eighty concubines,
      and maidens without number; but

9 Unique is she—my dove, my perfect one!
   Unique is she to her mother.

Pure is she to the one who bore her.

Women saw her and called her joyful;
   the queens and concubines praised her:

Solomon's compliments assure the princess of his complete understanding and forgiveness.

He likens her to Tirzah, a beautiful city in the north, and to Jerusalem, the splendid capital in the south. Just as these are the loveliest cities in their land, so she is the most beautiful woman. And his last compliment reaffirms that she is unique among the women of the palace. In Solomon's eyes no one compares with Shulamith.

He assures her he does not wish to be with anyone else. The problems in their relationship have not prompted him to look elsewhere for companionship.

Solomon praises her hair, smile, and lips in exactly the same way he did on the wedding night. He tells her again that she is his sister, darling companion, and dove. This is not for lack of creativity—it's a poetic way to communicate that his appreciation for her has not diminished since that time.

Yet Solomon avoids repeating the compliments from their wedding night that would be most sexual. He does not praise the milk and honey under her tongue, or her breasts like fawns. Nor does he introduce praise of her shapely hips and abdomen, as he will do in the future. Rather, Solomon asks the princess to turn her eyes from him so he will not be physically aroused as he had been on their wedding night.

The king wants to assure Shulamith of his motives. He wants to reconcile personally before expressing it physically. He knows that emotional bonding must precede sexual bonding. And what is her response? She opens her mouth to kiss him. "Like the sliced opening of a pomegranate are your parted lips," he whispers. Her mouth, open with fruit-like sweetness, speaks more than words.

Solomon's tender praise of the princess as his dove and perfect one assures her further of his adoration. And when he expresses as much love and affection as words can convey, she sees herself through his eyes and experiences his love again. The day which began in fear ends on a new plateau of happiness.

Since many of Shulamith's friends are aware of the difficulty that has arisen in her relationship, they also anxiously await the outcome. The same friends who had consoled her in her sorrow now share in the joy of her reconciliation.

Young maidens
6.10 "Who is this
    shining like the morning star,
      fair as the white moon,
    pure as the blazing sun,
      awe-inspiring as bannered hosts?"

Shulamith

6.11 To the garden of nut trees I had gone down,

to see the fresh shoots of the ravine,

to see if the vine had budded

and the pomegranates had bloomed.

12 Before I realized it,

my soul set me among the chariots

of my people of a prince.

Young maidens

6.13 Return, return, O Shulamith;

return, return, that we may gaze in awe upon you.

Solomon

6.13 How you gaze in awe upon Shulamith,

as at the dance of the two camps!

Shulamith has come to Solomon with confident hope that a new spring in their relationship might begin. She expresses this poetically by recounting that she had gone to the garden to see if—or that—the vine had budded or the pomegranates blossomed. Although *if* is often implied by the grammar of her original words, Shulamith omits saying it explicitly. She hints at the confidence that comes from knowing she and Solomon belong to each other.

The couple's courtship had flowered in spring. They harvested the fruit of marriage in early autumn. Now, having passed through a brief winter of indifference, Shulamith longs for a renewal of love similar to the renewal of life on the earth.

In the garden, once Solomon's praise had assured her of his love, she recalls, "Before I realized it, my soul set me among the chariots of my people of a prince." I love the sensitive touch of "Before I realized it" in describing the moment of reconciliation. It's psychologically perceptive of the experience of forgiveness. Shulamith would naturally not be aware of precisely when it happened. She was seeing herself through Solomon's eyes, and her focus was on his forgiving her.

I believe the women of Jerusalem are referring to the princess riding with the king, or at least riding past joyfully, when they describe her as a progressively brighter light. At a distance she's like the first glow of the morning star; then, coming closer, like the white moon; and finally, like the blazing sun. *Bannered hosts,* when preceded by mention of the moon and sun, is likely a reference to the most prominent stars in the heavens.

The image of Shulamith as the morning star signifies how wonderful her reunion with Solomon is. In the Song's original language, the word for this star is identical in pronunciation to the word for *darkened* that earlier described the effect of her labor in the fields. After her reconciliation with Solomon, the woman once darkened by the sun now shines like the morning star. Once the sun gazed down upon her—but now she is elevated with it in the sky.

His likening Shulamith to the sun, moon, and stars underscores the importance of what has happened because it alludes to one of the most important reconciliations in their nation's history. The image itself is from Joseph's prophetic dream in which the sun, moon, and eleven stars represented his family. The story of that dream was about the family's reconciliation.

Solomon makes it clear from the design of his praise, and by many other allusions to Joseph, that he draws his compliment from that dream. He began his praise of the princess by likening her to the pre-eminent cities of their land. Now the young women conclude by embellishing on that with imagery from Joseph's vision of their people. Tirzah, Jerusalem, and the bannered hosts of armies thus become the sun, the moon, and the bannered hosts of the sky—the stars.

In his dream Joseph saw the future reunion of his family. Apart from this event, no nation of Israel would have emerged. That's how important it was. And Solomon now tells Shulamith that their reconciliation is that important to him. The future of a nation may or may not be at stake, but the future of their love depends on it.

Solomon continues explaining how important their reconciliation is to him. "How you gaze in awe upon Shulamith, as at the dance of the two camps!" he says to the young maidens after they have pleaded with the princess to return. The people know she has reconciled with the king, perhaps because they've seen her in a chariot, riding past in a blaze of power and splendor. But Solomon tells them they're seeing the same kind of life-changing event that had happened to Jacob when he acquired the name of Israel and reconciled with his brother Esau.

I'll tell you the story. Esau had been angry twenty years earlier when Jacob deceived him out of his inheritance and then fled. Although Jacob had escaped alone, he was returning to the land with wives, children, flocks, servants, and wealth. Since he feared the retribution of Esau, he minimized the risk to himself and his people by dividing all he had into two camps. If Esau and his four hundred men attacked one camp, the other camp could flee with their lives and their half of the possessions.

The night before encountering Esau, Jacob slept fitfully. The people in the camps probably tossed and turned as well. All of their lives were at risk. As Jacob fearfully approached Esau the next morning, his people from the two camps followed, nervously awaiting the outcome. But instead of attacking Jacob, Esau ran forward and embraced him.

This event was so important in the history of their people that the site of the two camps was thereafter known as Mahanaim (pronounced *makh an ah' yeem*). This is the word in their language for *two camps*. Just as Gettysburg and Appomattox remind Americans of great events of the Civil War, Mahanaim stood for centuries as a reminder of where a possible battle became a heartfelt reunion. Not surprisingly, in the annals of a civil war in the beginning of David's reign, the historian notes that at Mahanaim peace finally came.

As Jacob and Esau embraced and wept together after years of unresolved hostility, an overwhelming sense of relief swept over those who, just the night before, had prepared to die or flee. How could they have kept from leaping and dancing for joy?

So the "dance of the two camps" might first have celebrated the reconciliation of the twins Jacob and Esau. In the Song, however, it refers to the joyful celebration of reconciliation between twin soul mates—Solomon and Shulamith.

The reunion that saved their love was as important to Solomon as the reunions that had saved their people. Jacob and Esau, then Joseph and his family, found forgiveness and hope. The effects of their experiences rippled out for centuries. Who could have foreseen what the effects of that would be throughout time? Had Esau attacked, there would be no Israel.

Another momentous event had also occurred at Mahanaim. During the sleepless night that preceded the meeting with Esau, a strange thing happened to Jacob. He encountered a divine messenger, with whom he struggled but reconciled, and who at the end of the ordeal gave Jacob the new name *Israel*. It was a defining moment in his life. And the new name would be the name of all his descendents and their country.

Shulamith's reconciliation with Solomon is a defining moment in their life together. As with Jacob, an anxious, sleepless night had preceded the meeting with her beloved. And afterward the princess, too, is given a profoundly significant new name. Although to identify her, I have called her by this name throughout the Song; it is here, for the first time, she is called Shulamith.

I think it's the most beautiful name in the Song.

Solomon is literally pronounced *Shulomoh* in the song's original language. *Shulamith* sounds like a feminine form of this. Both names likely stem from the same word, but *Solomon* has a masculine ending, and

Shulamith a feminine one. It's like making the words *actor* and *actress* from *act.* Her name implies that she is Solomon's feminine counterpart—the one who completes him.

That completeness is underscored by the word likely at the root of both of their names—*shalom,* which indicates wholeness and fulfillment. No wonder the Song says both have eyes like doves. The eyes are the windows to the soul, and since the two lovers' souls are alike, their eyes reflect the same qualities.

Perhaps they recognized this the first time they met. In recounting that moment, Shulamith says, "I became in his eyes as one who finds fulfillment"—*shalom* (8.10). What a wonderful play on words in the original language: Shulamith finds shalom in Shulomoh. They find contentment in each other.

The Song clearly presents the couple as soul mates. It is not simply a likeness in their names or their eyes. Everything about them shows an elegant compatibility: their equally artistic speech; their mutual desire for emotional and physical intimacy; their common interests and values; their mature love and devotion. They experience a wonderful oneness, and their names and eyes are but the artistic expression of that reality.

Contemporary culture has generated numerous "ideal" couples. The last generation had Gable and Lombard, Bogie and Bacall. We have Brad and Jennifer, the fictitious Ken and Barbie, or a vague Mr. and Mrs. Right. But even with time and cultural differences between us, I like Solomon and Shulamith best because they show me the elegant beauty of romantic love.

They also show the path to the richest experience of love. Only after passing through difficulties and pain is the princess recognized by others as the soul mate and companion of Solomon. The difficulties had a transforming effect.

When the young women call out to Shulamith after the reconciliation, Solomon observes that they look at her with awe. The word he chooses to describe their gaze is from the world of visions and prophets. It describes the transfixed look of complete absorption in a prophetic vision of ultimate truth.

It was a good word to use, because that's exactly what the maidens saw—a timeless truth cloaked in imagery from a prophetic dream. The image of the princess as sun, moon, and stars comes from Joseph's dream of his family. And Shulamith's new name alludes to the gift of a new name to Jacob. But the timeless truth is that reconciliation is the path to genuine fulfillment; that the journey to the full experience of life and love passes through Mahanaim.

Solomon and Shulamith know that finding the right person doesn't mean they won't face hardship and conflict, but that they'll face it together, in courage and forgiveness, and grow closer through it. That is the miracle of reconciliation. And it is the transforming power that gives us new names—the life-changing names that define our existence.

Earlier this year a woman called for advice about her pending divorce.

After discussing some legal issues, I asked her how she assessed the personal problems in their relationship.

"I've never felt that he valued me or my opinions," she said slowly and painfully. "I don't recall him *once* asking about my day or my thoughts or my feelings.

"It was worse than that, really," she continued. "He made me feel I had absolutely no value to him. He completely took me for granted."

I'm sad, but not surprised, that their relationship ended. They had come to their Mahanaim a long time ago and had turned back to the isolation of separate lands.

Sometimes, though, people do find their way back home. I knew a couple who were in a downward spiral. The husband told me his wife had recently moved out, and he needed a divorce. They had no children. "What should I do?" he asked. I was a law student at the time and not about to give legal advice from my position of inexperience. But I suggested to him as a friend to take some time to let things settle.

Unconvinced but willing, he reluctantly agreed. Two weeks later, as he was packing up a few things his wife had left behind, he came across photographs from their vacation in Colorado the previous summer. He lingered over the pictures of her against the backdrop of the Rocky Mountains. He remembered the freedom and happiness they felt hiking in the great outdoors. He thought of the passion they shared in the cabin where they had stayed.

Later he found some of her things in a drawer: random cosmetic items, her fountain pen, and a few credit-card receipts from the store where she had bought things for their home. A couple of days later, he picked up his clothes at the cleaners, which he had dropped off weeks earlier. A summer dress his wife often wore was mixed in with his shirts and slacks. When he got home, he started to pack it with her things...but he didn't want to let it go. In his heart, he realized, he didn't want to let *her* go.

She had gone back to her parents' home to sort out what to do. In that time apart from her husband, she remembered the reasons they first fell in love and many of the happy memories they shared. When he called her to suggest they give it another try, she wept. That was six years, two children, and many treasured memories ago.

They had come to their Mahanaim too; but like Joseph and his brothers, like Jacob and Esau, Solomon and Shulamith, and countless others, they embraced forgiveness and embraced each other.

True love is…a love that shall be

new and fresh each hour,

As is the golden mystery of sunset,

Or the sweet coming of the evening star,

Alike, and yet most unlike, every day,

And seeming ever best and fairest now.

—JAMES RUSSELL LOWELL (1819–1891)
"Love"

Passion and Paradise

People sometimes say, "In our family we seldom talked about sex." I would say that, but it might give the impression that we did, on rare occasions, actually talk about it—which would be misleading. Although my older brother claims to have had one such discussion with my parents, I've never been able to verify that, so his claim remains in dispute.

About the closest I ever came to such a conversation was by accident. In my story of the colonel and his wife, I mentioned that I remembered her visit to our home, in part, because we discussed their seven children. I'll tell you why I remember that so well.

The colonel's wife, my father and mother, and I sat around the dining-room table as they reminisced about the past and got caught up on the present. As they talked I gathered that she had quite a few children, which surprised me. In my teenage mind, she didn't seem like a mother because she was still very attractive.

After I had listened for quite some time, I wanted to let her know I could speak; and since I had discerned that she had several children, I decided to ask about that.

"So, you have how many children?"

"Seven in all," she replied.

"Wow! I'll bet that's a lot of work," I responded, trying to show that in my seasoned maturity, I understood the responsibilities of parenting.

She didn't seem overwhelmed by my insight; she gave an expression and shrug that said, "I suppose so."

Seeing I had failed to make much of an impression, I pressed on. "Gee, that's a lot of kids. How in the world did you have seven of them?"

With a look of amusement in her eyes, she said, "Well, neither of us could stand to wear pajamas, so we slept together naked every night. And I'll tell you," she continued emphatically, "if you do that, kids are going to happen." Then she smiled—not at me, but staring ahead as if fondly remembering one of those nights.

Whoa! My jaw dropped. Immediately, I had a vision of her, naked with her husband every night. The fear that she could look inside my mind and see that image froze me in embarrassment. I closed my mouth and forced a smile, but I probably looked like I had seen a ghost.

Without moving my head, I looked sideways to my mother for help, but she just looked away, repositioning a plate on the table, while my father sat pleasantly poker-faced, as if this were *not* the first time a man and woman naked in bed had been mentioned in our house—naked every night, in fact, for twenty years!

Incredible! What was still only a fascinating mystery to me, she had been experiencing for years.

Her casual, even cheerful appreciation of lifelong sexual intimacy shocked me, although I'm incapable of telling you all the reasons why. The truth is that such sexual intimacy *is* sometimes frightening, not only for adolescents but also for adults, because of the vulnerability and love required to experience it.

Brief comments such as those from the colonel's wife are often the most we're told of the passion that burns in private when lovers are alone. But in the Song of Songs we have a rare look at the experience of passionate love from the heart—a possibility for Solomon because he had chosen to exchange the safety of selfish pleasure for the vulnerability that can bring lasting love. A reality for both him and Shulamith because their appreciation for each other had grown even deeper through loving forgiveness.

In the privacy of their room, the conflict seems a million miles away. Shadows from the oil lamp flicker across Solomon and Shulamith as they stand beside their bed. The glow of the lamp and the moonlight silhouette their youthful bodies, and we hear Solomon passionately describe his enjoyment of Shulamith.

7.1 How beautiful are your feet in sandals,
>   O daughter of a prince.
> The curves of your hips are like ornaments,
>   the work of the hands of an artist.
2 Your navel is a round chalice.
>   It never lacks mixed wine.
> Your abdomen is a stack of wheat
>   surrounded with lotus flowers.
3 Your two breasts are like two fawns,
>   twins of a gazelle.
4 Your neck is like a tower of ivory.
> Your eyes are like pools of understanding
>   by the gate of a crowded city.
> Your nose is like a tower in Lebanon,
>   keeping watch over Damascus.
5 Your head crowns you like Carmel.
>   And the flowing hair of your head is like purple threads—
>   the king is held captive by your tresses.
6 How beautiful and how lovely you are.
>   Love flows through your tender affection.
7 This—your stature—is like a palm tree,
>   and your breasts are like clusters of fruit.

8 I say, "I will climb the palm tree,
    I will take hold of its stalks of dates."
  May your breasts be like clusters of grapes
    and the fragrance of your breath like apples.
9 And your mouth like the best wine…

Shulamith

7.9 …going down smoothly for my beloved,
    flowing gently through your lips
      as we fall asleep.
10 I am my beloved's,
    and his desire is for me.

The couple's lovemaking has deepened and matured. Their praise is more intimate and complete, more erotic and explicit. And unlike their wedding night, now Solomon has no need to address any fears in Shulamith, because she is secure in his love. Completely comfortable with each other, they fulfill their most romantic desires.

In the soft candlelight, Solomon cups her face in his hands as he compliments her with a royal name, "daughter of a prince." These simple words convey Solomon's admiration for Shulamith. He cherishes her regal dignity.

Then he kneels to touch her feet. Perhaps reflected in this compliment is their cultural imagery of steps reflecting moral choices. Certainly Solomon loves her completely, even the beauty of her feet. After telling her this, Solomon removes her sandals. And she removes her robe.

The king is not too proud to kneel at Shulamith's feet, and she is not too regal to cast aside her robe, unveiling herself to him. Whoever they are to the outside world, when alone in their bedroom, they are a man and woman in love.

Still kneeling before his beloved, Solomon lightly touches the graceful outline of her hips, which are as smooth as precious stones. He compares her thighs and hips to "ornaments, the work of the hands of an artist," perfectly curved and beautiful.

The two lovers then lie upon the soft sheets of their bed, and Solomon begins to kiss where he has praised—first her hips, but then more intimately. He likens her navel to a round chalice never lacking mixed wine, and her abdomen to "a stack of wheat surrounded by lotus flowers."

Artistically, the poetry of the Song has led to this moment. Solomon was first a shepherd grazing his flock, then like a gazelle among the lotus flowers. Later those magical flowers will surround her breasts, but now they surround her hips and abdomen.

Solomon is describing his erotic kisses of her body. He enjoys the nourishment of wine and bread among the flower petals of her abdomen, kissing her as gazelles would graze and nibble among lotus blossoms. On their wedding night, the lotus flowers had encircled and mythically imparted sexual power to her breasts, which Solomon embraced and kissed and caressed. Now the flowers surround her abdomen—the moist and tender garden she invites him to enjoy.

The response of her body delights him. On their wedding night, the primary symbol of her arousal was water—from a garden spring, then a well, then a stream from Lebanon—a steadily increasing amount. But now the symbol is wine—mixed wine, distinctively flavorful and strong. Solomon uses a poetic image common in their world to describe this: "Your navel is a round chalice. It never lacks mixed wine." Her sexual arousal intoxicates him.

Solomon moves upward to tenderly enjoy her breasts, next rising further to kiss the skin of her neck, smooth as ivory.

He then pulls slightly back to look into her eyes. He calls them pools of understanding, not simply because they are serene and wide open, but because they embrace him with love and understanding. As he gazes into the eyes of the woman who knows him well yet loves him completely, Solomon feels overwhelming appreciation. And when he sees her eyes open wide with arousal at his touch, he desires to express with his body what he feels in his heart—a joyful union with his beloved.

On their wedding night, one glance from Shulamith's eyes had stolen his heart, and during reconciliation their erotic effect completely interrupted his words to her. Now they excite more passion than ever.

He sees in Shulamith's demeanor the essence of the person he loves. She is like a military fortress keeping watch over the city that was Damascus, an adversary of their nation. On the wedding night, Solomon had seen this strength symbolized in her neck. Her bearing reflected a character that allowed no one across her moral boundaries.

Now he sees this strength in her capacity for appropriate anger—the nose represented this in their culture because it flares in response to injustice. She not only appears strong like a fortress, she is swift to respond to those who cross boundaries of what's right. Solomon loves her integrity. He can trust her completely, and therefore entrust himself to her completely.

As beautiful and erotic as her breasts and hips are to him, her face—expressive of all who she is—crowns her as majestic Mount Carmel crowns their land. Shulamith's personality and character do not culminate in her erotic body but rather in her lovely face, reflecting her entire person.

And Solomon loves her hair, as luxurious as royal tapestry. "The king is held captive by your tresses," he says. What a playful and sensual picture. Since he is the king, no one has authority to bind him. Yet the soft threads of her hair draped around him hold him captive.

As her hair softly brushes his bare skin, he whispers how wonderful her love is to him. It is "beautiful and lovely," like a colorful display of fruits and wines set before him.

Yet their lovemaking is not merely mutual delight in physical beauty. Shulamith delights to give pleasure because she loves Solomon. And he delights to give pleasure because he loves her. The language of their bodies is the language of their hearts. "Soul meets soul on lovers' lips," the poet Shelley wrote. Solomon would agree. So he thankfully whispers to

Shulamith, "Love flows through your tender affection." Her body is a passionate instrument, playing a song of love from her heart to his.

As he draws back from Shulamith to admire the willowy grace of her body, her hair once draped around him now floats down upon her breasts. She is as inexpressibly graceful as a palm tree swaying in the wind. Her naked breasts beckon him through her long, silken hair, like clusters of fruit protruding from overshadowing palm leaves. At a distance her breasts seem like clusters of dates on the palm tree. But held close, they are like supple, juicy clusters of grapes, inviting him to enjoy their delicious taste.

As he looks at her beautiful breasts, he feels a surge of desire to hold them and place them in his mouth. So he playfully tells her he will "climb the palm tree" of her body to "take hold of its stalks of dates" so her breasts can be "like clusters of grapes." Then he tenderly takes them in his hands and eagerly enjoys them, his mouth-watering kisses moistening her breasts, then his own face, like juice overflowing from grapes hungrily eaten.

As Solomon continues to celebrate this erotic feast, he enjoys the fragrance of her breath like apples, a scent he has come to know well. And after tasting all the fruits, he drinks deeply of his favorite wine—the kisses of Shulamith. Her mouth is like the best wine—fragrant, delicious, and intoxicating.

When he compares her kisses with wine, Shulamith describes the flow of it: "going down smoothly for my beloved, flowing gently through your lips as we fall asleep." Her response is as fluid as a dancer responding to the partner of a lifetime. As they rest in each other's arms, their last kisses linger like the aftertaste of fine wine. They fall asleep with that taste on their lips as the oil from the lamp burns lower, until finally flickering out.

Solomon and Shulamith's sexual love on the wedding night had been beautiful, sensual, and pleasurable. Solomon's description of it poetically celebrated the *beginning* of marriage in its dramatic buildup to consummation. But as he describes their lovemaking now, he celebrates its *nurture* of their marriage, accentuating the intimacy of their passion and the closeness it creates.

They experience that closeness not only in their more passionate lovemaking. They feel it even in sleep, when surrealistic dreams transform palm trees and grape clusters into delicious breasts and lips, and apples and wine become fragrant, wet kisses. And they feel it when half-awakened, touching affectionately in the night—when a movement awakens Solomon and he kisses her neck, reaches his arm around her, or moves his body close against her. And when she stirs, she traces her fingers across his arm, breathes in the scent of his chest, or kisses his hand that lightly cups her breast. In dreamlike slow motion, their loving continues all night.

But the nurturing from their intimacy does not end with the morning. Shulamith describes the contentment and warmth she feels throughout the day.

She tries to put into words how deep a union she feels: "I am my beloved's, and his desire is for me." It's easy to overlook the profound significance of this brief variation of a statement she has made twice before. She first said, "My beloved is mine, and I am his," placing her possession of him first. Later she emphasized her growing security by placing his possession of her first: "I am my beloved's, and my beloved is mine." But here she says, "I am my beloved's, and his desire is for me."

This day after their passionate lovemaking, she not only makes his possession of her primary, but she strengthens it by adding "his desire is for me"—carefully choosing the word for *desire* that describes the ideal love of a husband for his wife.

It is the husband's desire, according to their earliest sacred writings, to provide a place of beauty and safety for his wife—like the sun and the moon provide guiding lights for the day and night. It is his desire to provide everything she could possibly want or need for her happiness, to the same extent that the Creator provides for His people.

Shulamith understands the meaning of this word for *desire* from the most well-known literature of her day, and she has waited until this moment to use it. The absence of this desire, according to the story of Creation, is a sign of the primeval curse. The presence of this desire, however, signals a return to Eden. The experience of paradise that began on the wedding night has blossomed to an even deeper experience of ideal love.

So secure is Shulamith in Solomon's love that she omits "my beloved is mine." She has no need to hold on to him; his arms are securely around her. The passionate intimacy that arose from love has strengthened love as well.

Smiling, refreshed, and content, Shulamith goes about the day's activities, enjoying memories of the night before, anticipating pleasantly the night to come, and deeply thankful for the love she and Solomon share.

A return to paradise—is this why Solomon and Shulamith contradict contemporary stereotypes of romantic love? Like the idea that men seek only sexual satisfaction and women seek only emotional intimacy. Although this seems to me like an insult to both genders, the caricatures often contain a measure of truth.

But in the Song, the pattern is different. In the return to paradise, each partner fully enjoys both emotional and physical intimacy.

In fact, Solomon more frequently initiates verbal intimacy, and Shulamith more frequently initiates sexual love. Perhaps the extent to which a couple experiences this correction of stereotypes is a measure of their return to the kind of love the Creator intended.

I don't know if Solomon and Shulamith slept together naked every night like the colonel and his wife. I imagine the healthy intimacy of lovers can be expressed in many wonderful ways. But whatever the variations, I believe it's worth every effort to experience the kind of relationship that leads to such nights of passion—when only you and your lover exist, like the earth's first couple in a beautiful new world.

Come live with me and be my love,

And we will all the pleasures prove

That valleys, groves, hills, and fields,

Woods, or steepy mountain yields.

And we will sit upon the rocks,

Seeing the shepherds feed their flocks,

By shallow rivers to whose falls

Melodious birds sing madrigals.

—CHRISTOPHER MARLOWE (1564–1593)
"The Passionate Shepherd to His Love"

Freedom and Delight

My vision of romantic love is a collage of images from the world of art and the memories of experience. They are like a personal collection of impressionist paintings in my mind that capture aspects of ideal love.

I feel fortunate that some of my closest friends in adolescence and adulthood have been women with whom romance did not develop, but deep friendship did. Some of my favorite ideas of what a beautiful love might be come from those relationships.

I remember a picnic in the Black Forest of southern Germany. I had immersed myself for several months in the study of the German language to prepare for a graduate school at which that was the language of instruction. I lived in a small village south of Freiburg, and whether in class or in the market, I heard and spoke this new language.

When I first began the process, I learned that what we see of others comes a great deal from their words. The villagers seemed indistinct and blurry to me, since I understood so little of what they said. As the months passed, my German gradually improved, and the people came more into focus. But still I felt a lingering loneliness. I had been incapable of seeing clearly, since I understood so little, and incapable of being seen, since I could express myself even less.

One of my best friends had moved earlier to a city farther north to spend a year improving her German language skills for use in international business. We had talked on the phone since I arrived, but our demanding academic schedules had prevented our meeting.

On an early summer weekend, however, I drove the autobahn north and followed the map to her dormitory. Thankfully, she still spoke perfect English! I had expected her to show me around the university and the surrounding city. But as soon as I arrived, she brought out a picnic basket full of wonderful fruits and cheese and cheerfully instructed me to get back into the car and drive into the hills of the Black Forest.

We passed gingerbread houses that reminded us of Hansel and Gretel, then at last found the plateau she sought. We looked out over an entire valley of emerald green grass, encompassed by the soft, rounded mountaintops that characterize these stairsteps to the Alps.

I related all the news I could remember from home, and she shared much of what she had learned in her time at the university. We also discussed our difficulties in making the transition to a strange place and how homesick we sometimes felt, despite the adventure of it all. We talked for hours, until the sun began to set and the mountain air grew cold. Half shivering but still sharing stories, we walked back to the car and talked all the way home. I think we both felt a little like Hansel and Gretel ourselves: lost children in a fearful place, thankful for the comfort of each other.

It's one of the most wonderful conversations I can remember. And I still have the picnic basket she gave me.

My experience in the Black Forest was similar to the experience that Solomon and Shulamith have when she invites him to go into the country with her for a delightful picnic. They enjoy the enchantment of new surroundings, a beautiful world of verbal intimacy, and a feeling of belonging and familiarity. But in addition, Solomon and Shulamith share the special intimacy of lovers.

Shulamith surprises Solomon early one morning as he works. The weather is warmer, so she's dressed lightly and is playfully seductive. She leans forward so he can feel her warm breath on his ear when she makes her erotic proposal.

Shulamith

7. 11 Come,

> my beloved.

> Let us go out into the countryside.

> Let us spend the night among the henna blossoms.

12 Let us rise early to the vineyards.

> Let us see if the vine has budded,

its blossoms have opened,

> the pomegranates have bloomed.

There I will give my love to you.

13 The mandrakes send out their fragrance,

and at our doors are delicious fruits,

> both new and old,

which I have kept for you,

> my beloved.

In courtship Solomon had come bounding on the hills, inviting Shulamith outside to enjoy a spring day. Now it's her turn. She invites him to spend the night among the henna blossoms, to rise early and go to the vineyards, and in the midst of pomegranates and mandrakes, to make love in the beauty of spring.

Mandrake plants, like pomegranates, were well-known symbols of fertility and sexual love. Persephone, the goddess of spring, was symbolized by the pomegranate. Aphrodite, the goddess of love, was called "Lady of the Mandrake." Shulamith playfully pretends to be a goddess of spring love, offering Solomon the choice fruits she has prepared for him.

Perhaps in the privacy of her home, she pretended to be a sex goddess of their culture, much like a young woman today might teasingly pretend to be a contemporary sex symbol—women to whom much of our society attributes ideal sexuality and attractiveness. In the past these qualities were attributed to the gods of myth and song.

Shulamith longs to see if the vine has budded and its blossoms opened. The possibility of flowers in bloom not only discloses the time of year—the transition from winter to spring—but a new spring in their relationship too.

"Delicious fruits" echoes the description of the delights of her body enjoyed by Solomon on their wedding night. But the development of their relationship is unveiled in the description of these fruits she has saved for her husband—new and old. *New* refers literally to the fresh fruits of the new spring; *old* indicates the dried fruits of the previous spring. Shulamith poetically expresses her desire to give love freshly and creatively, yet also in ways familiar and memorable. Their lovemaking is not monotonous. It's expressive of the vibrant character of their intimacy.

Her teasing play on words is as creative as the lovemaking she promises, provocatively revealing her desire to entice Solomon to come with her. At our doors, she says, are erotic fruits. But the word for *doors* is also the word for *openings,* a variation in the form she has used to describe the opening of blossoms in the previous lyric. She uses this term instead of the more common one for *door* so she can give it an erotic double meaning. But she also infuses it with beauty, having just used it to portray the opening of flowers in spring. It's a lovely depiction of her sexuality—blossoms unfolding, revealing treasures of delicious fruit.

And to heighten Solomon's interest even further, Shulamith gives double meaning to the word for *kept*, which also means *hidden*. She beckons her beloved, telling him she has all kinds of choice fruits, which she has hidden and kept for him. She not only has the old fruits she has kept for him but also the new fruits she has hidden from him. Shulamith has surprises in store that Solomon no doubt tries to imagine. I think he packed his suitcase faster than a schoolboy dashing out for summer vacation.

Couples who experience boredom in their emotional intimacy will soon experience boredom in their physical intimacy as well. But when each continues to delight in the other, they will enjoy the same creative pleasures Shulamith promises Solomon. Love from the heart can express itself in many ways, and one of those ways is through sexual love.

Great love includes not only passionate romance but also heartfelt friendship. In my collage of impressionist images, one of my favorites of friendship comes from Norway.

One of my best friends invited me to her family reunion there. We met in Oslo, then journeyed to a small village from which her father's family had come. Norwegian names sometimes sound strange to me, and her last name was one of those unusual ones. In fact, I had never met anyone with her last name before—or anyone quite like her, either.

I knew I had entered a different world when I came to a quaint Norwegian farming community and half the people I met shared my friend's last name. We toured the area for several days, and I met scores of her relatives from the United States and Norway. They were an accomplished group of doctors, ministers, musicians, and educators.

The Norwegians appeared to me to be an adventurous people. My friend's father, a retired surgeon, had flown a single-engine plane alone to the reunion, skipping along from Michigan to Canada to Iceland to Ireland and on to Norway, just for the challenge and excitement of it.

I've never met a more interesting family, but my friend was to me the most interesting of all. She was brilliant without being pretentious. She was articulate. Yet the most attractive things about her were her integrity and kindness.

We had a similar curiosity about life, so we loved discovering the history of Norway and the legacy of her family in particular as we toured the central region of the country that summer week.

I have numerous snapshots in my mind of being in Norway together, but one stands out. Many of her relatives stayed in homes provided by the families that still lived in the original village. The houses were filled to the brim. And her relatives seemed to think that since she and I were such good friends, we must also be romantically involved—an opinion no amount of disclaimer on our part could sway. So on the plausible grounds of overcrowding and the suspicion that we secretly would prefer it, the family lodged us in the same quarters.

Romantic spirit met Norwegian propriety, however, and the uneasy compromise was narrow bunk beds in a room sandwiched between the rooms where my friend's father and uncle slept.

But it didn't matter to us, and we were amused by the attention given the arrangement. My favorite memory of our friendship, however, comes from this room. I slept on the bottom bunk and she on the top one. We talked late into the night. We discussed all we had seen in Norway and spoke of things at home in the States. We also talked about her boyfriend, about whom she could never quite make up her mind what to do, and about a girl I was dating back home. I've never felt more like I had a sister my age and temperament with whom I could share practically anything.

In the Song, Solomon and Shulamith experience this profound friendship too. But theirs culminates in open and intimate sexual passion.

❧❖☙

Breaking away from the palace has been wonderful—as refreshing as a shower under a waterfall. Now it is early evening. Shulamith and Solomon walk hand in hand as she leans upon him. She is anxious for the privacy of their bedroom, where she can express her affection. Then she has a playful thought:

> 8.1 Oh that you were like a brother to me,
> who nursed at the breasts of my mother.
> Then if I found you outside,
> I would kiss you,
> and no one would scorn me.
> 2 I would lead you to the house of my mother.
> You would instruct me.
> I would let you drink
> from the wine—the spiced wine—
> from the sweet wine of my pomegranate.
> 3 Oh, may his left hand be under my head
> and his right hand embrace me.

Public romantic affection was evidently frowned upon in that culture. But Shulamith wouldn't have to wait for privacy to express affection if Solomon were a brother by birth. She could kiss him in public, and no one would disapprove.

If Solomon were her younger brother, she says, "I would lead you to the house of my mother." The word translated *lead* was typically used for something like a general leading his army, a king directing his captain, or a shepherd leading his sheep. At the beginning of their courtship, Shulamith had asked Solomon to draw her after him. But now she reverses the roles and draws him after her. The princess amusingly assumes the role of older sister. She would lead her younger brother to their common home.

Romantic couples exhibit this kind of playfulness in many ways. I saw it once when I went driving through the mountains near Santa Fe, New Mexico, joined by a young woman with whom I had hoped to form a lasting relationship. We had difficulty finding time to be together, so I looked forward to talking as we traveled the long, scenic route.

As we drove down a mountain pass and the valley below opened before us, we saw that a herd of cattle had come through a broken fence.

My companion asked me to stop the car so she could chase the cows. "You can't chase the cows," I said. "Besides, you're not dressed for it. You'll scratch your legs in the high grass."

"But I've never chased cows before," she replied.

"For good reason," I answered.

"But I want to chase the cows now," she insisted.

"Why do you want to chase cows?" I asked foolishly.

"Because I've never done it before, and it will be fun."

"You've never jumped off a cliff either, and you don't want to do that."

"Of course not," she said. "That wouldn't be *fun*."

I would never win this one. In fact, I had clearly lost. "OK." I gave in and pulled over.

She was wearing a broad-brimmed straw hat, a blue blouse, white shorts, sandals, and sunglasses. I can still see her holding onto her hat and chasing those cows—stopping to take off her sandals so she could run faster, then tiring and walking back to the car.

I took a picture of her holding her hat on her head as she strolled back. She looked like a Hollywood star on a Western set: lovely, glamorous, and smiling triumphantly after the brave chase. I loved her free, spirited playfulness and told myself that even if she and I didn't eventually marry, I hoped to find that spirit in my life partner.

Shulamith displays this kind of spontaneous, joyful spirit in her relationship with Solomon. After she pretends to lead him to the home where they lived together as children, she says that rather than her teaching him, he will teach her. And since this teacher is also her husband and lover, she offers an erotic incentive: "I would let you drink from the wine—the spiced wine—from the sweet wine of my pomegranate."

She continues her playfulness in the word for *drink,* since it is precisely like the word for *kiss* in her previous lyric—differing only in the way it's pronounced. The princess also portrays her pomegranate as a chalice of wine, twice using *from* to draw attention to the imagery of drinking out of it: "from the wine…from the sweet wine." This fruit, of course, has represented the sensual delights of her body throughout the Song. Her body is a paradise of pomegranates; her kisses are like the sliced opening of this luscious fruit.

So Shulamith offers to let Solomon drink, with the transparent flirtation to let him kiss, from the chalice of her body.

I envision her with a teasingly seductive smile, looking out at Solomon from the top of her eyes and suggestively whispering to him, "I would let you drink from the wine—the spiced wine—from the sweet wine of my pomegranate." And he interprets her artistic and sensual poetry to mean, "Let my body be your wine chalice; drink kisses wherever you wish."

Since this chalice is filled with excellent wine, spiced and sweet, she has invited him to be a connoisseur of its delicacy. She wants him to drink slowly, each kiss like a sip; to completely enjoy; and to drink fully, inhaling her fragrance and tasting her skin, until passion intoxicates them both in dizzying, swirling desire.

Shulamith evidently intends her poetic invitation to include the most intimate of these kisses. Doesn't the image of drinking from the chalice of wine resume Solomon's image of drinking wine from her navel like a "round chalice?" The subtle change in Shulamith's description of the pomegranate suggests this.

She refers to "my pomegranate" for the first time, and to its juice as wine spiced and sweet. The pomegranate was a common symbol of lovemaking in the ancient world because of its apparent fertility. The apple, for a contrasting example, has a tiny cluster of seeds in its center; but the pomegranate is completely filled with them. Its hundreds of shining, ruby seeds, transparently cloaked in delicious juice, suggest new life and the lovemaking that precedes it.

The pomegranate no doubt alludes to all of Shulamith's sexual charms. But since its erotic symbolism arises from its abundance of seeds, and Shulamith refers to her personal source of this symbol, it seems likely that "my pomegranate" includes her abdomen among those charms. The fruit's nectar is then not only the wine of her kisses but the spiced, sweet wine of her sexual arousal.

If so, then the image of this fruit has evolved in the Song like the lotus flower. The lotus first described Shulamith herself. Next it was the place where Solomon grazed like a gazelle, its blossoms first surrounding her breasts, then her hips and navel. In a similar transformation, the pomegranate sliced open was likened to the taste of her kisses. Many pomegranates were compared with her entire body. Now her single pomegranate is also in the lotus blossoms encircling the bread and wine of her abdomen.

Such intimate kissing likely explains why Shulamith expects some would disapprove of it. She first wishes to kiss Solomon in public without scorn from others. But that anticipates her climactic proposal for erotic kisses in private, without scorn. In the style of the Song's poetic lyrics, the desire to kiss in public without disapproval implicitly requests acceptance for the most intimate kissing as well.

The first wish also recalls the reason for such acceptance to be granted. If Solomon were like a natural brother, she would be free to kiss him in public. Now that he is her "brother" by marriage—he called her "my sister, my bride" on the wedding night—they should be free to kiss as intimately as they please when alone.

This playful, innocent love is as much a return to paradise as anything else in the Song. Just like the pristine lovers in the first garden, Solomon and Shulamith are naked and unashamed in their sexual celebration.

Still, they experience their openness in joyful, gradual progression. During courtship Shulamith had longed for Solomon's affection but expressed it first only to herself. On the wedding night, she spoke just once in their poetry of passion. Yet later she can finish his sentences falling asleep in his arms, invite him to make love among the flowers of the countryside, or make this playful, erotic invitation.

Now she longs for him to respond to her sensual flirtation: "May his left hand be under my head and his right hand embrace me," she whispers in her heart. After all the play, she wants him to place his hand under her head, lie down beside her, and make love.

❧✳❧

Shulamith knows her husband as brother, teacher, lover, and friend. The easy transition from one role to the next in these lyrics implies a sensitivity and responsiveness that enable each to meet the other's particular need of the moment.

Great lovers realize that sometimes their partner needs a friend to share the experience of chasing cows. Other times they may need a brother or sister to talk with, like on a picnic during the day or on bunk beds at night. And sometimes they want to experience familiarity and playfulness in their sexual love.

These fortunate couples describe an experience of deep friendship, childlike play, and liberating freedom. It is a freedom, they say, that allows them not only to be who they really are, but also to become who they most want to be—and to do so while maintaining a heartfelt oneness with their mate on every level.

Such companions seem to have much of what others have only in part. I caught glimpses of such riches in the mountains of Santa Fe, in the rugged interior of Norway, and in the enchantment of the Black Forest. Intimate lovers, however, create a world more beautiful than these—one that the land and sea only faintly reflect.

Love is not love

Which alters when it alteration finds,…

O no! it is an ever-fixed mark

That looks on tempests and is never shaken;…

Love's not Time's fool, though rosy lips and cheeks

Within his bending sickle's compass come:

Love alters not with his brief hours and weeks,

But bears it out even to the edge of doom.

If this be error and upon me prov'd,

I never writ, nor no man ever lov'd.

—WILLIAM SHAKESPEARE (1564–1616)
 Sonnet CXVI

Devotion and Fire

How could I have known that one of the most profound lessons I would learn about love would come from eavesdropping on a conversation between my camp counselor and one of the high-school students in our cabin? The message earlier that evening from the head counselor had been about sex. The gist of it, as I recall, was that sex was not an evil that marriage permitted, but rather a gift that marriage protected. That sounds good now. But we mostly interpreted it as further efforts on the part of the staff to discourage any questionable activities between the boys and girls at the camp.

But one of the guys in the cabin was a little disturbed. I heard him address our counselor with a slight challenge in his voice: "Well, John, it's a little late for me to hear that message."

"Why is that?"

"Well, Sharon and I have already…you know…"

"'You know,' what?" the counselor asked.

"We, uh, you know—went all the way," the student said, speeding up his words at the end but expressing himself with a hint of pride.

"What do you mean, 'all the way'?" John pressed, drawing out the last phrase as if to make up for the speed with which it had been uttered. I couldn't believe the counselor was so dense. *What was he thinking?*

"You know, *all the way,*" the boy stressed, as if saying it with emphasis would clarify the meaning.

But the counselor didn't let him off the hook. "No, I don't know what you mean. What are you talking about?"

"You know, we had sex!" he blurted out, exasperated.

"Ohhhhh, *that's* what you mean," John said with a show of surprise. "And you think that's going all the way?"

"Well, yes."

"That's not going all the way at all," he explained. "I'll tell you what going all the way is. There's a guy in my neighborhood who has five kids, and his wife is now in a wheelchair. He gets the kids off to school each morning, sells insurance all day to make a living, then comes home and makes dinner for the family. And at the end of the evening, he looks his wife in the eye and tells her he loves her. I know he means it, too, because he tells me he's the luckiest guy he knows to have been blessed with her. *That's* what going all the way is."

I was stunned by the counselor's response. But Solomon and Shulamith wouldn't have been. They would have simply nodded their heads in agreement. Their love gave birth to this kind of devotion. They began in excitement and grew in devotion—through all the difficulties of life.

Shulamith and Solomon emerge happily from the privacy of the wilderness, his arm securely around her. They have made love, talked for long hours, and enjoyed peaceful silence. As they leave their enchanted world, the princess enthusiastically advises others to seize the opportunity for genuine love when it appears. Then they express passionate commitment to each other.

Shulamith

8.4 I want you to promise me,

O young women of Jerusalem,

that you will surely arouse, you will surely awaken love

when love pleases to awaken.

Songwriter

8.5 Who is this coming from the wilderness,

leaning on her beloved?

Shulamith

8.5 Under the apple tree I awakened you.

There your mother was in labor with you;

there she was in labor and gave you birth.

6 Make me a seal upon your heart,

a seal upon your arm,

because love is strong as death,

fervent love as relentless as the grave;

its flashes are flashes of fire,

the flame of the Lord.

7 Many waters cannot extinguish love,

and rivers will not drown it.

If a man offered all the possessions of his house for love,

they would utterly scorn him.

During courtship Shulamith twice counseled patience in their intensifying relationship. "Wait until the time is right," she seemed to be saying. "Don't try to force love before it's ready. Be as sensitive as a gazelle to the timing of love."

But she has also seen that when love is ready to awaken, it should be awakened! On their wedding night, she asked the winds to draw Solomon to the garden of her body to enjoy her. On a later night, when Solomon longed to be with her, she learned the pain of turning away love. Rather than awaken it, she had chosen to let it sleep.

Yes, Shulamith knows that waiting is necessary. But so is responsiveness to love's call. Thus she transforms her counsel of patience into counsel to respond: "Promise me...that you will surely arouse, you will surely awaken love when love pleases to awaken."

The princess had already hinted at this, of course. "Don't waken love until it is ready" implies "Do waken love when it is." Now she advises directly not to be so cautious that you let the rare and special moments of love pass you by. Shulamith knows that life offers no guarantees. You never know if the chance for love will come your way again, so respond to the opportunities you have.

No wonder she offers that wisdom at this moment in the Song. She has just depicted the joys of true love. She is about to describe its fire and devotion. Now is a perfect time to encourage us to open our hearts to love when the time is right. But what is this love like?

True love grows through the hardships of life. "Who is this coming from the wilderness, leaning on her beloved?" the songwriter asks. This scene recalls the historical foundation of their nation, when the people emerged from the wilderness newly dependent on the God who had brought them through the pain and hardship they experienced there.

This picture reminds us that traveling through difficulties, including places like Mahanaim, has brought Solomon and Shulamith into the maturity of their relationship.

True love begins with mutual delight. "Under the apple tree I awakened you," Shulamith says to Solomon. "There your mother was in labor with you; there she was in labor and gave you birth." Twice the princess has cautioned others not to awaken love until it pleases to awaken. But evidently she awakened love when she awakened Solomon under the apple tree.

Shulamith is alluding to their courtship, when their escalating dance of praise culminated in her appreciation of Solomon's protective care under the apple tree. Their love had begun when they recognized each other as uniquely special: She was like "a lotus flower among thorns"; he was like "an apple tree among the trees of the forest." At that moment in the Song, they knew their love was mutual.

True love can journey with the companion of pain. Shulamith reminds Solomon that he was born under the same symbolic tree as was their love. She is inviting a comparison of the two births. And she implies, since she repeats it twice, that the point of comparison rests in his mother's pain of labor.

Solomon's mother suffered pain in giving birth to her son. Solomon's wife suffered the pain of waiting and hardship in giving birth to her love relationship with him. If this begins a definition of love, the first point is that devotion occurs in the midst of pain. But the analogy reminds us that it is the fruitful pain of birth.

The mention of Solomon's mother introduces another famous person in the couple's literature and history. Solomon's mother was Bathsheba. And if ever a woman knew about the pain of love, she did.

She had been happily married. Not without problems, of course. Her husband was not a native of their country, so she may have felt outside the mainstream of social life. But his tender love and affection were more than sufficient to make up for it. One contemporary of theirs observed that her husband's care was like a poor man's nurturing of his one lamb, which was adored like a pet. The poor man treasured that lamb more than a rich man enjoyed vast flocks.

And Bathsheba loved him too. She was proud of her husband's character and bravery. He was loyal to his friends and fellow soldiers, never shirking his duty. Though he was a foreigner, he was widely respected.

But one day that world came crashing down. Solomon's father, King

David, saw Bathsheba and wanted her. In a selfish and egregious abuse of power, he slept with her, then sent her home dishonored and demeaned. And pregnant.

The king first attempted to conceal his treachery by bringing Bathsheba's husband home from military duty, hoping he would sleep with her. But the loyal warrior refused to enjoy the love of his wife out of respect for his fellow soldiers, still fighting.

Desperate, David arranged to have the man killed in battle, in such a way that he would appear to be a casualty of war. The plan succeeded. Bathsheba's honorable and tender husband was killed. And she mourned.

She mourned again not long after, when the baby David had fathered died. *What happened to the simplicity and love I once had?* she must have thought. *It's all gone. Forever.* Love is difficult to find and difficult to maintain—so many ways to get it wrong, and few opportunities to get it right.

She went on, probably numbly at first, but then with some awareness, and finally with the capacity to feel more deeply again. She found a measure of happiness in the birth of her second son—Solomon. Bathsheba felt hope again as she watched him play as a child, then mature into a handsome and competent young man. She was actually happy again. And as the years went by, she also began to love David— and he grew to love her as well, the pain and shame of the past receding like distant clouds whose rain has been long forgotten.

David had suffered terribly from his treachery with her, had agonized over his guilt, and eventually had come to terms with God about it. And Bathsheba respected him for that, even though he was still by no means perfect.

Then David died, and she mourned that loss too. But Solomon was still the joy of her life. And when she placed the wedding crown on his head on the happiest day of his life, surely her heart overflowed with happiness too. Out of all the pain and confusion of love gone wrong had come this beloved son who was king.

So when Shulamith compares the pain of love with the pain of Solomon's birth, she is well aware that love can bring incredible pain. But sometimes it is the pain of birth—the birth of a relationship, the birth of understanding, and the birth of forgiveness.

It seems impossible that in the Song, just two lyrics prior to this one about the pain of birth, Shulamith had made one of the most delightful, erotic promises of the entire Song—a playful promise filled with uninhibited freedom and pleasure. Is there a lesson in its close proximity to this observation about the pain of love? Perhaps what Shulamith would want us to see is that even the journey to the greatest pleasures is not without difficulties and sorrows along the way.

True love is constant and strong. Shulamith requests that Solomon make her a seal upon his heart and upon his arm. The seal, as we learned earlier, was valuable because it was the signature of its owner. With it he could identify all he owned and verify all he said. He regarded it as a possession from which he should never part. Shulamith desires to be the most important person in Solomon's life, from whom he would never part.

Solomon's heart is the source of his love, which is "as relentless as the grave." Just as the grave will never give up the dead, so he will never give up Shulamith. The heart, strongly and steadily beating, day by day, in sickness and in health, through every season, is the picture of his constant love.

His protective arm represents strength—strength as mighty as death. Just as death always prevails over mortal bodies, so the power of his love will always protect her. And just as death holds on to those it claims, so his love will never relinquish its caring for her.

In the beginning of their courtship, Solomon was like a pouch of myrrh on Shulamith's heart; now she is like a seal on his. She had cherished her thoughts about him, which had risen from her heart, more than anything in the world. Now Solomon cherishes Shulamith like a seal upon his heart—as the most important person in the world to him.

What a contrast to the sad story of Tamar, who had to trick her father-in-law into providing for her. When Judah thought she was a prostitute, he promised a young goat as payment and gave her his seal only to hold until his payment arrived.

The Song of Songs provides a poetic contrast to that story. Solomon does not offer some token gift to Shulamith. He gives himself as an oasis in her desert. He does not loan his seal to her; she *is* the seal over his heart.

True love is from the source of all fire. Shulamith says their fervent love is like "flashes of fire." This is the opposite of apathy. Neither of them is indifferent toward the other, but rather each longs for the best the other can experience. And this burning desire never ends.

She calls this fire "the flame of the Lord" and claims that those who experience it reflect the character of the One who is the eternal source of all love. In describing this passionate flame, Shulamith adds, "Many waters cannot extinguish love, and rivers will not drown it." Neither the waters of time nor a flood of problems can extinguish it. Its ultimate source is eternal.

When the Song presents Solomon and Shulamith emerging from the wilderness, it paints their relationship against the background of their nation's experience with God in the wilderness. Both the nation and Shulamith have learned through their difficulties.

Now Shulamith sets the flame of Solomon's love against the background of the nation again. The dangerous waters allude to famous events from the past: the triumph over the universal waters at creation; the rescue of Noah from the flood; the deliverance of the Israelites through the Red Sea.

Shulamith believes that the fire of her and Solomon's love is from the same powerful flame of God that conquered the waters of chaos, stopped the raging flood, and pushed back the Red Sea. In the beginning the

Spirit of God hovered like a dove over the waters that covered the earth. The Great Artist painted the canvas of the land, wrote the music of the sky, and set the stage for human drama so that one day the world would reflect the one who shaped it.

Solomon's love for Shulamith is a picture in miniature of this loving creation. Alone by streams of water, his eyes like doves at last look into the tranquil waters of the world he and she have made, and in the center of this new creation are her eyes, like doves, looking back.

Their ancient literature describes an encounter between a great leader and the source of love's eternal flame. When Moses saw a burning bush, he was astonished because the easily combustible branches were not consumed. He was awestruck by this energy that could blaze on without fuel.

No wonder Shulamith believes the love she shares with Solomon will never end. If it comes from the source of all fire, how could it ever burn out?

True love is two priceless gifts. Shulamith avows, "If a man offered all the possessions of his house for love, they would utterly scorn him."

Any attempt to buy love invites scorn. It displays ignorance of the nature of love, since no one can buy or sell the inner feelings from which love comes. It shows insensitivity to the one being propositioned, since it requests selling the privilege of love for a mere pretense of it. And it reveals disrespect for oneself, since it would deprive even the potential purchaser of life's greatest gift.

The Song has already shown us in part why no one can put a price tag on love. In courtship Shulamith and Solomon were like doves in the houses of nature. In the house of wine, his love was as conspicuous as a banner, making her faint from love. Such houses of love are worth far more than any literal house full of possessions.

But if you cannot give all the wealth of your house to gain love, is there anything you can give to attain it?

There is. But it's much more costly than the sum of one's possessions. It is the gift of oneself. Solomon and Shulamith gained love only when he gave himself to her and she gave herself to him in return.

Two priceless gifts made one priceless love.

My camp counselor was right. Going all the way is a lot more than having sex.

It begins with delight in the whole person and in the gift of each to the other. It matures through the journey of life, with the heart of love beating constant and strong. And it reflects the One who is the source of all fire.

I saw this kind of love when my mother was seriously ill. Dad rose early every morning to begin caring for her. He provided every healthy food, supplement, or medicine that might improve her health. And his tender nursing continued throughout the day, my brothers and sister and I helping under his guidance and direction. His gentle touch, his anguished concern, and his daily sacrifice to ease her pain never ceased.

Neither did her love for him, even during the almost unbearable pain of her illness. A friend once offered to come by to pray with us. He's a wonderful, vibrant African-American, which I mention only to explain in part why he reminds me of the deeply spiritual black man in *The Green Mile*. This friend's presence is always a blessing.

I asked Mother when a good time would be for him to come see us. Barely able to speak, she whispered to me as I leaned my ear close to her: "Ask him to come when your father returns from the store. I don't want your dad to miss seeing him."

Nothing could extinguish the flame of their love for each other.

Thou lovely and beloved, thou my love;

Whose kiss seems still the first; whose

   summoning eyes,

Even now, as for our love-world's new sunrise,

Shed very dawn; whose voice, attuned above

All modulation of the deep-bowered dove,

   Is like a hand laid softly on the soul....

—DANTE GABRIEL ROSSETTI (1828–1882)
   Sonnet XXVI: "Mid-Rapture"

Hope and Fulfillment

On Thanksgiving Day several years ago, we were in my parents' living room by the fireplace. My children and their cousins were scattered about the house. It was time to reminisce.

"What do you remember?" my brother asked.

"About growing up?" I asked.

"Yes, about Mom and Dad and growing up."

"Well, a lot is fuzzy. I remember playing sports. School is a blur. Summers in Georgia were great."

"No, tell me some things in particular that were important to you, about Mom and Dad."

I thought a moment as images began coming into focus. "I remember Dad on the sidelines of the football field. And not just for the games. Every practice! Then afterward he and I always played catch in the front yard until it was dark."

"How about Mom?"

"I remember something at my ninth birthday party. I was standing by the front porch, catching my breath from playing tag with the other kids, when Mom walked over and knelt beside me."

"Do you see Bill?" she asked, pointing to a kid standing alone by the elm tree, beyond the mimosa tree I had climbed when I was five.

"Sure."

"Do you *really* see him?" she asked. I didn't know what she meant. But then she opened my eyes: "How would you like it if you were at a birthday party and no one was playing with you?"

"I guess I'd feel bad."

"Why don't you go talk to him, then?" she suggested.

"That's the day Bill and I became friends," I told my brother.

Some of our older kids drifted into the living room. Then Mom and Dad came in, and my other brother and my sister, and we all shared stories. That Thanksgiving afternoon was as warm as the colors of autumn. Through the living-room window, I could see the elm that still stood where Bill had been alone years earlier and where Dad and I had played catch after every practice. For me it's a memorial to the compassion I learned from my mother and the companionship I shared with my father.

Solomon and Shulamith must have enjoyed family reunions too. I can picture them in these next few lyrics at one of their own. Cousins, aunts, uncles, and brothers-in-law—they all mix and mingle as children play and food is served. Soon Solomon and Shulamith drift over to where her brothers are sitting, and the stories start to flow about when the king's bride was merely their little sister. The brothers remember how they had taken care of Shulamith after their father died.

Brothers of Shulamith

8.8 We have a little sister,

    and she has no breasts.

  What shall we do to prepare our sister

    for the day on which she is spoken for?

9 If she is a wall,

    we shall build upon her an embankment of silver.

  If she is a door,

    we shall enclose her with planks of cedar.

The Song's opening lyrics mentioned these brothers and described Shulamith's work in the vineyards. Now the concluding lyrics return to that setting.

"We have a little sister, and she has no breasts," they recall to the group, almost embarrassing Shulamith about her childhood figure. But on that day in the past, her brothers had wanted to teach her lessons that would stand like the elm tree and prepare her for marriage. "What shall we do to prepare our sister for the day on which she is spoken for?" they recall asking themselves.

They resolved to reward her for good choices: "If she is a wall, we shall build upon her an embankment of silver." And they determined to restrict her freedom if she exercised poor judgment: "If she is a door, we shall enclose her with planks of cedar."

A door provides access; a wall prohibits it. The brothers encourage a "wall" between her and young men until she's ready for marriage. And if she's tempted to be too open, they'll step in to board up the door to a freedom she isn't ready to handle. They wanted her to be "a garden locked... a fountain sealed," for which Solomon praised her on the wedding night.

One of Shulamith's most treasured childhood memories is of a family that cared for her.

If her brothers have any mischievous hopes of embarrassing Shulamith with the reminder of her childhood figure, they've forgotten what a confident, playful woman she has become. The woman who confidently walked past Solomon's friends like a mare among Pharaoh's stallions is not bashful. So, like at most family gatherings where stories are a kind of free-for-all, Shulamith jumps into the fray.

Shulamith

8.10　I was a wall,

　　　　and my breasts were like towers.

"I was a fortress wall—not a door," she interrupts them.

Then *she* embarrasses *them:* "And my breasts became like towers on that wall." I picture Solomon roaring with laughter at his wife's quick wit and her brothers' shocked expressions as they quickly look away and start poking at their food.

Even before the laughter settles, Shulamith's thoughts shift from the brothers and her upbringing to when Solomon first saw her in the full bloom of womanhood. As if everyone else has suddenly vanished, her eyes rest on her beloved, and her words convey the excitement of a story she will never tire of telling.

Shulamith

8.10 Then I became in his eyes
        as one who finds fulfillment.

"Then I met Solomon!" she exclaims. "He found me, and I found fulfillment." I can imagine her looking tenderly at Solomon and whispering to him, "All my hopes and dreams I've found in you."

If the brothers are uncomfortable with this expression of love, they're about to become even more uneasy. Shulamith reminds them of the circumstances in which she met Solomon.

8.11 A vineyard belonged to Solomon
        at the Place of Plenty.

      He gave the vineyard to caretakers;
        each one was to bring for its fruit
          a thousand shekels of silver.

   12 "My own vineyard,
        which belongs to me,
          lies before me.

      The thousand are for you,
        O Solomon,
          and two hundred for the caretakers of the fruit."

At the beginning of the Song, Shulamith said her brothers had treated her harshly, making her caretaker of the vineyards. Now we learn that these vineyards really belonged to Solomon and had been leased from him by her brothers. They were under contract to bring Solomon, the owner, a thousand shekels of silver for the harvest, and like all such vineyard keepers, they counted on selling the harvest for more than the cost of the lease.

Next Shulamith recounts the occasion on which she said yes to Solomon's proposal of marriage. She remembers her inner struggle: *My own vineyard, which belongs to me, lies before me,* she thought. No matter how many vineyards Solomon owned, he didn't own her. Her love was hers to give or hers to keep.

And it lies before me, she affirmed to herself. Her entire life lay before her. That one decision would risk so much, change so much, hopefully bring so much. In her heart she heard *yes* growing louder until a resounding, beautiful *Yes!* burst out to her beloved: "The thousand are for you, O Solomon."

Shulamith is the owner of the vineyard that is her life, and she is due a thousand shekels of silver by analogy to the literal vineyards. But in telling Solomon he should receive the thousand for her vineyard, she shows she has given herself to him.

As Shulamith remembers this thrilling moment in her life, the forks become still and the brothers become noticeably uncomfortable. Their harshness had made her caretaker of the vineyards, forcing her to work long hours with no time for herself. Now she's in a position of power, second only to the king. Did she harbor a grudge toward them after all this time? One word from her, one negative comment about their earlier treatment of her, and they knew they'd face the anger not only of a brother-in-law but of a king.

Perhaps Shulamith senses their momentary uncertainty, since she quickly puts an end to their possible anxiety: "and two hundred [shekels] for the caretakers of the fruit." Her brothers cared for her as a child, and like caretakers of literal vineyards, they should be rewarded. What a gentle way to assure them of her forgiveness. She has left their mistreatment of her in the past, wishing only blessings on them in the future.

As Shulamith's family reunion mellows into the late afternoon, I can picture a brother off by himself, leisurely re-reading some of the favorite stories in their literature. Suddenly it dawns on him from what source Shulamith has drawn encouragement to be forgiving toward him and his brothers.

Her life had been like Joseph's! He, too, had been mistreated by his brothers, but he forgave them and later provided for them. And he was able to do so because he recognized that God had been taking care of him through all the hardship, working to accomplish the best for him and his family. Shulamith must have sensed the same hidden guidance in her meeting Solomon: It might never have happened if the brothers hadn't sent her to the vineyards.

When Shulamith's brother looks across the room at his sister, he realizes at least one reason she smiles so confidently. She feels God's care and direction in her life.

As her brother continues browsing through his favorite stories, he realizes that Shulamith's life also resembles that of Ruth. After Shulamith's father died, Shulamith had worked in the vineyards, unable to have a life for herself—just as Ruth, after the death of her husband, found herself humbly seeking leftover grain in someone else's fields. But like Ruth had found favor in the eyes of Boaz, Shulamith has found love in the eyes of Solomon. And both Ruth and Shulamith had been raised to places of honor by their new husbands.

Shulamith perhaps entertains similar thoughts as she sits smiling and half-listening to the stories shared around her.

She realizes that a common thread links her to the men and women of history to which the Song sometimes alludes. At one time they *all* felt unlikely to find love.

Tamar's husband had died, and she was driven to play the role of a prostitute. Rahab was a prostitute with little or no hope. Ruth's husband had died, and she was forced into poverty. And, of course, Bathsheba had had a beautiful love stolen from her and seemed destined for a life of grief.

The men had little hope either. Ruth's husband, Boaz, considered himself too old; Bathsheba's husband, David, felt too unworthy; Shulamith's husband, Solomon, seemed too hardened.

But God, Shulamith realizes, takes great delight in bringing love to those least expecting it.

As she contemplates God's guiding hand, she feels the sense of destiny that lovers often describe. The song "After All" captures this wonderful assurance.

> After all the stops and starts,
>> We keep coming back to these two hearts,
>> Two angels who've been rescued from the fall,
> And after all that we've been through,
>> It all comes down to me and you,
>> I guess it's meant to be,
> Forever you and me,
>> After all.

As their family reunion draws to a close, Solomon and Shulamith begin gathering their things. They kiss the children and hug their adult relatives, then walk hand in hand from the place where Shulamith grew up. Solomon has fond memories of his times there. It seems like just yesterday when he took Shulamith from her home during their courtship to enjoy a perfect spring day.

Now, as they walk in silent contentment, each reflects on the day and remembers the joys they've shared. Many seasons have passed since the beginning of their relationship. But their feelings have only grown deeper, like streams becoming a river.

Solomon

8.13 You who dwell in the gardens,

> with close friends listening attentively to your voice,

>> let me hear you.

Shulamith

8.14 Hurry,

> my beloved,

and be like a gazelle

> or a young stag

>> on the mountains of spices.

Solomon's last words echo a desire he whispered long ago. He likened Shulamith then to a bashful dove whose voice he yearned to hear. The voice of the dove was a love song of spring, as the voice of Shulamith was a love song to him, revealing the hidden beauty within her. He still longs, with the same intensity as in courtship, to enjoy the melody of her heart. "You who dwell in the gardens," he says, "let me hear you."

Shulamith's last words also ring with a desire first expressed on that past spring day. She longed then for the time Solomon would be like a gazelle on the divided mountains, the mountain of myrrh and hill of frankincense he caresses on their wedding night. She still longs with that same fervor to offer her fragrant breasts to him, like the invitation of a mountain meadow to a playful gazelle. "Hurry, my beloved," she urges him, "and be like a gazelle…on the mountains of spices."

Her voice is a song in the gardens, dovelike music in a paradise. When she sings from her heart, her words touch his heart, and the melody resonates through his soul.

His touch is a dance in the mountains, gazellelike delight in a wonderland of spice. When he loves from his heart, he touches her body but reaches her heart as the warmth radiates through her soul.

The voice of love. The touch of love.

Delight in the one follows the joy of the other in a rhythmic heartbeat of love. Love pulses life into the marrow of their souls. It's the wellspring that creates an oasis in the desert, and the fertile place that grows an apple tree in a forest. It is the mystical power that enlivens the gazelle and brings forth the lotus.

And it is the primordial power that makes two hearts sing as one in a song of love and beat as one in a dance of love.

Theories of love change with each new month's magazines. But the hearts of lovers remain the same. And since love songs arise from the heart, they reflect similar, beautiful themes—even if in different melodies from various times and places. So the love songs from all time speak to our hearts for all time.

I'm not surprised, then, that the song of Solomon and Shulamith speaks to us. It's fascinating, however, to realize also that our contemporary songs would speak to them. If they had been at the festival in Stockholm, "The Rose" and other songs might have mesmerized them with a medley of tunes telling their story.

Songs like "All by Myself" may have reminded Solomon of the days before he met Shulamith. The reference to the cruel sun in "It's All Coming Back to Me Now" might have evoked Shulamith's memories of working in the fields. The lyrics of "The First Time Ever I Saw Your Face" could have applied to the moment Solomon first saw Shulamith there.

Perhaps "Truly, Madly, Deeply" and "Through the Eyes of Love" would remind them of the happiness of courtship. And "All Out of Love" might remind them of the time love had waned in their marriage. "Everything I Do, I Do It for You" could express Solomon's assurance of love to Shulamith during that time. And wouldn't "My Heart Will Go On," the theme song of *Titanic,* express their lifelong devotion to each other?

As Shulamith and Solomon enjoyed these songs, the images of their past would swirl in memories of desire and delight—fruit trees and cedars, palm trees and wine, doves and gazelles, leopards and lions.

Lotus flowers and fortress towers, eyes like doves, mystical powers. Palaces and paradise; gardens and fountains; long, flowing hair; and spice-laden mountains.

Winters of longing and spring days of love, clusters of dates and clusters of grapes, lips dripping myrrh and breasts like young fawns, bodies of splendor and bodies aflame, with a fire flowing through them of love without end.

Unforgettable images. Irresistible beauty. Undeniable insight. The Song of Solomon and Shulamith.

Its melody lilts through the centuries, untouched by trend and time, to sing its song to us. It is a story of love to inspire us and a vision of love to guide us.

A gift from their hearts to ours.

Once upon a Song of Songs,

Soul touched soul when lovers kissed,

And winter blushed to spring.

Her eyes like his were doves in love,

And hearts like doves arose to sing

A Song of Solomon.

So gentle sounds caressed our dreams,

And wakened gentle wishes dreamed,

And when all hope was gone, it seemed,

Gave us the love that was our dream

From long ago,

When soul touched soul on lovers' lips,

And winter blushed to spring.

—CRAIG GLICKMAN
  "Once upon a Love Song"

Epilogue

Shulamith told us to seize the moment when love appears. The colonel certainly did so during World War II, and my father did the same. Even my five-year-plan friend found the courage when it seemed his chance had passed. But the moments don't last forever.

When I was a teenager, I learned how fragile those moments can be and that I must live them well. I was still enjoying the memories of my first picnic with the sophomore princess when a call woke me early on a Sunday morning.

"Where is she?"

"St. Paul's Hospital," he said.

"How bad is it?" I asked.

He hesitated. "I don't know."

"Is she going to die?"

"I don't know," he said.

I shuffled into the kitchen, and my family breakfast was a blur. I was too confused to talk when they asked what was wrong, so I retreated back to my room. After driving to the hospital and wandering from one information desk to the next, I found her room. Her parents were there, and other adults too, praying for her. That scared me—I had never seen so many adults praying who weren't in church.

I stood to the side and helplessly looked at the sophomore princess, immobile in the bed, in traction to relieve the pressure on her spinal cord that had been severed when the car flipped over. She would always be paralyzed, I later found out. She was like a beautiful flower with a broken stem.

A religious leader once told me I shouldn't wish anything were different about the past. But I sure wish that accident had never happened.

I also wish I had told her how beautiful she was when we were on that picnic. It didn't feel right to tell her after the accident, even though she was still beautiful, because I worried it might make her sad to think of the life she'd had before.

I would never have the opportunity to tell her at a picnic again. And the stars she would now set her eyes upon were in a world I couldn't yet see, where broken hearts are healed and broken bodies mended.

I know how a long time can seem like a moment, too, and how important it is to live that moment well. My father and mother loved each other for fifty-eight years. But even all that time seemed like too short a moment when she was gone.

Healthy and beautiful throughout her life, she looked as though she could live forever. But no one does, of course—not in this life, in these bodies.

She was diagnosed with cancer in the fall; she died in the spring.

The landscape of the world changed for all of us that day. At first the terrain looked like the wasteland from a forest fire, all bleak and ashen and empty. But just as the healing seasons restore life to the land, time has brought healing to us.

Many things will never be the same, of course. And certain things are still changing. Dad is learning to cook. That's sure different. And Mother is praying for us from a loftier place. That's different too.

But Dad's love for Mom isn't different.

I see it in his eyes when he looks at her pictures in that time-weathered album on the living-room table. I hear it in his voice when he tells his favorite stories about her and how they met. And I feel it in his heart, when he hugs me good-bye. That's a subtle thing. But his hugs are just a little bit longer than before. And I know that he's missing Mom then.

Last week when I checked in on Dad, he remarked that since it was getting colder with the approach of winter, he had made himself some chili.

"Dad, I didn't know you had learned to make Mother's recipe for chili," I replied, remembering how every winter she used to keep a plentiful supply for us.

"Well, I never *have* learned to make it." He hesitated.

"Last winter when she was still able to be up for a few hours a day, and we were all hoping and praying she'd pull through, one of the last things she did was fill up the freezer with it. Now that winter is coming on, I thought I would begin to thaw some."

When Dad sits at the kitchen table, as the steam rises from the chili, he eats in silence. But he savors the memories of Mother sitting there with him.

A long time can be like a moment. But lived well, that moment of love never ends, and the rivers of death do not extinguish its flame. "My Heart Will Go On" is not only the theme song from *Titanic*. All true lovers sing a song of a love that lasts forever—even beyond this life, when death has claimed the body but love has claimed the soul and gained the greater prize.

Most of us want to find the best of romantic love, but it's easy to lose our way. I've certainly lost direction at times in my life. And sometimes I've stumbled around in the darkness a long time trying to regain it. I'm thankful for the light of the Song that guides me back like a constellation of stars in the night.

Solomon and Shulamith provide that constellation. They give hope when I need to pick up the pieces and encouragement to resume the journey. When I look at them, I see stars to follow and a destination to seek.

I see emotional intimacy, sensitive communication, and delightful sexuality. I see profound companionship, common perspective, and willing forgiveness. I see respect, integrity, security. And I see love's devotion through bleak seasons of winter and love's renewal in new seasons of spring.

Those are some of the ideals that touch my heart most deeply.

But find the stars in the Song that touch your heart deeply. Let them inspire you and guide you. Measure your love by the ideals you treasure, and sing the Song's melody in your life more and more.

⌘

Even now it warms my heart to remember how Mother helped me reach out to Wendy. Mother helped compose the letter and stood under the tree in case I fell. And by secretly retrieving the letter, she let me glimpse the joy of knowing that the person I loved received a message from my heart.

The Song tells of a Great Songwriter who wants us to know the joy of love too—who wants us to reach out in love bravely; who stands by to catch us if we fall; and who yearns for us to know the heartfelt love of our dreams.

If you listen closely, you may hear his music, or even his voice, whispering hope on the way. In the sounds of the wind rustling leaves on a picnic, in the song of the wind whistling notes through the trees, in the breath of the wind bearing the fragrance of sea, you may sense him gently urging: *Fly on these winds. Fly like the doves, through the leaves, over trees and the sea. Let your heart feel the ways of love.*

Dear Reader,

If you'd like to explore the relationship between the Song of Songs and Christian faith, I encourage you to read my thoughts on that in the following appendix.

If you're curious about the discoveries that culminated in unlocking the meaning of the Song, then I recommend perusing the appendix on the design of the Song and the appendix on the translation. The notes to the translation will also give you more detailed explanations about my understanding of particular lyrics of the Song.

In any case, let's stay in touch.

If you have any comments about the book, I'd love to hear them. If the book inspires your own romantic story, I'd love to hear about that too.

And if you'd like to know about other books in the works or where I'll be speaking on the Song, I'll be glad to keep you informed.

You can reach me through my Web site, http://www. craigglickman.com/.

I hope you enjoyed the Song and that you sing its melody in your life.

Sincerely,
Craig Glickman

When we see the face of God

we shall know that we have always known it.

He has been…within,

all our earthly experiences of innocent love.

All that was true love in them was,

even on earth, far more His than ours,

and ours only because His.

—C. S. LEWIS (1898–1963)
   The Four Loves

APPENDIX A

The Song and Christian Faith

The Christian faith regards Old Testament literature as sacred, making the Song of Songs part of its Scripture. And although the teachings of the New Testament don't add a great deal to the understanding of romantic ideals, they certainly place them in a broader context. Perhaps more than any one teaching, Jesus' way of forgiving and restoring broken people gives hope to those seeking the best of love.

Jesus once forgave a woman caught in adultery. The religious leaders had thrown her in front of him and asked if they should stone her for her misconduct. Jesus uttered a since-famous answer: "Let him who is without sin among you cast the first stone." Beginning with the oldest (who were the most honest and wise), they all walked away. Then Jesus said, "Neither do I condemn you. Go, and sin no more."

On another occasion the New Testament records a conversation with a woman who had been married five times and was living with another man. Jesus gently confronted her with her broken romantic history and offered her the "living water" of forgiveness and life.

On yet another occasion, Jesus extended forgiveness to a prostitute, whose thankfulness led her to wash his feet while he was at a gathering of disapproving religious leaders.

Neither the woman caught in adultery, nor the woman married five times, nor the prostitute had achieved the ideals of romantic love in their lives. But each met the great Songwriter who forgave her past and empowered her for the future.

So the Christian message points our eyes to one more guiding star in the sky—the one the wise men saw. In doing so it offers new hope for all who seek romantic ideals, especially those who feel unworthy of them. And that includes most of us at one time or another.

The message of hope for all, of course, is also in the Song. It provides pictures of love occurring especially where it seems most unlikely. Look at the main characters: Shulamith was working in the fields; Solomon had been immersed in himself. And consider the images: Fruit trees appear in a dangerous forest; lotus flowers arise out of water; oases flourish in the desert; gazelles thrive there too.

Look at the women in the supporting cast. At one time Tamar, Rahab, Ruth, and Bathsheba felt they were on the outside looking in, disqualified by their birth, behavior, or misfortune from experiencing the best of God's design.

Yet they were not disqualified in God's eyes. He not only showed his special care for each of them, but he also made them central in his plan to bless the entire earth.

Through many centuries God orchestrated the grand event of bringing his Son into the world. The Father's mysterious hand guided the human line of descent that would culminate in the Word becoming flesh—when the music of the great Songwriter would be sung with a human voice.

The New Testament allows a glimpse of that hidden guidance in the first chapter of its first book. There Matthew unveils the line of descent that led to Jesus' birth. In accordance with custom, the descent is traced through men. But it also breaks tradition to include four remarkable women. And guess who they are.

Tamar. Rahab. Ruth. Bathsheba.

God had not simply given them token parts in his unfolding drama. He gave them starring roles! Far from being embarrassed by their failures, God embraced them in his grace. And through them he delighted to bring the birth of his Son.

Matthew could scarcely endorse more strongly what was already clear in the Song—that God reaches out to all, especially to those who feel most excluded.

The stories of these women, and also of Solomon and Shulamith, even hint at the way it might happen. God not only overcame the deaths of Ruth, Tamar, and Bathsheba's husbands, he even accomplished his plan through those events to bring good out of tragedy. And he not only overcame the deaths of Shulamith and Solomon's fathers, but through those deaths he enabled them to meet as Shulamith worked in Solomon's vineyards.

These stories foreshadowed how God would transform Jesus' death into the foundation for new life. He not only overcame his Son's death with resurrection but through that death offered forgiveness and resurrection to all.

Many of the New Testament authors were as equally disqualified to write what they did as Solomon was to write the Song.

Solomon was in many respects the *least* qualified person to write it. He was immersed in power and selfish pleasure before love broke through his life. But then he wrote one of the most beautiful love songs ever written.

The apostle Paul was thoroughly immersed in self-righteous, judgmental hatred. But love broke through and opened his eyes to the message of grace and mercy. He became the follower of Jesus who, of all New Testament writers, talked most passionately about the undeserved forgiveness of God.

John was prone to be the most angry among the twelve original disciples, and his natural response was to call for divine punishment on those who rejected Jesus. But he later became known as the apostle of love because of his life and writings.

Peter was the disciple who most resisted the unjust suffering of Jesus, declaring he would never allow it. And when the time came for Jesus' arrest, Peter indeed resisted with his sword, injuring a Roman soldier. But Peter became known as the apostle who most embraced the necessity of willingness to suffer unjustly, and he wrote a famous letter with that as its primary theme.

So the New Testament writers were, at one time, as uniquely disqualified as Solomon to write what they did. But again, God was not embarrassed by their failures. He embraced them in his grace and transformed them with his love.

The ultimate source of the romantic love in the Song is described as the "flame of the Lord." And that is the foundation of the Christian's relationship to Christ— the burning love that offers us forgiveness and life and sustains the new life he gives.

"Nothing will have the power to separate us from the love of God that is in Christ Jesus our Lord," Paul wrote in a letter. "Neither death nor life, nor angels, nor demons, nor things present, nor things to come, nor powers, nor height, nor depth, nor any other created thing."

Quite a remarkable statement from someone who once lived in constant guilt over every imperfection in his life and in constant fear he would fail again. But his life changed forever when he realized that nothing could extinguish the flame of God's love for him.

I've been told that Paul believed in a God of second chances. I'm thankful that's not completely true. Paul believed in a God of *countless* chances, and that gives me hope. Because I've lost count of the times I've needed another.

"Better yet," I think Paul would tell me, smiling as he placed his hand on my shoulder, "God was never counting in the first place. That stopped on a hill outside Jerusalem a long time ago.

"And if you think the Song's renewal of love in spring is beautiful, wait till you see the renewal of life planned for the future. I'm talking about a brand-new world and bodies that last forever!

"The Great Songwriter will be there too, singing and celebrating like at the Song's wedding—living, laughing, and loving among us!" Paul would laugh heartily, then say, "Now, friend, I want you to go live—really live—and laugh and love so that people catch a glimpse of what that new world will be like."

The Song of Songs

A New Translation

1.1[1] The Song of Songs, which is Solomon's.[2]

Shulamith[3]

1.2 How I wish he would kiss me with the kisses of his mouth![4]
    because your lovemaking is better than wine.

3   For fragrance your perfumes are wonderful,[5]
    and perfume poured fragrantly[6] is your name.[7]
    Therefore young maidens love you.

4   Draw me after you! Let us run together!
How I wish the king would bring[8] me to his chambers!

Young maidens[9]

    We will rejoice and delight in you.
    We will celebrate[10] your love more[11] than wine.

Shulamith

    How right they are to love you.

1.5 Dark am I,
    but lovely,
        O young women of Jerusalem,
    like tents darkened,[12]
        but like curtains of Solomon.

6 Do not stare at me
    because I am dark,
        because the sun has gazed upon me.
The sons of my mother[13]
    burned in anger toward me.[1]

They appointed me caretaker of the vineyards,
　　but of my own vineyard,
which belongs to me,[15]
　　I have not taken care.[16]

7　Tell me,
　　you whom my soul loves,[17]
where you graze your flock,[18]
　　where you rest them at noon;
for why[19] should I be like a veiled woman[20]
　　by the flocks of your close friends?[21]

Young maidens[22]
　1.8　If you do not know,
　　　　O fairest among women,[23]
　　　go forth on the trail of the flock
　　　and graze your flock of female kids[24]
　　　　by the dwellings[25] of the shepherds.

Solomon
　1.9　To my mare[26] among the chariots of Pharaoh
　　　　I liken you,
　　　　　my darling companion.[27]
　10　Lovely are your cheeks with ornaments[28]
　　　and your neck with strings of jewels.

Young maidens
　1.11　Ornaments of gold we will make for you
　　　　with beads of silver.

Shulamith
　1.12　While the king was in his realm,[29]
　　　　my nard gave its fragrance.
　13　A pouch[30] of myrrh is my beloved to me,
　　　which lies all night between my breasts.[31]
　14　A cluster of henna blossoms is my beloved[32] to me
　　　in the vineyards of En Gedi.[33]

Solomon
　1.15　Behold, you are beautiful,
　　　　my darling companion.
　　　Behold, you are beautiful.
　　　　Your eyes are doves.

Shulamith

1.16 Behold, you are beautiful,[34]
        my beloved.
    Indeed, you are delightful,
        and our resting place is in the flourishing branches.[35]

17 The beams of our houses are cedars,
        our rafters cypresses.

2.1 I am a flower[36] of the Sharon plain,
        a lotus[37] flower of the valleys.

Solomon

2.2 As a lotus flower among thorns,
        so is my darling companion among the young women.

Shulamith

2.3 As an apple tree[38] among the trees of the forest,
        so is my beloved among the young men.
    In his[39] shade[40] I longed[41] to stay,
        and his fruit was sweet[42] to my taste.

4 He has brought me to the house of wine,[43]
        and his banner[44] over me is love.

5 Sustain me with raisin cakes
        and refresh me with apples,
            because I am faint from love.[45]

6 Oh, may his left hand be under my head
        and his right hand embrace me.[46]

7 I want you to promise me,
        O young women of Jerusalem,
    by the gazelles and by the does of the field,
        not to arouse, not to awaken[47] love[48]
            until love pleases to awaken.[49]

8 The voice[50] of my beloved!
        Behold!
    He comes,
        leaping over the mountains,
            bounding[51] over the hills.

9 My beloved is like a gazelle or a young stag.
        Behold!

He is standing behind our wall,
> gazing through the windows,
>> peering through the lattice.

10 My beloved responded and said to me,
> "Arise, my darling companion,
>> my beautiful one; come away.
11   For behold, the winter has passed.
>> The rain is over and gone.[52]
12   The blossoms have appeared in the land.
>> The time of singing[53] has come,
>>> and the voice of the turtledove is heard in our land.
13   The fig tree ripens its figs,
>> and the vines in blossom give off fragrance.
> Arise, my darling companion,
>> my beautiful one; come away.

14   O my dove,
>> in the clefts of the rock,
>>> in the hiding places of the cliff,
>> let me see your form;[54]
>> let me hear your voice;
> for your voice is pleasing,[55]
>> and your form is lovely."

Solomon and Shulamith[56]

2.15 Let us catch the foxes,
> the little foxes who ruin vineyards,[57]
>> because our vineyards are in blossom.

Shulamith

2.16 My beloved is mine,
> and I am his,
>> he who grazes among the lotus flowers.[58]

17 When the day[59] breathes[60]
> and the shadows flee,
turn;[61]
> be like,
>> my beloved,
> a gazelle or a young stag[62]

on the divided mountains.[63]

3.1 Upon my bed in the nights,[64]
      I sought him whom my soul loves;
    I sought him but did not find him.

2   I will arise now and go about in the city,
      in the streets and in the squares.
    I will seek him whom my soul loves.
     I sought him but did not find him.

3 They found me—
    the watchmen who go about in the city.
      "Have you seen him whom my soul loves?"

4 Scarcely had I passed from them
    when I found him whom my soul loves.
  I held on to him
    and would not let him go
  until I had brought him to the house of my mother,
    to the place[65] of the one who conceived me.

5 I want you to promise me,
    O young women of Jerusalem,
  by the gazelles and by the does of the field,
    not to arouse, not to awaken love
      until love pleases to awaken.[66]

Songwriter

3.6 Who is this[67]
    coming from the wilderness[68]
      like columns of smoke,
    filled with fragrance of myrrh and frankincense,
      from every scented powder of the merchant?

7 Behold!
  It is the carriage of Solomon,
    sixty mighty men around it
      from the mighty of Israel;

8   all of them holders of the sword,
      trained for battle;
  each, his sword at his side[69]
    for the terror of the nights;[70]

9 A royal carriage King Solomon made for himself
    from the timber of Lebanon.

10 Its posts he made of silver,
>   its back of gold,
>>   its seat of purple,
>   its interior inlaid with love
>>   by the young women of Jerusalem.

11 Go forth, O young women of Zion,
>   and look upon King Solomon,
>>   with the crown with which his mother has crowned him
>   on the day of his wedding,
>>   on the day of his heart's rejoicing.[71]

Solomon

4.1 Behold! You are beautiful,
>   my darling companion.
Behold! You are beautiful.

Your eyes are doves
>   behind your veil.[72]
Your hair is like a flock of goats
>   moving briskly[73] down Mount Gilead.

2 Your teeth are like a flock of newly shorn sheep
>   which have come up from the washing,
each one bearing twins
>   and bereaved of not one of them.[74]

3 Like a scarlet ribbon[75] are your lips,
>   and your mouth is lovely.
Like the sliced opening of a pomegranate are your parted lips[76]
>   behind your veil.

4 Like the tower of David is your neck,
>   made for strength;[77]
a thousand shields hang upon it,
>   all the shields[78] of the mighty men.

5 Your two breasts are like two fawns,
>   twins[79] of a gazelle
>>   which graze among the lotus flowers.

6 Until the day breathes[80]
>   and the shadows flee,
I will go my way
>   to the mountain of myrrh[81]
>>   and to the hill of frankincense.[82]

7 You are completely beautiful,
  my darling companion,
    and there is no blemish[83] in you.

8 With me from Lebanon,
    O bride,[84]
  with me from Lebanon come.
  Descend from the peak of Amana,
    from the peak of Senir and Hermon,
  from the dens of lions
    and the mountains of leopards.[85]

9 You have made my heart beat fast,
    my sister, my bride.[86]
  You have made my heart beat fast
    with one glance of your eyes,
      with one strand of your necklace.

10 How beautiful is your lovemaking,
    my sister, my bride.
  How much better is your lovemaking than wine
    and the fragrance of your perfumes than any spice.
11 Honey from the comb[87] your lips drip,
    my bride,
  Honey and milk are under your tongue.
    And the fragrance of your garments
      is like the fragrance of Lebanon.

12 You are a garden locked,
    my sister, my bride.
  You are a garden[88] locked,
    a fountain sealed.[89]
13 Your tender shoots[90] are
    a paradise of pomegranates
      with delicious fruits;
    henna blossoms with nard plants,
14   nard and saffron;
    fragrant reed[91] and cinnamon,
      with all trees of frankincense,[92]
    myrrh, and aloes—
      with all the best spices.
15 A fountain of gardens[93] you are,

a well of fresh [94] water
>> and streams flowing from Lebanon.

Shulamith

4.16 Awaken,[95] O north wind,
>> and come, wind of the south.
> Blow upon my garden
>> and cause its spices to flow like a stream.[96]
> May my beloved come to his garden
>> And eat its delicious fruits.

Solomon

5.1 I have come into my garden,
>> my sister, my bride;
> I have gathered my myrrh with my spice.
>> I have eaten my honeycomb with my honey.
>> I have drunk my wine with my milk.

Songwriter

>> Eat, O darling companions.
>> Drink and be drunk, O beloved ones.[97]

Shulamith

5.2 I was asleep, but my heart was awake.
>> A voice![98]
> My beloved knocking,
> "Open to me,
>> my sister,
>>> my darling companion,
>> my dove,
>>> my perfect one,
> for my head is filled with dew,
>> my hair with damp of the night."

3 I had taken off my cloak;
>> must I put it on back on?
> I had washed my feet;
>> must I get them dirty?

4 My beloved extended his hand through the latch opening,[99]
>> and my heart deeply longed for him.

5 I arose to open to my beloved,
>> and my hands dripped with myrrh,

and my fingers with liquid myrrh,
    upon the handles of the bolt.[100]

6   I opened to my beloved,
        but my beloved had turned and gone.
    My soul went out[101] when he spoke.
        I sought him but did not find him.
    I called out to him, but he did not answer me.

7   They found me—
        the watchmen who go about in the city.
    They struck me;
        they bruised me;
    they took my shawl from upon me—
        those watchmen of the walls.

8   I want you to promise me,
        O young women of Jerusalem,
    if you find my beloved,
        that you will tell him
            that I am faint from love.[102]

Young maidens

5.9   How is your beloved better than another beloved,
        O fairest among women?
    How is your beloved better than another beloved,
        that you so earnestly ask us to promise this?

Shulamith

5.10   My beloved is radiant and lustrous,
        distinguished among ten thousand.

11   His head is purest gold.
    His hair is like palm leaves,
        but black as a raven.

12   His eyes are like doves
        beside streams of water,
    bathed in milk,
        perched over a pool.[103]

13   His cheeks are like a bed of spice,
        towers of perfumes.
    His lips are lotus flowers,
        dripping liquid myrrh.

14   His hands are cylinders of gold
        set with golden topaz.

His abdomen is a plate of ivory
  covered with sapphires.[104]
15 His legs are marble pillars
  set upon pedestals of purest gold.
His appearance is like Lebanon,
  distinguished as its cedars.
16 His mouth is sweetness itself.

Everything about him is desirable[105] to me!
This is my lover[106] and companion,[107]
  O young women of Jerusalem.

Young maidens to Shulamith
6.1 Where has your beloved gone,
  O fairest among women?
Where has your beloved turned,
  that we may seek him with you?

Shulamith
6.2 My beloved has gone to his garden,
  to beds of spice,
to graze in the gardens
  and to gather lotus flowers.

3 I am my beloved's,
  and my beloved is mine—
    he grazes among the lotus flowers.

Solomon
6.4 You are as fair,
  my darling companion,
    as Tirzah,
  as lovely as Jerusalem,
    as awe-inspiring as bannered hosts.[108]
5 Turn your eyes from me,
  because they arouse me.[109]
Your hair is like a flock of goats
  descending from Mount Gilead.
6 Your teeth are like a flock of ewes[110]
  which have come up from the washing,
each one bearing twins
  and bereaved of not one of them.

7   Like the sliced opening of a pomegranate are your parted lips
        behind your veil.

8   Sixty queens there are,[111]
        and eighty concubines,
            and maidens without number; but

9   Unique is she—my dove, my perfect one!
        Unique is she to her mother.
    Pure is she to the one who bore her.
        Women saw her and called her joyful;
            the queens and concubines praised her:

Young maidens

6.10   "Who is this[112]
            shining like the morning star,[113]
                fair[114] as the white moon,[115]
            pure as the blazing sun,
                awe-inspiring as bannered hosts?"[116]

Shulamith

6.11   To the garden of nut trees I had gone down,
            to see the fresh shoots of the ravine,
        to see if[117] the vine had budded
            and the pomegranates had bloomed.

12   Before I realized it,
            my soul[118] set me among the chariots
                of my people of a prince.[119]

Young maidens

6.13   Return, return, O Shulamith;[120]
            return, return, that we may gaze in awe upon you.

Solomon

6.13   How you gaze in awe[121] upon Shulamith,
            as at the dance of the two camps![122]

7.1   How beautiful are your feet[123] in sandals,
            O daughter of a prince.[124]
        The curves of your hips[125] are like ornaments,
            the work of the hands of an artist.[126]

2   Your navel[127] is a round chalice.[128]
        It never lacks mixed wine.
    Your abdomen is a stack of wheat
        surrounded with lotus flowers.[129]

3 Your two breasts are like two fawns,
    twins of a gazelle.
4 Your neck is like a tower of ivory.
    Your eyes are like pools of understanding[130]
      by the gate of a crowded city.
    Your nose[131] is like a tower in Lebanon,
      keeping watch over Damascus.
5 Your head crowns you like Carmel.
      And the flowing hair of your head is like purple threads—
        the king is held captive by your tresses.

6 How beautiful and how lovely you are.[132]
      Love flows through your tender affection.[133]
7 This—your stature—is like a palm tree,
    and your breasts are like clusters[134] of fruit.
8 I say, "I will climb the palm tree,
      I will take hold of its stalks of dates."
    May your breasts be like clusters of grapes
      and the fragrance of your breath like apples.
9 And your mouth like the best wine…

Shulamith

7.9 …going down smoothly[135] for my beloved,
      flowing gently through your lips
        as we fall asleep.[136]

10 I am my beloved's,
    and his desire is for me.[137]

11 Come,
    my beloved.
  Let us go out into the countryside.
    Let us spend the night among the henna blossoms.[138]
12 Let us rise early to the vineyards.
    Let us see if the vine has budded,
  its blossoms have opened,
    the pomegranates have bloomed.
  There I will give my love to you.
13 The mandrakes[139] send out their fragrance,
  and at our doors[140] are delicious fruits,[141]
    both new and old,
  which I have kept[142] for you,

my beloved.

8.1 Oh that you were like a brother to me,
   who nursed at the breasts of my mother.
  Then if I found you outside,
   I would kiss you,
    and no one would scorn [143] me.
 2 I would lead you to the house of my mother.
   You would instruct me. [144]
  I would let you drink [145]
    from [146] the wine—the spiced wine— [147]
     from the sweet wine [148] of my pomegranate. [149]
 3 Oh, may his left hand be under my head
   and his right hand embrace me. [150]

 4 I want you to promise me,
   O young women of Jerusalem,
  that you will surely arouse, you will surely awaken love
   when love pleases to awaken. [151]

Songwriter
 8.5 Who is this coming from the wilderness,
   leaning on her beloved?

Shulamith
 8.5 Under the apple tree [152] I awakened you.
   There your mother was in labor with you; [153]
    there she was in labor [154] and gave you birth.

 6 Make me a seal upon your heart, [155]
   a seal upon your arm,
  because love is strong as death,
   fervent love [156] as relentless as the grave; [157]
  its flashes are flashes of fire,
   the flame of the Lord.
 7 Many waters cannot extinguish love,
   and rivers will not drown it.
  If a man offered all the possessions of his house for love,
   they would utterly scorn him.

Brothers of Shulamith
 8.8 We have a little sister,
   and she has no breasts.

What shall we do to prepare our sister
for the day on which she is spoken for?

9 If she is a wall,
we shall build upon her an embankment[158] of silver.

If she is a door,
we shall enclose her with planks of cedar.

Shulamith

8.10 I was a wall,
and my breasts were like towers.

Then I became in his eyes[159]
as one who finds fulfillment.[160]

11 A vineyard belonged to Solomon
at the Place of Plenty.

He gave the vineyard to caretakers;[161]
each one was to bring for its fruit
a thousand shekels of silver.

12 "My own vineyard,
which belongs to me,[162]
lies before me.

The thousand are for you,
O Solomon,
and two hundred for the caretakers of the fruit."

Solomon

8.13 You who dwell in the gardens,
with close friends[163] listening attentively to your voice,
let me hear you.

Shulamith

8.14 Hurry,
my beloved,
and be like a gazelle
or a young stag
on the mountains of spices.[164]

Notes to Appendix B

1. The lyrics of the Song were originally like those of modern song, lacking identification by numbers or sections. Later readers imposed chapter and verse numbers upon the Song, accentuating its appearance as a poem. Whatever we may think about this treatment of the lyrics, at least we may now conveniently identify them by reference to chapter and verse.

2. The name *Solomon* appears seven times in the Song: twice in the first of seven sections (1.1, 5); three times in the central section (3.7, 9, 11); and twice in the last of the seven sections (8.11–12). In light of the significance of number in the sevenfold and tenfold praise, and in the tenfold occurrences of the abstract word for love (2.4–5, 7; 3.5; 5.8; 7.6; 8.4, 6–7 [twice]), perhaps the name *Solomon* has been symmetrically balanced in its sevenfold mention as a kind of signature on the Song. The symmetrical design of the Song is presented in Appendix C, "The Elegant Design of the Song."

3. The original Song does not explicitly state the speaker before the lyrics like a modern play might do. But it identifies the speaker in several ways. Sometimes the term of address does so. For example, when the speaker addresses "darling companion," Solomon is speaking; but when the speaker addresses "beloved," Shulamith is speaking. Other times, the gender of the second-person pronoun is the indication. In the original language, the pronoun "you" is either masculine or feminine. So if a lover says, "I love you," and "you" is feminine, Solomon is likely speaking; but if "you" is masculine, Shulamith is likely speaking. If neither the term of endearment nor the gender of the pronoun identifies the speaker, then various aspects of the context normally do so.

The name *Shulamith,* which occurs in 6.13, is one of many terms of endearment given to the princess bride by Solomon. I use it throughout the translation when identifying her as the speaker.

4. Although several words for "mouth" and "lips" occur in the Song, this is the only place this particular word occurs. This word connotes an open mouth and is perhaps used here to suggest passionate kisses and to show the depth of Shulamith's longing for Solomon. The repetition of "fragrant oils," passionate kisses, and "lovemaking better than wine" in 4.10 shows her longings fulfilled.

5. The words for "better" in verse 2 and "wonderful" in verse 3 are identical in the original language. It is tempting to translate this something like, "for your kisses are *superior* to wine; for fragrance your oils are *superior,*" to capture the repetition of the original.

6. The translation "poured fragrantly" attempts to capture the alliteration of the word for "fragrance" *(rayak)* at the beginning of this lyric, and the word for

"poured fragrantly" *(turak)*. Literally, the word translated "poured fragrantly" means "poured out."

7. This is a wordplay on "name" *(shem)* and "perfumes" *(shemen)* in the original language. I have tried to capture the sounds of the underlying Hebrew words without using conventional forms that represent every aspect of the word in the original. The unusual marks necessary to show Hebrew vocalization sometimes interfere with a grasp of the sounds, unless someone is familiar with the conventions of academic transliteration.

The name of the father of their nation, Abraham, means "father of a multitude"; David means "beloved"; Joshua means "deliverer." So if Solomon's name is like perfume, he has a pleasant, "fragrant" character.

8. Many translators render this, "The king has brought me to his chambers." The form of the verb is most frequently translated in the simple past tense like that, rather than as a wish, as I have rendered it. But the use of the form to indicate a wish may be more likely here because of the grammatical parallelism of this to the wish of the opening line. The third-person "How I wish he would kiss me" parallels the third-person "How I wish he would bring me" with direct addresses (second-person verbs) in between. Bruce Waltke points out that the use of this form to express a wish (the "precative") can be recognized contextually by its parallelism with the other volitive forms (Waltke-O'Connor, *Hebrew Syntax*, 30.5.4d). If one translates this in the simple past, then the meaning would apparently be that Solomon has brought Shulamith to the palace "rooms" (note the plural) so that in the palace environment he may (literally and figuratively) "court" her. But the atmosphere of a wish to be with Solomon pervades the entire first chapter of the Song, and that broader context, coupled with the grammatical parallelism and Shulamith's wish that he would kiss her, makes the relatively rare use of the verb as a wish the more likely use here.

9. The young maidens to whom Shulamith refers in 1.4 are likely the same group of young women more frequently called "young women" of Jerusalem. "Young maidens" is set in parallel to "young women" in 6.8 and 6.9.

10. The word for "celebrate" means literally "cause to be remembered," expressing the belief that this love between Solomon and Shulamith is a love story for all time.

11. This could perhaps be translated, "We will celebrate your love [which is] better than wine."

12. Many translate this "like the tents of Kedar." But the name of the tribe means "darkened," either from their skin or their tents darkened from wear. And that association is the reason for the use of the phrase here. The translation "like the tents of Kedar" is still a good one but requires more explanation than "like tents darkened."

13. Some have regarded the phrase "sons of my mother" as odd and signifying perhaps a reference to stepbrothers. But the other six occurrences of this phrase in the Old Testament show it is simply a poetic reference to natural brothers. Its occurrence in the Song is likely to set them in parallel to the "daughters of Jerusalem." "Sons" and "daughters" in the original language are quite similar words (*banim* and *banot,* respectively). The daughters of Jerusalem stared at her in disdain. Her brothers "burned" in anger and then placed her in the vineyards, where the burning sun "gazed" on her and darkened her skin. So the daughters' "staring" disdain parallels the sun's burning "gaze," which is, in turn, the expression of her brothers' burning anger.

14. The Song not only has clever plays on words but colorful allusions to people and events in the primary literature of Israel. Allusions to famous people enable a writer to say a great deal in few words. Instead of describing at length the characteristics of a person, one might simply say he is as creative as Albert Einstein, or as articulate as Winston Churchill, or as attractive as Marilyn Monroe. To describe famous love scenes in chapter one of this book, I found I could communicate exactly what I wanted with brief references to characters in movies or to a classic play like *Romeo and Juliet.*

The reference to angry brothers who mistreated Shulamith is the first of several allusions to Joseph, the eleventh of twelve brothers, ten of whom mistreated him too. At the end of that story, Joseph forgave his brothers and cared for them just as Shulamith will forgive her brothers and care for them at the end of the Song.

In fact, Shulamith's question—in the verse following the reference to her brothers—about the location where Solomon rested his flocks, may allude to Joseph's question as to the location where her brothers graze their flocks (Genesis 37.16).

When the watchmen of the walls mistreat Shulamith as she wanders about the city seeking Solomon (5.2–8), the mention that they take her cloak from her immediately suggests another allusion to the story of Joseph.

Joseph's cloak was twice taken from him and used wrongfully against him: His brothers stripped it from him, sprinkled blood on it, and with it persuaded their father that Joseph was dead (Genesis 37.31–33); later Potiphar's wife took his cloak and deceitfully used it to substantiate her accusation that he tried to sleep with her (Genesis 39.13–19).

In the night of conflict described in 5.2–8, Shulamith also refers to the removal of her cloak twice: once by her and once by the watchmen of the walls. It is interesting that the phrase "to strip off the tunic," describing her removal of her cloak in 5.3, uses the same words that describe the action of Joseph's brothers, who stripped his cloak from him.

When Shulamith reconciles with Solomon, she is described in terms that allude to a dream of Joseph's. She is like the sun, the moon, and the prominent stars—an allusion to the dream's symbol for Israel. And in the context of that lyric, her experience of reconciliation replicates that of the first person named Israel, confirming the allusion to Joseph's dream (see note at 6.10).

Finally, the allusions to Tamar (see note at 1.7) strengthen the allusion to Joseph, since the story of Tamar and Judah (Genesis 38) artistically contrasts the story of Potiphar's wife and Joseph (Genesis 39). Judah went to a prostitute; Joseph refused Potiphar's wife. Judah willingly gave away his seal; Joseph had his cloak taken from him. Judah feared his household would become a laughingstock; Potiphar's wife claimed Joseph had made a laughingstock of their household. Judah's personal possessions (seal and staff) were used to justly acquit Tamar; Joseph's personal possession (cloak) was used to unjustly imprison him. If Shulamith is like the noble person in the story of Tamar and Judah, she is implicitly like the noble person in the story of Joseph and Potiphar's wife, since the author of Genesis sets both stories in parallel to one another.

To summarize, the fundamental allusion to Joseph by Shulamith is her reference to the mistreatment she received from her older brothers and her ultimate forgiveness of them. That allusion is strengthened by the twofold removal of her cloak and the allusion to Joseph's dream of Israel as represented in the sun, the moon, and twelve stars. The allusion to Joseph is further strengthened by the allusion to Tamar, who is parallel to Joseph in Genesis 37 and 38.

Genesis, A Commentary, by Dr. Bruce Waltke (Zondervan, 2001), was to me the most helpful commentary on Genesis. His presentation of literary patterns and multiple levels of meaning honors this fascinating literature.

15. The phrase "my own vineyard, which belongs to me" is identical in the original language to its other occurrence in 8.12.

16. The pattern of this verse is *abb ′a ′*: "caretaker, vineyards, vineyard, taken care," since the words for "caretaker" and "taken care" are from the same verb in the original language.

17. The address to "you whom my soul loves" may imply that Solomon is not actually present and explain why the young maidens answer. In 3.1–4 the expression "him whom my soul loves" occurs first when Solomon is absent. The identity of the speakers who answer her is confirmed by the term of address they use for Shulamith—"most beautiful among women"—which they also use in 5.9 and 6.1.

18. "Your flock" it is not explicitly in the text but is implied by the verb "to graze" and the following phrase, "where you rest them at noon."

19. The word for "why" in the original, while common, appears in this particular form only here in the Old Testament and is a play on Solomon's name. So the word functions almost as a term of address to Solomon, but then its pronunciation and order in the sentence reveals the word to be not "Solomon" but "why."

The songwriter teases the reader with the foreshadowing that this young girl will one day speak directly to the great king, but she does not call him Solomon directly until the very end of the Song (8.12).

20. The reference to "a veiled woman" whose activity could be misunderstood is the first of several allusions to Tamar (Genesis 38). Her husband had died. Her husband's brothers had the responsibility to impregnate her so the family line would not cease. One of the brothers shirked his duty, and her father-in-law refused to permit the second brother to come to her.

The only other man who could continue the family name was the father-in-law himself—Judah. After Judah's wife died, and as he traveled to a celebratory shearing of his sheep, Tamar put a veil around her, pretending to be a prostitute, and enticed him.

When he promised Tamar a young goat in payment for her service, she requested and received his seal and staff as collateral. Judah later attempted to deliver the goat but could not find the veiled woman he had encountered.

When Tamar's pregnancy began to show, it was brought to the attention of Judah, who decreed punishment for her immorality, bursting out that she should be burned. But when she showed him his seal and staff, he realized it was he who had been wrong in not instructing his son to provide a child for her; Tamar had been right to continue the family name through the closest relative to her husband.

Shulamith's activity outside as a "veiled woman" could be misinterpreted, but the allusion to Tamar tells us Shulamith has noble character. The praise of Shulamith includes imagery from a celebratory sheep shearing (4.2), and her praise of Solomon as the henna blossoms in the vineyards of "En Gedi" ("Spring of a Young Goat") may be subtle associations with the story of Tamar also.

Shulamith's request to be a "seal" (8.6–7), which structurally parallels the association of Solomon with the "Spring of a Young Goat," (see Appendix C, "The Elegant Design of the Song") offers further allusions to the story. Solomon, unlike Judah, would not part with his "seal," which is Shulamith. He is better than the "young goat" offered to her, since he is like henna blossoms in the "Spring of a Young Goat." Instead of the sheep-shearing being the occasion for a desperate subterfuge by Tamar, it is its primary association with joy and happiness that describes Shulamith's smile. And unlike Judah, who exclaims that Tamar should be burned for her apparent immorality, Solomon has a flame of love from God for Shulamith.

No wonder Solomon delights to liken Shulamith to a palm tree in 7.7. The word for "palm tree" is "Tamar."

21. This particular word for "close friends" occurs only here and at 8.13. In the beginning Solomon is portrayed with companions, and Shulamith—perhaps outside his social circle—is among the daughters of Jerusalem and among his companions.

At the end of the Song, she is among companions that fully accept her and are eager to hear her voice.

22. Some interpreters believe Solomon is the speaker here. But since Shulamith has just addressed the daughters of Jerusalem in the previous lyric, and in two later lyrics, they address her as "fairest among women," it seems reasonable to conclude they are speaking to Shulamith here. The evidence that Solomon speaks is that Shulamith has just addressed him: "you whom my soul loves." This is significant. But in 1.2–4, it appears that she can address him in a form similar to a soliloquy.

23. Only the daughters of Jerusalem call her by this name, and they do so three times (1.8; 5.9; 6.1).

24. Only here in the Old Testament is the female form for goat kids used. The songwriter portrays Shulamith as the shepherd of a flock of young female goats, which is likely a figurative representation of the feminine charm of her hair.

25. Although these dwellings may be tents, the translation as "dwellings" distinguishes this word from a different word used for "tents" in 1.5. This word rendered "dwellings," which sounds like *mishkanot*, may be a play on "kisses" at 1.2 (*minshakot*) and/or "draw me" (*mushakeni*). The intent of such a play might be to contrast Shulamith's initial desires with disappointment. She wanted kisses and time with him; she's offered a place by the tents of his friends.

But the young maidens' response also paves the way for Solomon's name for Shulamith. The "close friends" of 1.7 are set parallel to the "shepherds" of 1.8. So when the daughters of Jerusalem suggest to Shulamith that she go shepherd her flock by the dwellings of the shepherds, they are suggesting she go among Solomon's friends. The word for "shepherd" *(rayah)* sounds very much like "darling companion" *(raayah)* in the original language, which name he gives her in 1.9. So his first name for her accentuates a foundation of companionship they share. She is his shepherdess companion.

26. Interpreters often point out that the horses of Pharaoh's chariots are stallions, and that a mare among them would stir them up. While that is true, it is also noteworthy that the image of ornaments on her cheeks and necklaces around her neck is likely a continuation of the metaphor and portrays a mare decorated with jewels, which were common on the bridles of the horses. This could also be translated, "To a mare among the chariots of Pharaoh I liken you."

27. I have consistently translated this term of address as "darling companion" throughout the Song. The songwriter prepares the reader for it with the parallelism of "companions" and "shepherds" in the previous verses, and then presents Shulamith as Solomon's preeminent companion in this lyric.

28. The gifts given to Shulamith would remind her of the rewards and punishments promised to her by her brothers in 8.8–9. Her brothers promised her an

"embankment of silver" to reward her if she were a "wall" resisting suitors, and in 1.11 the young maidens promise her a necklace with silver in it. Her brothers also promised if she were a "door," they would enclose her with planks of cedar. But in contrast to the restrictions had she disobeyed, a few lyrics later she is completely unrestricted among the cedars of nature (1.17), just as she was unrestricted in her freedom to seek Solomon by the tents of the shepherds.

The words for "ornaments" *(torim)*, cypresses *(rotim)*, and "strings of jewels" *(charuzim)* sound very much like the reward of an "embankment" *(tira)* and the punishment of "planks of cedar" *(luach aruz)*. Since the strings of jewels are *not* planks of cedar but symbols of reward, they serve to say implicitly what is shown in her freedom in nature—that she had displayed responsible behavior for which she is now rewarded. "The ornaments *(toray)* of gold" (1.11) exceed even the rewards promised by her brothers. The correspondence of 1.7–11 with 8.8–9 in the literary structure of the Song (see Appendix C) increases the likelihood that these are intentional wordplays.

29. The phrase "in his realm" is often translated "at his table," but I believe the lexical evidence favors "in his realm" or "in his surroundings," similar to its meaning in 1 Kings 6.29 and 2 Kings 23.5, the only other places where the word for "surroundings" or "table" occurs in the Old Testament. In addition, the meaning of the preposition is much more commonly "in" than "at."

30. In this alliterative phrase, "pouch of myrrh" *(zaror hamor)*, the word rendered "pouch" refers to a bag in which valuables are carried, like the bags of money found with Joseph's brothers in Genesis 42.35. Shulamith's valuable possessions are her fragrant thoughts of Solomon carried over her heart.

31. Occasionally translators and interpreters will render this in a way that it is not a bag of myrrh between her breasts all night, but Solomon lying there. However, the parallelism of verses 13 and 14 make it clear that just as the cluster of henna blossoms are in En Gedi, the pouch of myrrh is between her breasts. It is true that the verb "lies" means to "spend the night," and it creates a warm image of the pouch of myrrh "spending the night between her breasts." The image personifies the pouch of myrrh and pictures Shulamith holding it like a young girl would hold on to her pillow, pretending it is her lover.

32. "My beloved" is Shulamith's most frequent term of address for Solomon in the Song. I have translated it "my beloved" throughout, except in 5.16.

33. This name means, literally, the "Spring of a Young Goat."

34. Shulamith uses the same word Solomon has used twice to describe her in the previous lyric. He twice calls her beautiful, and she responds, "*You* are beautiful." In the original language, the word for "beautiful" can be used appropriately for a male or female, whereas in English "beautiful" is much more commonly applied to females. Consequently, many translations of her response to him translate this

word as "handsome." However, in translating it that way, one loses the precise sense of her returning the compliment with the same word.

35. Although I found one translation of this as "our couch is in a bower," most translate this as something like, "our bed is verdant." However, in the other eighteen usages in the Old Testament, the word describing the "bed" describes trees every time but once (and then it is the product of a tree).

The pattern of the dialogue supports the imagery of the trees here too. Three comparative images are introduced: Solomon likens her eyes to doves (1.15); Shulamith likens herself to a "lotus flower of the valleys" (2.1); Shulamith likens him to "an apple tree among the trees of the forest" (2.3). Then each image is embellished: Solomon embellishes the second image by adding "as a lotus flower among thorns" (2.2); Shulamith embellishes the third image with, "In his shade I longed to stay, and his fruit was sweet to my taste" (2.3). But how is the first image embellished?

Solomon opens the dialogue by twice saying, "You are beautiful," and then adds, "Your eyes are doves." She echoes with two compliments of his attractiveness: "You are beautiful....Indeed, you are delightful"; and in parallel to his, "Your eyes are doves" is her, "Our resting place is in the flourishing branches. The beams of our houses are cedars, our rafters cypresses." The natural interpretation of the embellishment is that she is extending the metaphor of doves. Since the eyes portray the essence of the heart, and her eyes are doves, she knew already what he would say in 2.14, that she is a dove, as later his "eyes like doves" show he is a dove as well. The plural "houses" (1.17) confirms that she speaks of nature, just as in one later scene in nature, corresponding to this in the design of the Song, she refers to the plural "doors" in their outdoor house of erotic fruit trees and aphrodisiacal plants (7.13).

So after Solomon calls Shulamith's eyes doves in 1.15, she continues the imagery with, "Yes, our resting place is in the trees, and the beams of our houses are cedar trees, and our rafters are cypress trees." It is a beautiful image of the young lovers like playful doves flitting from branch to branch in the trees, since their love has given them wings.

36. Many translations render this flower a "rose." Although its identity is uncertain, it is certainly not the rose with which modern readers are familiar.

37. The identity of this flower is likely either the lily or the lotus. Othmar Keel argues convincingly that this word, *shushan*, is the lotus—the water lily with beautiful flowers of blue or white. (1) The word is borrowed from Egypt, where it indisputably refers to the lotus. (2) The *shushan* at the top of certain columns in Solomon's temple likely means "lotus" (1 Kings 7.19, 22); archaeological discoveries include many examples of lotus flowers at the tops of columns, but no examples of lilies there. (3) The *shushan* in Solomon's temple on the rim of a great bowl called The Sea, which was the water supply for temple services, was likely the lotus flower;

archaeological discoveries in Israel and Egypt include many examples of water vessels either in the shape of lotus flowers or with their representation but do not include examples of lilies used in this way. (Othmar Keel, *The Song of Songs,* Fortress Press, 1994.)

In addition, the symbolic meaning of the lotus water lily arising from the water and resting upon it is more harmonious with their placement over the water of The Sea in the temple, memorializing the triumph of God over the waters of chaos in the beginning (Genesis 1).

Some scholars have argued that no lotus flowers existed in Israel. As Keel points out, however, not only do they exist in Israel today, but when the plain of Sharon was marshy in the past, they would have existed in abundance. In the ancient world, Sharon was filled with sand dunes and watery marsh, and it was a habitat for crocodiles even into the nineteenth century.

The primary argument against identifying the *shushan* as the lotus here is the implication from its context that it is "among thorns," which are imagined to be away from the water. But the bramble bush is quite common along river banks and so could be in proximity to lotus flowers.

But if "lotus flower" is the right meaning, how does one explain the references in the Song to grazing "among the lotus flowers" by the gazelles or by the king? Even the figurative picture of a gazelle, or anyone else, grazing among lotus water lilies arising from the water is hard to imagine.

But this is not a decisive objection. Lotus blossoms appear in all sorts of places in art where one would not find them in nature: not only in the architectural designs already mentioned but as designs around food, either around the outer rims of plates where food is served, or in drawings, where the lotus blossoms surround fruits and other foods. So eating among lotus flowers took place all the time in their world: The lotus blossoms frequently surrounded their food.

Certainly the *shushan* functions like a lotus flower in the Song. It refers first to the life giving princess (2.1); to the source of life that bonds Solomon to her (2.16); to the erotic setting of her breasts (4.5); to his lips flowing with liquid myrrh (5.13); to flowers picked before their reconciliation (6.3), which are likely words of praise communicating forgiveness and love; and last, to the flowers that surround her abdomen and navel offering Solomon the erotic renewal of life from her most intimate sexuality (7.2).

Finally, the word *shushan* is apparently a play on Solomon's first compliment of Shulamith as "like a mare" *(susa)*. The actual letters are different, but the sounds of the two together are similar and alliterative. The artistic significance of this might be similar to the escalating praise of each other in 1.15 to 2.3, where each one embellishes the other's praise. His first praise of her as a mare *(susa,* 1.9) leads to her playful reference to herself as a *shushan* (2.1) and makes it seem less like a concept out of the blue. And the meaning that emerges has artistic simplicity. She is not only like a mare that *receives* the attention of all the stallions, but she is also like a life-giving lotus flower who *gives* attention as well.

In any case, the numerous associations of the lotus in the region from Egypt to Syria during this time provide illuminating possibilities for its meaning in the Song. Keel's discussion of these possibilities is consistent with his creative and scholarly consideration of relevant literature and archaeology that is the broad background to the Song.

Although scholars debate the botanical identity of the *shushan,* and the "flower of the Sharon plain," all can agree that these two flowers, whatever they are, describe part of the blossoming of the land of Israel from God's blessing (Isaiah 35.1–2; Hosea 14.6–8).

38. The apple tree or its fruit appears four times in the Song (2.3, 5; 7.8; 8.5). Solomon's company refreshes Shulamith like sweet apples (2.3) and nourishes her longing (2.5), and she returns his love with kisses scented with apples (7.8). Her response to his uniqueness among all men perhaps further arouses his love for her (8.5).

39. Or, "in its shade," "its fruit."

40. The most common figurative meaning of the shade or shadow of a tree or a bird's wings is "protection." It arises from the simple analogy of shade under a tree providing protection from the sun, or shade of the wings of a bird providing protection of its young. Perhaps the most well-known use of the metaphor occurs in Psalm 91.1. The word rendered "to sit down" or "to dwell" in Song 2.3 also occurs in this verse: "You who dwell ["stay"/"sit" in the Song] in the shelter of the Most High shall abide in the shadow ["shade" in the Song] of the Almighty." "Shade," meaning "protection," occurs elsewhere, for example, in Isaiah 25.4; 30.2; Ezekiel 17.23.

41. The verb normally takes an object and so is transitive. But an object is not clear in this verse, since it would be unusual for "to sit" to function as an object or an infinitive here. But it is possible for it to do so, similar to the grammar of Deuteronomy 1.5, where "undertook, explained" seems to mean "undertook to explain" (Bloch and Bloch, *The Song of Songs,* Random House, 1995.) Then the translation would be, "I longed to sit/dwell/stay."

The verb translated "longed" is the intensive form of the verb meaning "to want something very much." A noun can be made from this verb that means "something longed for." That noun is used in 5.16 when Shulamith concludes her praise of Solomon by saying "everything about him is desirable." The only other place where this verb of "longing" is followed by the verb "to sit" (although it is a different form of the verb) is in Psalm 68.16, in describing God's "desire" "to dwell" in his holy mountain.

42. The word rendered "sweet" is an unusual term to describe fruit. In its other twelve occurrences in the Old Testament, the only food it describes is the sweetness

of honey. But this is one more example of whimsical wordplay in the Song. The word for "forest" *(yaar)* is precisely like one word for "honey" or "honeycomb" *(yaar)* and almost exactly like another for "honey" *(yaarah),* and so since Solomon is the preeminent tree in the "forest," which sounds like honey, Shulamith can play on that word to describe his fruit as "sweet" like honey.

Such sweetness also figuratively describes a person's pleasant speech: "Pleasant words are a honeycomb, sweet to the soul and healing to the bones" (Proverbs 16.24 NIV). In 5.16 Shulamith describes Solomon's mouth with this same word for "sweet." Since in that praise section she has already described his lips as "dripping with liquid myrrh," which is a clear reference to his passionate kisses, the second reference to his mouth in her praise seems clearly a reference to his speech. If "sweetness" describes his speech in 5.16, then it becomes more likely that the fruit that is "sweet" to her taste in 2.3 includes his speech too. The most common reference of "fruit" outside the Song is to literal fruit; but it frequently refers to speech, the "fruit of the mouth" in Proverbs 12.14; 13.2; 18.20.

In certain lyrics of the Song, fruit clearly has erotic connotations. However, several images in the Song begin with a comprehensive association and then become erotic: fragrance (1.3; 4.16); lotus flower (2.1; 4.5; 7.2); grazing (1.7; 2.16; 6.3); gazelles (2.9; 2.17; 8.14); pomegranates (4.3, 13; 8.2). Fruit seems also like this (2.3; 4.13): first describing the "sweetness" of his speech and then of the banquet of her body (4.13, 16; 7.13). It is a beautiful way to show erotic affection arising out of appreciation for the whole person.

43. The phrase "house of wine" is the literal translation of the words and probably refers to a banquet hall. I have retained the literal translation because of its natural connection and contrast to the "houses" of nature in nearby 1.17 and the contrast invited by the literary structure of the Song with the house of wealth in 8.6–7. The concept of a prominent banner of love implies a public place where Solomon's love for Shulamith is apparent to all.

44. Symbols are frequently found on banners in the drawings found by archaeologists in other cultures of the ancient Near East. The symbol may show the purpose of the group holding the banner, much like a football banner may have a symbol of a mascot on it to identify its purpose. One banner held by a group of wrestlers, for example, simply shows two wrestlers. Anyone could see who they were when looking at the banner. Anyone can see that Solomon loves Shulamith when looking at the figurative banner of love he holds over her. His public behavior toward her shows it.

A few translations render this, "He looked on me with love," in dependence upon a similar word in Akkadian. But it's unlikely the Song would borrow a word for "to see" from another language when its own language offered so many common and specialized words for that already, unless perhaps for some special purpose of alliteration or wordplay, which I don't see in the context. But the normal meaning in the Hebrew of "public banner" makes good sense here. And the use in the Song of words derived from its root always depends upon the original meaning of "public banner" (5.10; 6.4, 10), though derivative words naturally develop meaning and nuance.

45. The word order in the original language is literally, "Faint from love am I." This is significant because the "I" pronoun, relatively uncommon since it is most often simply implied by the form of the verb, begins this poetic subsection at 2.1 ("I" am the flower of the Sharon plain) and concludes the last words of the subsection, thus functioning as poetic markers of the boundaries of the subsection.

46. This refrain occurs here and in 8.3. Translators sometimes render it a fact instead of a wish: "His left hand is under my head," etc. In the original language, only the one verb "embrace" appears. There is no "is" or any verb after "left hand." The translator must imply the verb and its tense, after determining the tense and mode of "embrace." The immediate and broader context of the Song suggests that the sense of "embrace" is of a wish.

The opening lyric of the Song, "How I wish he would kiss me with the kisses of his mouth," sets a pattern for wishes when, in the context of affection, Shulamith speaks of Solomon in the third person. Even on the wedding night, when Shulamith speaks of Solomon in the third person, she expresses a wish: "May my beloved come into his garden," etc., (4.16). Since she is a "garden locked" and "fountain sealed" on her wedding night, it appears that 2.6 follows the precedent of the opening lyric in being a wish.

More decisively, the public setting favors the concept of wish. The preceding lyrics, with the imagery of a public banner of love that everyone could see, imply a public setting in which only a wish could be appropriate. When this refrain reappears in 8.3, Shulamith is longing for Solomon to respond to her enticing proposal of 8.2, and consistent with previous references to him in the third person during lovemaking, it is likely a wish.

In addition, the phrase immediately preceding this, "I am faint from love," implies a longing for love that is not being experienced, just as it does when it is precisely repeated during their separation in 5.8: Shulamith asks the young women of Jerusalem to tell Solomon, "I am faint from love."

47. The words for "arouse" and "awaken" are different forms of the same verb; perhaps each one having a slightly different nuance. The sense seems to be, "Don't try to make the feelings of love begin or the actions of love to start until love desires it to happen." Love is personified as the director of their relationship.

48. Some translate this "my love." But personal pronoun "my" is in the original language, and the word for "love" does not imply it. It is not the same word Shulamith often uses to refer to her "beloved." In fact, it is an abstract form of a dif-

ferent word for love that suggests the translation given here.

49. This is literally "until it pleases." Although some translations make "she" the subject, that would mean that "love" is a reference to Shulamith. But she is the speaker. Also, the word for "love" used here is never used of a specific person (see note at 7.6). The subject, therefore, is "love," which I have included in my translation. The word rendered "pleases" implies "pleases to do something," and since the action contemplated is "to awaken," I included that in the translation too. "Love" has its own sense of timing, and the lovers who participate in love must be sensitive to it. This use of language is similar to saying something like "nature" guides the harvest. A farmer may plant and his workers cultivate, but the rules of nature guide the harvest, and the farmer must be aware of those principles.

50. The word for "voice" could also be translated "sound," which may be the sense of it here. However, since this lyric begins a series of carefully crafted lyrics that includes a reference to the "voice" of the turtledove in 2.12 and concludes with Solomon's desire to hear Shulamith's voice in 2.14, I wanted the reader to be aware of the artistic balancing of this section (2.8–14). The beginning, middle, and ending of it refer to a "voice." His voice begins the section; the voice of the turtledove is the central part of the spring day; the desire to hear her voice concludes it.

51. The word for "bounding" sounds like the word for "delights to do so" in the previous verse that admonishes patience in waiting for love. Now love comes "bounding delightfully" in response to Shulamith's patience, in the manner of the gazelles, whose behavior is an example for the behavior of lovers.

52. Keel points out that both London and Israel average 21.45 inches of rain a year, but in London it rains three hundred days a year, whereas in Jerusalem the same amount is concentrated in fifty days (Keel, 100).

53. The word for "singing" can also mean "pruning," and some have thought that this may be a play on both those meanings, each being a possible translation. This kind of wordplay appears, for example, at 7.13. However, the time of pruning is before the flowers blossom, so pruning would not be the likely translation. In addition, this lyric parallels the following reference to the voice of the turtledove, which necessitates the meaning of "singing." Perhaps the meaning of "pruning" is still in the background of the lyric in a different way. When the original reader saw this word, he realized when rejecting the meaning of "pruning" that the time for pruning was not only past literally but figuratively as well. The time of preparation to blossom was also in the past for Solomon and Shulamith, and now was their time to blossom.

54. The word for "form" could also be translated "appearance." It is plural in the original and suggests the appearance of her from every angle. The second time it appears in this verse, it is singular.

55. The word rendered "pleasing" could also be translated "sweet" or "melodic."

56. The speaker could be Solomon, Shulamith, or both.

57. In 1.6 and 8.12 the "vineyard" refers to Shulamith. In 2.15 the "vineyards" seem to refer to both Shulamith and Solomon.

58. The concept of grazing among the lotus flowers unfolds beautifully in the Song. Shulamith is a lotus flower (2.1–2); Solomon grazes among lotus flowers (2.16); her breasts are like fawns that graze among lotus flowers (4.5); his lips are like lotus flowers dripping with myrrh (5.13); he grazes in the gardens and gathers lotus flowers (6.2–3); her abdomen is encircled with lotus flowers (7.2).

The "lotus flower" first describes the whole person of Shulamith, and then becomes more erotic, and evidently associated with tenderness—her breasts, his kisses, her abdomen. The grazing refers to the nourishment Solomon draws from this. The association of lotus flowers with magical, life-giving power seems always appropriate to the context.

"Graze" is first more literal in describing Solomon and Shulamith each grazing their respective flocks (1.7 8). But soon Solomon embodies the gazelle grazing among lotus flowers (2.16), which flowers are then more specifically around her breasts (4.5) and then hips, abdomen, and navel (7.1 2).

Not only is the whole person and his or her sexuality life-giving, so are words of forgiveness and praise, which are the lotus flowers he gives her when they reconcile (6.2–9).

59. "Day" occurs five times in the Song, and the other four occurrences are clearly linked to the wedding day and night. In 3.11 the lyric refers to the "day of his wedding, …the day of his heart's rejoicing." In 4.6 Solomon promises lovemaking until the following "day." And in 8.8 Shulamith's brothers prepare for the "day on which she is spoken for," which is likely her wedding day but possibly engagement. It would be consistent with the artistry of the Song for the first occurrence of "day" in 2.17 to refer to the wedding day, as well.

60. Here and in 4.6 this is literally "the day blows" or "the day breathes," an idiom either for the break of day when the morning breezes blow and the shadows of darkness flee, or when the new day "breathes," which means "comes to life," and the shadows of darkness flee.

The beginning of the phrase is either "when" or "until" (or remotely possible as "before"). Almost all translations will render the introductory phrase the same way in both 2.17 and 4.6: either as "when the day breathes" in both verses or "until the day breathes" in both verses. But it does not appear necessary to translate them the same way if the translation of the underlying conjunctive compound rendered "when" or "until" is governed by the action of the main verb and the broader context.

Let's agree on some terms to sort this out. In the sentence, "He shopped at the store until he fainted," let's say "shopped" is the *primary verb* of the primary clause; "until" is the *subordinating conjunction* introducing the *adverb clause* that *modifies* the primary clause; and "fainted" is the *subordinate verb* of the adverb clause. So in the sentence, "turn; be like a gazelle when (or until) the day breaks," the *primary verb* is "turn," and the *subordinating conjunction* introducing the adverb clause is "when."

The action a verb describes may be characterized as either completed or ongoing. Completed action is like, "He broke the window when he passed the ball" or, "Jump once in the air when the clock strikes noon." Ongoing action is like, "He passes the ball until he's too tired to throw" or, "Jump in the air until I say stop."

This distinction in the conception of the action of a verb is helpful in determining the meaning of certain words that modify primary verbs. For example, if the action of the primary verb is conceived as completed action, and the subordinating conjunction introducing the modifying adverb clause can otherwise mean either "when" or "until," then the only meaning in the context would be "when." It would make little sense to say, "He broke the window until he passed the ball" or, "Jump once in the air until the clock strikes noon." "When" is consistent with the primary verb in introducing something conceived as a point in time, but "until" imagines a duration of time. (The only alternative to "when" is sometimes the translation "before." But the underlying meaning of the subordinating conjunction and the context disfavors this choice in 2.17. And even "before" is precluded by the context in 8.4: It would make no sense to say, "Surely arouse love before it pleases to awaken.")

Since "turn" appears to be a verb of completed action in the sentence "Turn, be like a gazelle," it would similarly make little sense to translate the subordinating conjunction as "until." So in 2.17, the translation should likely be, "Turn; be like, my beloved, a gazelle or a young stag on the divided mountains *when* the day breathes and the shadows flee away.

However, in the sentence in 4.6, "When/until the day breathes…, I will go my way to the mountain of myrrh," the possibility emerges that "until" could introduce the modifying clause. And that possibility becomes a probability if the underlying subordinate conjunction favors duration in time, and the context suggests it. Since the underlying compound conjunction means literally "unto the point," and the context of "I will go my way" is that of action that has already begun and will continue, it becomes probable that the proper translation is, "*Until* the day breathes…, I will go my way to the mountain of myrrh and to the hill of frankincense."

So it does indeed appear that the action of the primary verb and the broader context govern the translation of the subordinating conjunction that can be translated either "when" or "until." And the grammatical rule is fairly straightforward. The subordinating conjunction is most likely translated "when" when it introduces a relative clause modifying a primary verb of *completed action*. It is most likely translated "until" when it introduces a relative clause modifying a primary verb of *ongoing action*, especially when the context suggests that the action has already begun.

If we apply this rule to the refrain of patience and its counterpart, the refrain of responsiveness, the following translations emerge: patience—"Do not arouse, do not awaken love [*ongoing action* of restraint] *until* love pleases to awaken"; and responsiveness—"Surely awaken love [*completed action* "awaken"] *when* love pleases to awaken."

This rule is consistent with the traditional translation of the subordinating conjunction in 3.4 as well: "Scarcely had I *passed* [*completed action*] from them *when* I found him whom my soul loves."

The songwriter may be teasing the reader in 2.17 with the two verbs following "until the day breathes": "turn" and then immediately next, "be like," abruptly appearing before the term of address, "my beloved." Since the introductory clause modifies the first verb, which is a verb of completed action, the clause begins with "when"; but if it had modified the second verb of ongoing action, then the clause would begin with "until," like in 4.6 when it modifies "I will go." The songwriter seems to foreshadow artistically the lovemaking all through the wedding night.

It is still quite possible that the phrase beginning 2.17 could be translated "until the day breathes" and that it is left to the poetry of the Song to show us that this request is not answered until the wedding night in 4.6. A precise grammatical rule for the conjunctive compound of these verses lacks mathematical certainty.

And even if the rule is reliable, it is often as much art as science to determine whether the action of the main verb is completed or ongoing. For example, is "I will go" in 4.6 conceived as a single step in time or an ongoing action? Fortunately, here we have help from 2.17, where Shulamith asks Solomon not only to "turn" or "turn back," which is completed action, but she also asks him after that to "be like" a gazelle, which is ongoing. And the action of lovemaking is already ongoing in the context. So 4.6 is most likely translated, "Until the day breathes and the shadows flee, I will go my way."

The conjunctive compound, incidentally, occurs ten times in the Old Testament: Judges 5.7; Psalm 123.2; Song 1.12; 2.7, 17; 3.4 (twice); 3.5; 4.6; 8.4. It is a compound of the common word for "until" and the archaic relative pronoun for "which, who, that" which can even function conjunctively. That archaic relative pronoun appears frequently in the Song and in Ecclesiastes but not often elsewhere.

61. This could *possibly*, but not likely, be translated, "When the day breathes and the shadows flee, *return* [or *turn back*]; be, my beloved, like a gazelle or a young stag on the divided mountains."

62. The phrase translated "gazelle or a young stag" is identical in the original language to that phrase in 2.9.

63. This is literally the "mountains of Bether," which means "the mountains of separation," later clarified as Shulamith's breasts in 4.6 and echoed with changes in 8.14.

64. The word for "nights" is plural in the original, as in 3.8, and may suggest repeated nights of longing.

65. The word for "place" appears in the plural in 1.4, "I wish the king would bring me to his chambers."

66. See notes at 2.7.

67. The word for "this" is feminine in gender, suggesting that Shulamith is in the carriage being brought to Solomon.

68. "The wilderness" suggests two complementary allusions. One allusion is to the experience of Israel in the wilderness after leaving Egypt. God led them by a pillar of a cloud by day, to which the "columns of frankincense" may refer. This allusion to Israel's time of testing in the wilderness would remind the reader of the times of difficulty experienced by Solomon and Shulamith that prepared them for marriage. It would also alert the reader to the life-changing experience of the wedding day that brought Solomon and Shulamith to a new land, upon which they would build their life together.

"The wilderness" also alludes to the story of Adam and Eve, who, beginning in paradise in the Garden of Eden, created a wilderness by their departure from God's will. Solomon and Shulamith begin the wedding procession emerging from the wilderness but conclude in a celebration of her paradisal garden. The Song thus poetically portrays a return to paradise in their experience of love.

69. "At his side" is literally "on his thigh."

70. In the anxiety of Shulamith's search "in the nights" for Solomon, she "went around" the city and encountered the watchmen who "went around" in the city. When she found Solomon, she "held on" to him and took him to the room of her mother. Now the mighty of Israel are "around" (same root word) the carriage; they "hold" (same root word) swords; and they protect her from the terror "in the nights" (same phrase); Solomon's mother has crowned him with a special crown for the wedding. The wedding day is described in a way that portrays Solomon's responses to the fears of Shulamith.

71. The "day of his wedding," the "day of his heart's rejoicing," is likely the day Shulamith asked him to turn when the "day breathes and the shadows flee" and to "be like…a gazelle or a young stag on the divided mountains" (2.17). The "turn" in 2.17 suggests his departure in that context, and the shadows fleeing suggest the coming night of anxiety in 3.1–4.

72. Some evidence exists for translating this word for "veil" (4.1, 3; 6.7) as "hair," but I agree with most translators that "veil" is more likely, lexically and contextually.

I am more puzzled, however, by the prepositions I've translated "from behind," and the preposition "to" *(lamed)* preceding "veil." I'm not aware of anywhere else in Old Testament literature where the combination of "from" and "behind" merge to form the single "from behind." This could simply be poetic license, accentuating the movement coming forward of her eyes like doves and lips like a scarlet ribbon. But I am also a little puzzled by the purpose of the preposition "to" preceding "veil," which I and others most frequently leave essentially untranslated.

Again, perhaps these unusual prepositions accentuate the movement from the veil or hint at its removal during the praise. I would welcome any help on this from other translators.

73. The word describing this movement down the mountain is from a root for "bubbling" or "boiling" and pictures the small movements within the whole, which are like bubbles from boiling water. Some, therefore, have translated this verb "hopping"; but the whole flock does not hop at once, so "moving briskly" tries to capture the smaller movements within the whole, like the bouncing of curls of hair cascading to her shoulders.

74. This lighthearted statement has a clever play on words in the original language. "Each one" *(shekulam—*literally, "all of which") in "each one bearing twins" sounds like "is bereaved" *(shakulah)* in "and bereaved is not one." Both "bearing twins" and "bereaved" of offspring in the lyric are terms from the language of birth and loss.

75. The phrase "scarlet ribbon" could also be translated as a scarlet "thread," "cord," or "strand." The phrase occurs elsewhere in the Old Testament only at Joshua 2.18, where it refers to the scarlet strand Rahab would hang from her window as a sign to the invading Israelites to protect her home from any violence. The imagery is reminiscent of the Exodus plagues, wherein if the Israelites placed the blood of the lamb over their doors, the angel of death would "pass over" them.

The scarlet thread may well link Rahab to Tamar as well. When Tamar gave birth to twin boys, the midwife identified the firstborn son by placing a scarlet thread on his wrist. Perhaps the image of two sons coming from Tamar with a scarlet thread, identifying the chosen firstborn, is in the background of the two spies in Rahab's house emerging from the window with the scarlet cord. Tamar and Rahab would both be seen as chosen by God to bring the fulfillment of his design for the earth (Warren Gage, unpublished).

In any case, Solomon's praise alludes primarily to the scarlet strand of Rahab. The significance seems to be that Shulamith's speech, which expresses her character, is her protection and indicates she belongs to God, just as Rahab's scarlet ribbon indicated she belonged to God and his people. Just as God chose Tamar and Rahab to fulfill his plans for the earth, Solomon chooses Shulamith to fulfill God's plan for his life.

When the emphasis of the word falls on the "strand" or "thread" of the lips, then the focus is on the slit of Shulamith's lips where they close, a natural contrast to the next compliment of her lips open like a slice into a pomegranate.

76. This is normally translated, "Like the half [or slice] of a pomegranate is your brow [or temple]." The more precise sense of the word rendered "slice" is "split," but not a cut all the way through like a "slice." So a more accurate translation would be "sliced opening." This conforms to the way the pomegranate customarily was eaten in the ancient world. One normally cut into it and picked or sucked out the seeds surrounded by crimson juice. It is, in fact, highly unlikely that someone would make "slices" of a pomegranate. Keel points out that this cut into the fruit, or the fissure where the cut would be made, is virtually always present in the Egyptian representations of pomegranates discovered by archaeologists.

Next, what is the meaning of the word that this split pomegranate describes? Almost all translations indicate a reference to the "brow" or "temple," since that is the most common meaning given to this word in the two other occurrences of it in Judges 4.21 and 5.26. And that is certainly a possible meaning.

But even if this word, *rakkah,* derives from the same root as that in Judges, it may suggest the softness of the lips or thinness of the opening of the lips. More importantly, it may derive from a root word identical in form, which has the root meaning of "saliva" and, therefore, refers to the moisture of her mouth. A translation like "parted lips" would be close to this meaning. Keel regards this as a reference to the softness of the interior of the mouth (Keel, 146).

The context of the manner of praise supports this meaning too. Solomon is proceeding from the top of her head to her breasts—eyes, hair beside her cheeks, teeth, lips, *rakkah,* neck, breasts—it would be a clear break in the direction to descend to the teeth, then rise to the brow or temple. Consequently, some have rendered this "cheeks," but the word in the singular doesn't support this. After praising "eyes," "teeth," and "lips," it would be awkward to praise a "cheek" in the singular. And it is a reversal of direction to go to her brow or temple.

Contextually, the reference to the whiteness of her teeth, then the redness of her lips, seems best to conclude with the moist opening of her parted lips—open like the pomegranate to him, offering him sweet, moist kisses. The immediately preceding description of her lips like a scarlet thread pictures her lips as closed. It is a natural sequence now to portray them as open.

A play on words supports this meaning too. The play on this word (*rakkah:* "moist inner mouth" like a pomegranate) in 8.2 (*rekak:* "spiced wine" of her pomegranate), when Shulamith promises Solomon she will "let him drink" (with the play "let him kiss" from 8.1) from the wine of her pomegranate, is much more consistent with the meaning of *rakkah* as "parted lips" or "moist interior" of her mouth than a meaning of "brow" or "cheeks." On her wedding night her lips parted to the moist interior of her mouth are like the sliced opening in a pomegranate, but on the later night, the moisture of her pomegranate is like flavorful mixed wine.

The weakness of any view of the meaning of this word (rendered "parted lips") is inadequate linguistic data. It does not literally mean parted lips, in any case, but refers to the soft, moist inner mouth. Perhaps a translator should take consolation in the fact that both the translation of it as the "brow" or the "lips parted" are at least consistent with the concepts elsewhere in the Song. We know elsewhere he loves her overall beauty, which includes the glow of her brow, and he specifically describes in passages easy to translate, the "honey and milk under her tongue." So even if not in this text, both concepts appear in the Song. Although the translation indicating a reference to the moisture of the interior of her mouth is the less common translation in current translations, I am convinced the evidence favors it.

77. The phrase "made for strength" in the original seems to describe the manner of building the fortress in careful layers for strength and stability.

78. The word for "shields" in its second occurrence in this lyric may possibly be rendered as "quivers."

79. A slight play on words occurs in "two" (shuney) and "teeth" (shiney) and the repetition of the same word for "twins" in the description of her teeth and her breasts. Solomon appreciates the perfect symmetry he sees in her.

80. The prepositional phrase beginning this statement is identical to the phrase beginning 2.17, but in 2.17 it modifies "turn" (or "return"), whereas here it modifies "I will go." So in 2.17 the prepositional phrase means "when the day breathes," according to the grammatical analysis discussed at 2.17, but here it means "until the day breathes." In 2.17 the morning shadows that flee anticipated the anxiety of 3.1–4 and the day of the wedding in 3.6–11. Here the morning shadows that flee suggest any lingering fears or anxieties that his love will lay to rest. In 2.17 Shulamith asks Solomon to return on the day of the wedding and make love to her. In 4.6 Solomon responds by saying he will make love to her until dawn.

81. The "mountain of myrrh and…hill of frankincense" are a poetic reference to Shulamith's breasts. The literary design of the Song shows that this image is introduced at the conclusion of the first two sections (2.17), at the conclusion of the last two sections (8.14), and then here in the center of this central section. So it functions like a refrain. In both the first and third usages of this image, it clearly refers to breasts: "Be like…a gazelle or a young stag on the *divided mountains*" (2.17); "Be like…a gazelle or a young stag on the *mountains of spices*" (8.14). So in this central use of the image in 4.6, it most likely refers to her breasts as well. In the immediate context, Solomon has just described her breasts like fawns among the lotus flowers. Now he poetically answers the request Shulamith made in 2.17.

82. The words for "frankincense" (lebonah) and "Lebanon" (lebonan) sound alike, so when these words appear in proximity, a transitional play on words occurs.

83. The word for blemish refers to both inner and outer flaws. Solomon compliments Shulamith's complete perfection to him.

84. An alliterative transition occurs concluding 4.6 and beginning 4.7 with "frankincense. All of you" (*lebonah cullak,* rendered, "You are completely"), and then beginning 4.8 with "Lebanon, O bride" *(lebanon callah),* which draws attention to the root word of "bride," which is "completion," so that the term for "bride" connotes a "completed one." Such alliteration, of course, also serves to provide poetic transition and unity in the smooth flow of the lyrics.

85. Many interpreters regard this image of Shulamith in the mountains surrounded by the wild animals as indicative of her inaccessibility before this night, as depicting her remoteness, surrounded by wild animals that protect her. It is a beautiful and intriguing image and may, in fact, be the picture intended by the songwriter. However, in previous lyrics before the wedding night, Shulamith has not been inaccessible or protected by anything like this but rather longing for Solomon from the very beginning of the Song. I think it is more likely the image captures her fears, from which Solomon calls her. But perhaps the picture of wild animals protecting her is indeed in the background, suggesting that in her fear she places the figurative barriers of lions and leopards between them.

86. The phrase "my sister, my bride" occurs four times, appearing at each stage of lovemaking: arousal (4.9); kissing (4.10); consummation (4.12); and after consummation (5.1). It is given a prominent position in the lyrics by the poetic device of placing it between beautiful lyrics repetitive of or parallel to each other.

87. This is literally "honeycomb your lips drip," accentuating the freshness and newness of the honey. It is melodic and alliterative, perhaps even onomatopoeic, Keel notes, so that the sounds seem to be those of honey dripping: *nophet titphenah shiphtotayik* (Keel, 165).

88. This might be translated "a fountain locked." The underlying word is rare and may be a transcriptional error in the word for "garden." The pattern in 4.1 to 5.1, whereby the terms of endearment for Shulamith are bordered on each side by the same or similar phrases, favors the intended word to be "garden."

89. The word for "sealed" *(chatum)* is from the same root word as "seal" *(chatom)* in 8.6.

90. The subject of this lyric is easier to understand than to translate. Literally, the subject is "your shoots" or "your extensions," an image of the plants and trees that extend from a garden. So some translations have maintained the figurative element and rendered this "your shoots" or "your branches." But "shoots" is a relatively uncommon word and encompasses too little, and "branches" does not include the smaller flowers and plants or the entire trees of this vast oriental garden. The meaning of the *phrase* is something like "The garden of your body." It is also possible,

however, that the meaning of the *word* is "watered fields," which some lexical evidence supports.

91. The particular plant to which this refers is most likely the calamus reed, which grows in marshes and by streams. The phrase "fragrant reed and cinnamon" is alliterative in the original *(qineh and qinnamon)*.

92. This could be translated "with every kind of aromatic tree."

93. Most translations have "fountain" in the singular here, but the original is clearly plural and, poetically, a continuation of Solomon's praise spiraling upward: Shulamith is not merely a beautiful garden but a fountain of many gardens. Then he proceeds to embellish the water imagery with the imagery of the well and the flowing streams.

94. The word for "fresh" means literally "living" or "flowing," and the meaning is "fresh," healthy water from a clean, flowing source.

95. This is the same word for "awaken" used in the refrains for patience: "not to arouse, not to awaken love" in 2.7; 3.5 and its variation, to seize the moment in 8.4.

96. The same verb for flowing water is used to refer to "streams flowing from Lebanon" in 4.15 and Shulamith's spices that "flow like a stream" in 4.16.

97. The songwriter addresses Solomon and Shulamith with the names each has most frequently called the other. He has consistently called her "darling companion," and she has consistently called him "my beloved." The Song accomplishes at least three things with this address to both of them by the songwriter.

On one level it affirms the goodness of sexual love, since the creator of it is blessing them with encouragement.

On another level it tells us that each of them is a friend to the other, and each of them is beloved to the other. This corrects any implication that there is one-sidedness to either of these two aspects of their relationship.

On a third level, it reveals the poetic artistry of the songwriter. In ruling out any implications of one-sidedness by an address to both of them in those names by a third party, the songwriter preserves the poetic device of identifying speakers by each calling the other favorite names.

98. This could be translated "A sound!" But to draw attention to the contrast with earlier responses to Solomon's sound or voice, as in 2.8–14, I have translated this "A voice!"

99. This is literally "My beloved extended his hand from the opening," and seems to portray an opening in the door through which Solomon either tried to reach a latch, or more likely, as the text says, he extended his hand though the door to leave a reminder of his presence there. The extension "from the opening" is from her perspective inside the room, where the hand is reaching out from the opening. Instead of a modern possibility of a letter pushed beneath the door, he leaves fragrant oil on the handle of the door.

100. Some interpreters believe that the myrrh left on the bolt is intended to be an erotic reminder of the lovemaking Solomon desired.

101. The sense could be either (a) her soul went out *to him,* or (b) her soul went out *from her,* leaving her weak. I have tried to retain this ambiguity in my translation. The occasional translation of "when he spoke" as "upon his departure" has little lexical support.

102. The phrase "I am faint from love" is identical in word and sequence to its occurrence in 2.5, which represented a peak of longing during their courtship.

103. The underlying language could depart from the dove imagery and perhaps be translated "set like jewels." However, part of the motivation for this departure is the perception that "doves beside streams of water" is inconsistent with doves "perched over a pool."

But the imagery of "bathed in milk" is the transition between the two and suggests a movement from "streams" to "bath" to "pool." Since this is by far the lengthiest expansion on a metaphor in Shulamith's description of Solomon, it is likely pregnant with meaning. The eyes are the only aspects of Solomon and Shulamith described alike, and the reflections of the doves in the pools of water (accentuated by their contrast with streams incapable of reflection) suggest that the image is intended to show doves and their reflections. It is a beautiful picture of Solomon and Shulamith each having eyes of love for each other.

Solomon evolves this image in the tenfold praise of Shulamith corresponding to this tenfold praise section in the design of the Song. He likens her eyes to "pools of understanding" by the gates of a city. When he looks into her eyes, he sees her understanding eyes of love, reflecting the same eyes of love he has for her.

104. This gemstone is either the red sapphire or the blue lapis lazuli.

105. See note on "longed" at 2.3.

106. The word I have translated "lover" here, I have elsewhere in the Song rendered "beloved." But in this particular verse, the linking of the word with "companion" captures the ideal of "friend and lover." I did not want to obscure in any way the Song's presentation of that ideal.

107. This word for "companion" is from the same root as one of Solomon's favorite names for Shulamith, "darling companion." It may simply be a feminine form of that word.

108. See note at 6.10.

109. This might also be translated "your eyes overwhelm me." The form of this verb does not often appear, but its use in Psalm 138.3 suggests the action of the verb arouses strong emotions in the one affected by the action. The meaning of the word as "arouse" is consistent with the repetition of the praise of the wedding night, from which most of the praise in this section comes, when "one glance of her eyes" arouses him.

110. This compliment differs slightly from its first occurrence in 4.2, where on the wedding night, Solomon added the point that the sheep were "newly shorn," coming up from the washing. Perhaps this signifies that on the wedding night, Shulamith first gave herself to him. In imagery similar to the harvest of the vineyard (2.15; 4.12 to 5.1) that had matured through the spring, on the wedding night he harvested the new wool of the sheep.

111. The "sixty queens" may refer to the wives of the sixty mighty men (3.7). Perhaps, just as "gods" diminishes the stature of "God," "queens" may diminish the stature of "queen" and refer to royal aristocracy, not the wife of a king. But it seems just as likely that these women are part of a harem forsaken by Solomon for Shulamith.

112. "Fair...as Tirzah, as lovely as Jerusalem,...as awe-inspiring as bannered hosts" begins the praise in 6.4 and parallels the conclusion of the praise "fair as the white moon, pure as the blazing sun, awe-inspiring as bannered hosts." In light of the similarity in content of other beginnings and conclusions, as in 2.10 and 2.13; 4.1 and 4.7; 5.2 and 7.9 in Appendix C; one must consider how similar the content is here. Since Tirzah was a magnificent city in northern Israel (at one time the capital of the Northern Kingdom after the division after Solomon) yet not deemed as glorious as Jerusalem, it seems natural to see the moon describing Tirzah, the sun describing Jerusalem, and the bannered hosts bringing balance to both descriptions but taking its specific meaning from the different contexts (see note on "bannered hosts" at 6.10). So both the beginning and ending of this section praise Shulamith as representing the best of Israel in its glory.

The symbolism of the moon, sun, and eleven stars (or twelve, counting Joseph—Revelation 12.1) in the dream of Joseph, where they represent the Israel comprised of Jacob, his wive(s), and Joseph's eleven brothers, adds further support to this view (Genesis 37). Allusions to Joseph appear elsewhere in the Song: in Shulamith's mistreatment by older brothers; in the removal of the shawl twice, once very roughly (see note at 1.6, "burned in anger toward me"); and in the forgiveness and care of her brothers at 8.12. The sun, moon, and stars appear often in the negative context of their worship elsewhere in the Old Testament. So the most likely origin of a positive connotation to them is the reference in the dream of Joseph.

Moreover, the likely meaning of "bannered hosts" when referring to stars is not to all the stars but to those "bannered" hosts, those *prominent* stars—a restricted number, as scholars who take this view often observe. Since literal banners identified the twelve tribes of Israel in Numbers, and eleven stars plus one for Joseph represent the twelve tribes of Israel in Joseph's dreams, a poetic convergence of the two in the "bannered hosts" of stars in 6.10 seems quite possible.

Finally, a clear allusion to Jacob, who is given the name *Israel* at the event to which 6.13 alludes, supports the compliments of 6.10 as embellishment on the praise imagery of Shulamith in 6.4. The dance of the two camps recalls a celebration of the reconciliation of Jacob and Esau, just as this chapter concludes with the celebration of the reconciliation of Solomon and Shulamith.

113. The word rendered "morning star" could well be translated "dawn." In either case, it could be the beginning of a short chiastic structure: morning star/dawn; moon; sun; stars (if "bannered hosts" in this context refers to the hosts of heaven). The pattern of *abb´a´* proceeds on the premise that the moon and sun govern the night and the day. The movement from *a* to *a´* is progressive: one star/dawn to many stars. The movement from *b* to *b´* is also progressive: from the lesser to the greater light—from moon to sun.

A clever play on words occurs once again with the choice of this word in conjunction with Shulamith's description of herself in the beginning as "dark" (1.6). The root of the word for "dawn" (or "morning star") is identical to the root for "dark." The forms in which the root words appear differ slightly but clearly preserve the similar sound of "dark" *(shekorah)* and "morning star"or "dawn" *(shakar)*. The young girl "darkened" by the sun now "shines" like the morning star.

114. This is the same word for "fair" beginning the compliments in 6.4. The repetition of it here in 6.10 begins a set of three comparisons which conclude in the identical way those of 6.4 conclude—"awe-inspiring as bannered hosts."

115. The word for moon *(lebanah)* is alliterative with frankincense *(lebonah)* and Lebanon *(lebanon)* and connotes the whiteness of the moon.

116. The term for "bannered hosts" is ambiguous. The word occurs in the Old Testament only in the Song at 6.4 and 6.10. The word "bannered" refers to prominent flags, and interpreters and translators have speculated that the meaning in the Song is probably to "awe-inspiring" troops with banners (drawing upon the use of "banners" in Numbers) or to awesome "stars" prominently seen (drawing upon the context of 6.10, where it follows mention of the dawn—or morning star—and the moon and the sun, which in the Old Testament is frequently followed by reference to stars.)

The translation "bannered hosts" preserves the flexibility of the original word. I suggest that it is a word that draws its specific meaning from its context, as "bright lights" means one thing when said in the context of "This year's movie stars are the 'bright lights' of the industry." But it means something else when in the context of "The astronomer loved the 'bright lights' of the sky."

The repetition of the same word in 6.4 and 6.10 concludes an artful parallelism in the opening and closing of Solomon's praise during the reconciliation sequence. The different contexts suggest that the first occurrence of "bannered hosts" in 6.4 could possibly be different from "stars" and be something like "hosts of troops with banners," but the second context gives it the meaning of "the hosts of heaven" and refers to prominent stars.

117. The word for "if" is not present but is allowed by the structure of the

sentence. However, when a lyric much like this occurs in 7.12, the "if" is explicitly present. It is possible that Shulamith hints at her confidence in the outcome of her visit to the garden. So she would go to see that "the vine had budded and the pomegranates had bloomed." She has just said before going to see Solomon that she knows they belong to each other (6.3), in a passage that is structurally parallel to this one (see Appendix C); perhaps the absence of "if" is a further expression of that confidence.

118. The word for "soul" might also be rendered "desire."

119. This is a notoriously difficult verse to translate. Some render it, "My desire set me among the chariots of my noble people" or "over the chariots of my people, a prince." The implication of almost every translation, however, is that Shulamith is in a place of authority and notoriety. Perhaps the reference to chariots is meant to recall the chariots of Pharaoh, where as a mare, she stirred up quite a response (1.9). Some translators simply transliterate the phrase "my people of a prince" as a personal name and render it "Amminadib" (*ammi* is "my people"; *nadib* is "a prince"). This sounds very much like the name of one of Solomon's ancestors, "Amminadab," (Ruth 4.19) and so perhaps is an allusion or even a direct reference to him.

120. Shulamith is preceded in the original language by an article, "the," that functions to introduce a vocative case—a noun or name directly addressed (e.g., 2 Samuel 14.4; 2 Kings 6.26). Some interpreters have rightly pointed out that since this article precedes Shulamith, it is likely not a "pure" personal name but more likely a descriptive personal name, something like "Solomoness."

One of the more subtle disputes about *Shulamith* debates the conclusion that it is a feminine form of *Solomon* and suggests rather that it is a name derived independently from *shalom*. But since *Solomon* clearly is based on *shalom*, the ultimate result is essentially the same: a masculine and feminine version of the same word.

Although some translations abandon the derivation from *shalom* altogether by translating the name "Shunammite," no textual evidence in the original language supports this.

121. This word translated "gaze in awe" differs from the normal word "to see" and from other words in the Song rendered "stare" (1.6a) or "gazed"(1.6b) or "behold" (2.8). The fundamental meaning of it is "to see in a vision"; secondarily, "to see or recognize God's work"; and occasionally, it is used of God "to see." Later usage of this word after the Song broadened its meaning to include simple visual perception apart from the connotations of insights about God and his activity in daily life.

The connotations from its early primary meanings appear to be retained in the two usages in 6.13. A prophetic vision often invested earthly events with symbolic meaning, just like a prophetic dream might do: seven healthy cows can refer to seven years of prosperity (Genesis 41.26), or three branches of grapes poured into a cup can refer to three days before a man resumes his role as a cupbearer to Pharaoh (Genesis 40.12). Since these symbols are obscure, Joseph, an interpreter specially gifted by God, must explain their meaning.

When the young maidens ask Shulamith to return so they might "gaze in awe" upon her, as at a vision, they grasp that something is divine about what has taken place with Shulamith, but they don't fully grasp what it is.

Perhaps Solomon interprets that "vision" for them, just like Joseph interpreted the dreams in Genesis. They gaze in awe upon her, he says, as if looking at the "dance of the two camps." This likely refers to the celebration of the reconciliation of Jacob and Esau that accompanied the dramatic change of Jacob's name to *Israel,* just as Shulamith's reconciliation with Solomon accompanied the dramatic change of her name to *Shulamith.* (The next note explains this more fully.)

In addition, if the reconciliation of Solomon and Shulamith recalls the restoration of the relationship of Esau and Jacob, and Jacob's restored relationship with God the night before, then another meaning of the "vision" emerges. The restoration of Solomon and Shulamith illustrates the reconciliation possible between God and his people and among his people with each other.

122. This is literally "the dance of the Mahanaim," which means "dance of two camps." Many interpreters speculate on what such a dance would be like. However, it is not the manner of the dance but the meaning of it that explains the reference to it here. It is quite likely any dancing that celebrates reconciliation. This meaning arises from the origin of the name: Jacob's division of all his people and property into two camps, and their likely celebration when the twin brothers Jacob and Esau reconciled (Genesis 32).

Esau had been angry with Jacob when Jacob had deceived him (Genesis 27.41) and then fled from him years earlier. Although Jacob had fled alone, he was now returning to the land with wives, children, many servants, large flocks, and a wealth of possessions. Since he feared the possible retribution of Esau, Jacob minimized the risk to himself and those with him by dividing all he had into two camps. If Esau attacked one camp, the other camp could flee with their lives and half of the possessions. Jacob named the place of the two camps "Mahanaim."

While Jacob wrestled all through the night before his confrontation with Esau, the people of the camps no doubt tossed and turned as well. All of their lives were at risk. As Jacob fearfully approached Esau the next morning, his people came with him, anxiously awaiting the outcome. Instead of attacking Jacob, Esau ran forward and embraced him. Just as Jacob and Esau wept for joy after years apart, a vast sense of relief and joy must have swept over the others too. How would they have expressed their happiness? Could they have kept themselves from dancing for joy? Not likely.

Their earlier division into two camps forever reminded them of the genuine danger they had faced. The "dance of the two camps" first celebrated the reconciliation of the twins Jacob and Esau but now refers to a dance that celebrates the reconciliation of Solomon and Shulamith.

An unusual thing had happened to Jacob during the sleepless night preceding the reconciliation. He encountered "the messenger of God," with whom he "struggled" but reconciled, and who at the end dramatically gave him the new name *Israel*, which would become the most important name for his people in their history.

Similarly, an anxious, sleepless night preceded the reconciliation of Solomon and Shulamith; but as a consequence of the reconciliation, she first receives the highly significant new name of "Shulamith," which is perhaps the most important name for her in the Song.

Even with these parallels, one might still wonder why dancing was not mentioned in the Genesis account. Probably, it would simply be assumed. Often details of this kind of event persisted in the tradition of the people, even if not included in the official written account. For example, in the story of Ruth, we do not read that Rahab was Boaz's mother, but the memory of that fact was preserved and finally recorded in the New Testament document of Matthew. And in reading the story of Ruth, such a fact would give depth and clarification to aspects of the story. For example, Ruth asked Boaz, "How is it that I, a foreigner, have found favor in your eyes?" He certainly answered her question, but the answer doesn't tell us the origin of his compassion. Perhaps growing up with a mother who had been an outsider—one whose very name was an insult—had given him a heart of compassion for people rejected for the wrong reasons. Boaz in his character certainly reflected the noble character and courage seen in the speech and behavior of Rahab (Joshua 2.8–21).

Interpreters often miss the significance of Mahanaim to the meaning of the dance. Many commentaries explore the numerous occurrences of the word in all its forms but fail to see that every time this particular form of the word occurs, it refers either to the event that gave rise to the name or to the place name itself.

The original language presents this word in three forms: singular, plural, and—distinctive to Hebrew and uncommon in English—a dual form referring to two of the camps. The word in singular and plural occurs about two hundred times, and commentators dutifully look for help in all these occurrences. But it is the dual form that occurs in the Song that should be investigated. In the dual form, it occurs only thirteen times outside the Song and once within it. Every time it occurs outside the Song, it refers to the place where Jacob reconciled with Esau (Genesis 32.2; Joshua 13.26, 30; 21.38; 2 Samuel 2.8, 12, 29; 17.24, 27; 19.32; 1Kings 2.8; 4.14; 1 Chronicles 6.80), and the meaning of that event is often in the background: Mahanaim is the place where civil war within Israel ends (2 Samuel 2.8, 12, 29), and is the place of rest and sustenance within civil war (2 Samuel 17.24, 27; 19.32).

Most scholars acknowledge that we don't currently know precisely where this is now. So it is interesting to me that all the references to it occur in books of the Old Testament purporting to be prior to the time of Solomon and his Song. Sometime after this era the exact location became unclear. But the location and the significance it represented was evidently still known in the time of Solomon, just as it had been known at the time of his father, David.

123. One could possibly translate this "steps" instead of "feet." Perhaps it refers to the dance steps of Shulamith, whose happiness overflows into her steps after the reconciliation. But it would not be odd to praise her ordinary steps. Even the Egyptian love songs occasionally compliment the "steps" of the beloved (W. K. Simpson, *The Literature of Ancient Egypt,* 316).

124. Only here at 7.1 and at 6.12 does the word "prince" occur. Perhaps one reason they occur here is to draw attention to the separate realms of authority and prestige that both Shulamith and Solomon bring to the reconciliation, which is like the reconciliation of two equally powerful brothers—Jacob and Esau—at Mahanaim (Genesis 32 and 33).

125. The word for "hips" refers to the upper part of the thighs, inclusive of the side of the hips, which would bear the shape of the curve to which Solomon refers.

126. The word for "artist" is literally "master craftsman." Perhaps this is a lingering allusion to the hip of Jacob, "touched" and injured by the messenger of God during the night of struggle before the reconciliation with Esau. God had formed the hips of Shulamith just as he had also touched the hip of Jacob.

127. Some lexical evidence from Arabic suggests the possibility that this word translated "navel" means "vulva." However, the other two occurrences of this word in the Old Testament refer to the body in general (Proverbs 3.8) and to the umbilical cord (Ezekiel 16.4). "Navel" seems the likely meaning in 7.2, since it is a more likely image of a wine chalice or bowl, to which it is compared.

On the other hand, the image of wine and wheat coupled with the reference to the pomegranate in 8.2, with its wordplay on "drink" and "kiss" and the prior wordplays on "love" and "mandrakes" and then on "doors" and "openings," suggests that the word for "navel" may be a euphemism for her more intimate sexuality.

This euphemism would be consistent with the texts on lovemaking from Sumerian literature, which predate the Song. In that literature a woman's sexual arousal is praised as an intoxicating drink to the lover. In ancient Egyptian and Syrian art depicting lovers, the vulva and the navel are often interchangeable in their schematic representations. But consistent with the difference in tone from this other literature, the Song expresses such eroticism more beautifully and indirectly.

128. The container could also be translated "bowl" and be reminiscent of ancient schematics of the female body with the navel (and sometimes vulva) represented as a bowl. The adjective "round" may allude to the roundness of the moon

and thus bring a beautiful association to the beauty of the chalice.

129. In Egyptian archaeology the lotus flowers often appear offered to one's lover along with other aphrodisiacal plants and fruits and with the suggestion of eroticism in the seductive dress or actions of the one offering. But the lotus appears surrounding food offered as well. For example, in the tomb of Ramose is a mural with fruits surrounded by lotus flowers. Or one can find plates with lotus flower designs around the outer edge, like the designs on china plates, suggesting the life-giving power of the food (Keel, 233). Solomon portrays the wheat and wine of Shulamith's abdomen and navel as surrounded by life-renewing lotus flowers.

130. This could be translated the "pools in Heshbon, by the gate of Bath Rabbim." But "Heshbon" means "explanation"; the gate in view is one of the large gates of entrance to a city; and "Bath Rabbim" is literally "daughter of many," which seems to allude to the many people either in the city or passing through the gate. Just as travelers contemplated by pools of water away from the city, so Solomon found understanding and communication in the eyes of Shulamith.

131. The word for "nose" is a common word for anger, an association arising from the flaring of the nostrils in anger. If Shulamith's "nose" is like a military tower looking toward an adversary, then she has the same capacity for anger as the soldiers of the tower fortress and is as protective of her boundaries as the tower is of the country's boundaries. Anyone seeking to violate either one will meet swift resistance.

132. The words for "beautiful" and "lovely" are in their verb form here, unlike, for example, where they appear together as adjectives in 1.16. The word for "beautiful" may offer a clue to the significance of the distinction between the verb and adjective use. The adjective occurs in 1.15 (twice); 1.16; 4.1 (twice) 4.7; 6.4; and once in 6.10 from the daughters of Jerusalem. The verb occurs at 4.10 describing Shulamith's caresses, at 7.1 describing her steps or feet in sandals, and then at 7.6 in describing her giving. It appears the verb is chosen when the description is of action, but the adjective when it is of something more static. So when Solomon describes her basic appearance in 1.15, the adjective is chosen; but the first time the verb appears is in his description of her lovemaking as they begin to make love on their wedding night. The connotation is "How beautiful you are *being* in your love-making." Similarly, in 7.6 Solomon describes how beautiful she is *being* in her tender giving, or how beautiful her steps are in 7.1.

133. This is literally "Love is in the tender [or comforting] things delighted in." Sometimes this is translated "O love, in your delights," with "love" as a term of address. But the word for love occurs ten times in the Song, and nowhere else is it a personal name of address (2.4–5, 7; 3.5; 5.8; 7.6; 8.4, 6–7). It occurs twenty-two other times in the Old Testament, never as a term of address or name. In the structural parallelism with 5.8, which you can observe in Appendix C, the word for love occurs in the same sense as here, as the abstract word for love.

Additionally, the parallelism of content in 1.16 supports the reading of "love" as a subject rather than as a term of address. In 1.16 the same root words for "beautiful" and "lovely" appear, albeit in their adjective form; it is the only other place in the Song where they appear together in *any* form outside of here at 7.6, and in particular the only other appearance of any form of "lovely" in the Song. As here, they are the basis of two compliments which precede a brief two-word sentence in the original language. In light of that parallelism, one might expect a two-word sentence with subject and predicate here as well.

So the literal translation must begin with "love" as the subject. The predicate is a relatively uncommon noun but with a more common root. The verb of this root means "to take pleasure in" or "to delight in." The adjective of the root refers to "tender" or "comforting" pleasures, like a "comfortable" home. The noun refers to those "tender" or "delightful" comforts Shulamith gives to Solomon, "the things delighted in."

Thus when Solomon says simply, "Love is in the tender things delighted in," he is saying that the feelings and intentions of love flow through all of the tender affection she gives to him. Her inner love prompts outward expression. Her heart and body are integrated in her giving. And her tender giving from love comforts and delights him.

134. Some translations read "its clusters" of fruit. But the "its" is intentionally absent in the original, since the lyric will liken her breasts to *two* kinds of clusters: first to "date clusters" of the palm tree and then to "grape clusters" from the vine.

135. The word translated "smoothly" is the same word rendered "how right" or "rightly" in 1.4. The connotation of "smoothly" is the "rightness" of their comforting love together, so that "appropriately and rightly" do their kisses linger in their hearts as they drift off to sleep.

136. Some translations read "and teeth" instead of "as we fall asleep," but the most reliable early manuscripts of the Song support "as we fall asleep." The original language reads literally "of sleeping ones." This word is then played upon a few lyrics later when Shulamith tantalizes Solomon with erotic fruits that she has in store for him (7.13). In her description of the "new" and "old" fruits, the word for "old" (*yeshanim*) sounds like the word for "sleeping ones" (*yeshenim*). If the "old" fruits metaphorically describe their familiar ways of making love, and the "new" describe fresh and creative ways to make love, then the significance of the play on words is perhaps that the comfortable and familiar lovemaking brings the peacefulness of sleep together.

137. The word for "desire" in 7.10 occurs only twice elsewhere in the Old Testament: at Genesis 3.16, in God's words to Eve in the context of describing the consequences of disobedience ("Your desire is for him, but he must [or "shall"] rule over you"); and in God's words to Cain in Genesis 4.7, describing sin personified as

a lion crouching at the door ("It's desire is for you, but you must rule over it").

Many interpreters agree that since Genesis attributes the "desire" to Eve but the Song attributes the "desire" to Solomon, the ideal relationship of the Song is a picture of romantic love that reverses the consequences of disobedience. Now the husband has the desire, whereas after the first disobedience, the wife had the desire, and so this implies a return to paradise in some way in 7.10.

The nature of that return to paradise has been interpreted in three ways. One interpretation is that a consequence of disobedience is that Eve and future wives will desire their husbands—sexually and otherwise—but that Adam and future husbands would seek only to dominate their wives. So in the Song of Solomon, the interpretation continues, Solomon and Shulamith equally desire each other, and neither seeks to rule the other. And that is the nature of the return to paradise. But this meaning of "desire" is contrary to its meaning in Genesis 4.7.

Another interpretation points out that the exact phrase in Genesis 4.7, about sin seeking to control Cain ("Its desire is for him, but he must rule over it"), implies that the "desire" is a desire to rule or control, and that therefore a consequence of disobedience is that Eve and future wives will seek to control their husbands, and Adam and future husbands will retaliate by seeking to dominate their wives. So in the Song of Solomon, the interpretation proceeds, Shulamith does not seek to control Solomon, and he does not retaliate by seeking to control her, and so neither seeks to rule the other. In this interpretation Solomon's "desire" is not a desire to rule but simply a desire to love. But that is a different meaning of "desire" than in Genesis 4.7.

A third interpretation affirms the meaning of "desire" as a "desire to rule," accepting the meaning in Genesis 4.7 as a guide to the meaning of Genesis 3.16. But it also points out that in 4.7 the need to "rule" or "control" sin was not a retaliation but a moral requirement. So, they argue, if you accept 4.7 as a guide to the meaning of "desire," how can you not accept it as a guide to the meaning of "rule"?

After all, the proponent continues, in the account of the consequences for the first acts of disobedience, moral duties are affirmed that simply must be done with greater difficulty: Eve shall have children, but now with pain; Adam shall work to eat, but now with pain; and Adam shall "rule" his wife, so it concludes, but now with resistance. Before the disobedience, there was childbirth, work, and husbands "ruling" wives; and after the disobedience these facts remain, but now each of these broad areas of life are met with resistance: man resists God; children resist their parents; the ground resists those working it; and wives resist their husbands. That is the argument.

On this view, a consequence of disobedience is that Eve and future wives will seek to control their husbands, but Adam and future husbands must still fulfill their moral duty to resist this control and "rule" the household. So it may be wrong for

Eve to "desire to rule" Adam, but it is virtuous for Solomon to "desire to rule" Shulamith. So in the Song of Solomon, this interpretation concludes, Shulamith resists the desire to rule Solomon, and he desires to "rule" her, which is his moral duty.

I find the third interpretation most logically compelling of the three, although I am personally uncomfortable with much emphasis on the moral obligation of a husband to rule a woman or his house with some kind of kingly authority.

But a closer look at the third view makes me more comfortable with a variation of that view. The word for "rule" does not mean "rule" with an iron fist. In fact, the word is first used in Genesis 1.18 to describe the "rule" of the sun and the moon over the day and the night. Many translations capture the meaning of this by saying the sun and the moon "govern" the day and the night. They demarcate those time periods and provide the light of guidance during them.

This is not the same word for "rule," incidentally, that is used in the command to Adam to "rule" the earth. That word much more often bears a negative connotation of ruling harshly (even though it certainly does not always mean that).

Rather, the word describing the "rule" of Adam for Eve is used quite neutrally of responsible government and leadership. It describes responsible and caring political leadership (2 Samuel 23.3–4), messianic rule over the earth (Micah 5.2; Zechariah 9.10), and God's loving care for his people (Psalms 22.28; 59.13; 66.7; 89.9).

It appears the meaning of Genesis 3.16 is that Adam and future husbands should provide a "guiding light" to the household—as the sun and moon do for the day and the night—and provide the same kind of sacrificial care and provision that God provides for his people. If Genesis 3.16 is requiring that of Adam and future husbands, even in the face of possible "desire" from Eve and future wives who (out of fear their husbands will not do as they should, or out of a selfish desire to control) seek to take matters into their own hands, then the third view is consistent with the spirit of the Song and the rest of biblical literature as well.

On this third view, the interpretation would then mean that Solomon has as deep a desire to care for Shulamith as God has to care for his people.

Does this imply that the husband in the biblical perspective should have legal "authority" if he and his wife desire to follow the guidelines of the Bible? I personally think that is very risky to make legally statutory, even if some aspects of authority are implicit in the word "to rule." Here's why. In an ideal world, a student of biblical literature might acknowledge that a monarchical government is the ideal form of government, since that is the ideal picture given of a messianic king ruling the earth. But until that benevolent king is here to rule, many of us would agree that a democracy of checks and balances that limits the potential for the abuse of power is the best option. Similarly, the potential abuse of power by a husband, legally invested with more rights than his wife, is a societal risk not to take.

In addition, the context of a love relationship requires this sort of thing to be voluntary. A woman may choose to accept the leadership of a loving and responsible husband who delights to give the same care and concern for his wife that Solomon desired for Shulamith. But legislation or recommendation that would seek to force that seems a terrible mistake. Love must be given and the leadership from love voluntarily accepted. The husband and wife are in a family, not a monarchy.

138. The only other use of the word for "to spend the night" in the Song occurs with the first mention of henna blossoms in 1.13–14, where after saying Solomon is a "pouch of myrrh" which "lies all night between her breasts," Shulamith says he is a "cluster of henna blossoms…in the vineyards of En Gedi." The contrast with courtship is clear. Then her fragrant thoughts of him, who is like henna blossoms, spent the night in her heart. Now she proposes they spend the night together among the henna blossoms he is like.

139. The word for "mandrakes" sounds very much like the word for "love" in the preceding lyric. This is one of many places where the songwriter poetically uses similar sounding words. Shulamith offers her "love" under the aphrodisiacal "love plant."

140. The word for "doors" derives from the verb "to open" and can mean "opening." It is likely that this is a wordplay on "doors" and "openings" and suggestive of the erotic lovemaking Shulamith proposes in the next lyric. The songwriter certainly could have used the word for "door" he used in 8.9, but in 8.9 the word is derived from the verb for "close" and so didn't have the possibility of play on "door" and "opening." The word is then a play on the same root word for "open" in the previous lyric describing the "opening" of the blossoms. A beautiful play on words emerges which suggests her sexual "openings" and "openness" are like the "opening" of the flower blossoms.

The preposition is sometimes translated "over," so that the phrase is "over our doors," which is grammatically possible (Exodus 12.23); but "at our doors" has grammatical precedent too (Job 31.9) and is more consistent with the image of provisions available to them in the romantic houses of nature.

141. This word translated "delicious" is the same word translated like this in 4.13 and 4.16, where it describes erotic fruits.

142. The verb translated "kept" means both "stored" and "kept secret" or "hidden." In a very clever play on words, both meanings of the verb are its meaning in this context! Shulamith has "stored" the old fruits and "hidden" the new fruits for their love in the countryside. I have rendered this word "kept" because it, too, can bear the double meaning of "stored" and "hidden."

143. This word for "scorn" occurs in two forms in 8.7 to strengthen the intensity of the disapproval, and suggests the translation "they would utterly scorn" of a

man who attempts to buy love.

144. Some translations have Shulamith's mother as the subject here: "She would instruct me." The form of the verb allows this translation, but no relative pronoun "who" is in the original language of the Song. Sometimes a writer may omit the relative pronoun and only imply it. That is certainly a possibility here. But since Shulamith addresses Solomon in the lyrics before and after this, a change to a statement about a third person would likely require the relative pronoun. Since it is lacking, Solomon is the likely subject.

On the other hand, perhaps it is intentionally ambiguous—a kind of play on the form of the verb which allows either the mother or Solomon to be subject. If that is the case here, then Shulamith has implied that the lovemaking she expresses to Solomon has the endorsement of her mother who taught her, and such instruction reinforces the propriety of it so that no one should scorn her.

145. The words for "I would kiss you" *(eshakakka)* and "I would let you drink" *(ashkeka)* are from different roots; but the verb forms in which they occur cause them to be identical in the consonants that appear and to differ only in the way they are pronounced. It is one more of the many examples of wordplay in the Song. Shulamith offers to "let him drink," with the playful suggestiveness of "let him kiss" the wine of her pomegranate.

I have noted other wordplays like this, for example, in 1.3: "name" *(shem)* and "perfumed oils" *(shemen),* "fragrance" *(rayak)* and "oil poured out" *(turak);* in 1.5: a possible play on "dwellings" *(mishkanot)* with "draw me after you" *(meshakeni)* and "kisses" *(minshacot);* in 1.5 and 6.10: "dark" *(shekorah)* and "dawn" or "morning star" *(shakar);* in 1.5–7: "why" *(shalamah)* and "Solomon" *(Shulomoh);* in 1.8–9: "darling companion" *(rayat)* and "shepherd" *(rayah);* in 1.10–11 and 8.9: see note at 1.10 for the numerous plays on the brother's reward and punishment; in 2.3: "forest" *(yaar)* and "honey" *(yaarah),* which is always "sweet"; in 4.6–8: "frankincense" *(lebonah)* and "Lebanon" *(lebanon),* "all of you" *(cullak)* and "bride" *(callah);* in 7.9, 13: "sleeping ones" *(yeshenim)* and "old" *(yeshanim)* fruits; in 7.12–13: "love" *(doday)* and "mandrakes" *(dudaim)* and "doors" *(pitakenu),* which means both "our doors" and "our openings" and "have opened" *(pitak)* in reference to flower blossoms; and 8.10–11: "fulfillment" *(shalom)* and "Solomon" *(Shulomoh).*

I have tried to capture the sounds of the underlying words without using conventional forms that represent every aspect of the word in the original. The unusual marks necessary to show Hebrew vocalization sometimes interfere with a grasp of the sounds unless someone is familiar with the conventions of academic transliteration.

146. The preposition "from" precedes "the wine" and also precedes "sweet wine," presenting the image of drinking from a container holding wine in an image consistent with the container of the "navel" in 7.2. It is misleading to translate "the

wine" or "the sweet wine" as direct objects, as in the common translation, "I will give you wine to drink and pomegranate juice." Customarily, the original language provides the preposition "from" when drinking from a container and omits it before the direct object (Genesis 24.43; 2 Samuel 23.15).

147. This probably refers to wine spiced with ground herbs for flavor. This word, *rekak,* is likely a play on the word for the moist interior of Shulamith's mouth in 4.3, *rakkak.* On the wedding night, the moisture of her mouth (*rakkak:* her "parted lips") is like the sliced opening of pomegranate; now the moisture of her pomegranate is like spiced wine *(rekak).* The wordplay would make little sense if on the wedding night the reference is to her cheeks or brow.

148. This word refers not to mere juice but to sweet wine elsewhere in the Old Testament (Isaiah 49.26; Joel 1.5).

149. Some translations have "pomegranates" instead of "pomegranate." Sometimes the motivation for this translation is partly because the translators think Shulamith is referring to her breasts, and so the plural is more appropriate. Other times the motivation for this may be because the singular "pomegranate" suggests something too erotic for the translators. Although there is some evidence for the plural from early *translations* of the Song, "pomegranate" is singular in the original *language* of the Song.

The imagery of the pomegranate here seems to include the most intimate of their kisses. Although the image of drinking from the chalice of wine can refer to Shulamith's kisses like wine, it also likely resumes the image of drinking from the chalice of her "navel like a round chalice." The subtle change in Shulamith's description of the pomegranate suggests the resumption of this image since it is slightly different from its mention elsewhere.

It is not the "sliced opening of a pomegranate" likened to the moisture of her mouth on the wedding night. Neither is it a "paradise of pomegranates" that described all her sensual beauty on that night. Nor is it pomegranate trees, whose spring blossoms signified renewal in their life together.

Rather, she refers to "my pomegranate" in the singular and to its juice as wine "spiced" and "sweet." The pomegranate is a common symbol of lovemaking in the ancient world because of its apparent fertility. Shulamith's reference to her personal source of this fertility apparently focuses on her intimate sexuality and arousal.

An implication from a literary device in the section supports this interpretation, since it suggests that Shulamith is describing that which some might scorn—not a likely response if she is referring to less intimate kissing. On the first spring day, Solomon initially invites her to enjoy the beauty and voices of spring. And that anticipates his climactic proposal to her—"Let me see *your* form; let me hear *your* voice." The wonders of spring implicitly illustrate the wonders of Shulamith he wished to see.

Now Shulamith communicates in a similar way. It is a spring day symmetrically balanced with the first one in the Song. And initially she describes her wish to kiss Solomon outside without scorn from others. That anticipates her climactic proposal to him—"come drink kisses of wine from the chalice of my body." The desire for kissing without scorn in the first lyrics implicitly illustrates the acceptance she wishes for the most intimate kissing too.

Her wish that she might kiss him outside seems intended to recall why acceptance of such intimacy should be granted. If he were like a natural brother, she would be free to kiss him even in public. Now that he is her "brother" by marriage—he called her "my sister, my bride" on the wedding night—she should be free to offer him kisses in private as intimate as they please.

The pomegranate imagery has evidently evolved in the Song like the lotus flower. The lotus first described Shulamith herself. Next, it is the place where Solomon grazes like a gazelle, its blossoms first surrounding her breasts, then later her hips and navel. In a similar transformation, the slice into a pomegranate first was likened to the taste of her kisses, then many pomegranates to her entire body. Finally, her single pomegranate is also in the lotus blossoms encircling the bread and wine of her abdomen.

150. Some translations make this a statement of fact rather than a wish: "His left hand is under my head," etc. When this refrain first appeared during courtship, the setting supported following the precedent of wish—when speaking of Solomon in the third person, as in the wish for Solomon to kiss her. When it now appears in an outdoor setting, where Shulamith wishes privacy to make love, the public setting and third person perspective again favors the translation as a wish (see note at 2.6).

151. This might be translated "Promise me you will not arouse...love until it pleases to awaken." But that seems unlikely. This refrain appears in a slightly different form than in 2.7 and 3.5 where it is translated that way. The comments on the subject of the verb "pleases" in the notes at 2.7 are not affected. But I believe the new form of the refrain at 8.4 makes the translation much more likely to be "Promise me you will surely arouse," etc.

The refrain at 8.4 omits the phrase "by the gazelles and by the does of the field" and replaces the word rendered "not" *(im)* that precedes "arouse" and "awaken" in the earlier refrains with a different word *(mah)*. Omission of the phrase does not require the replacement of the word.

Most translations note that this new word preceding "arouse" and "awaken"*(mah*—"what, why, that") *can* on rare occasions indicate negation. Then they translate 8.4 like before: "Do *not* arouse...until it pleases." But in light of the subtle but very instructive differences in the reoccurrences of other refrains ("unity": 2.16; 6.3; 7.10; "invitation to breasts": 2.17; 4.6; 8.14), the translator must consider whether the variation in this refrain yields a change of meaning as well.

The grammars and lexicons that suggest this new word may imply negation can cite examples only where the negation arises out of a rhetorical question like, "How can I do this wrong?" meaning "I can't do this wrong." But that rarely occurs, and it would be awkward that the imperative "promise me" (or "swear to me") would introduce it. Furthermore, if Shulamith had wished to request a promise "not to arouse," she could simply have used the same word for "not" she used in the earlier refrains.

Elsewhere in the Song the word *mah* indicates only adverbial intensity: "how very much" (4.10; 7.1, 6); an introductory question (5.9); or the conjunctive use as "that" (5.8). In 6.13 it either introduces the question or indicates adverbial intensity. Quite significantly, the only other place where it follows the verb "promise me" (in 5.8), it bears the sense of "that."

That is also the only other occurrence of "promise me" outside of these refrains. The word "if" *(im)* that precedes "arouse" and "awaken" in the first two occurrences of the refrain and the word "that" or "what" or "how" *(mah)* that precedes the verbs in the third refrain each follow the request of "promise me" in 5.8. And neither word indicates negation there! "Promise me if *(im)* you find my beloved, that [or "what"—mah] you will tell him that I am faint from love." The songwriter appears to intentionally prepare the reader for the different sense of the refrain in 8.4, when *mah* occurs twice.

So the primary options for its meaning here are either adverbial intensity or some kind of conjunctive use, since it is unlikely introducing the rare rhetorical question. Either of these lead to similar translations. The adverbial intensity would render the lyric "Promise me you will surely arouse, you will surely awaken love." This use of adverbial intensity with verbs is illustrated, for example, in Psalm 119.97, when the psalmist says, "How I love your teaching!" The conjunctive use would render it simply "Promise me that you will arouse, you will awaken love." In both cases the admonition is to seize the opportunity when it comes.

If the first part of the refrain is "Promise me you will surely arouse and awaken love" or "promise that you will arouse," then the principle guiding the translation of the last phrase would render it *"when it pleases"* (see note at 2.17), since "awaken" appears to be a verb of completed action. Thus one would translate the entire refrain "I want you to promise me, O young women of Jerusalem, that you will surely arouse, you will surely awaken love when love pleases to awaken."

Perhaps this seems like a lot of translation work simply to detect a change of emphasis. After all, the customary translation "Do not arouse, do not awaken love until it pleases" clearly implies that one *should* arouse love when it *does* please. But it's difficult to resist the grammatical evidence that leads to the positive statement of the refrain in 8.4.

Perhaps in light of the obvious benefit of acting when the time is right and Shulamith's unfortunate experience on the night recounted after the wedding night, she desires to state the refrain in its positive form here. In light of the instructive transformations of other refrains in the Song, the resounding encouragement to seize the opportunity for real love when the opportunity arises is a climactic conclusion to this refrain.

In its prior variation, incidentally, when Shulamith says, "Promise me...you will not arouse or awaken love," she requests the listener literally to promise "by the gazelles or the hinds of the field, if I arouse, if I awaken love, before love pleases to awaken." From these words it is implied from the "if" that if such a thing is done, then may adverse consequences come to the person who does it.

The old oath formula was "If I do such and such, may 'punishment come upon me.'" Then in the history of the language, the consequence of punishment was dropped. "If I do such and such" remained and "I will *not* do such and such" was understood.

152. In the poetic structure of the Song presented in Appendix B, one may see that the mention of the apple tree in 8.5 corresponds to its occurrence in 2.3. Evidently, Solomon and Shulamith knew they were in love when they each revealed their delight in the other.

153. The word for "to labor" in birth may also mean "conceived" or simply "to be pregnant." The noun derived from the word means "labor pains," which favors the meaning of the verb as "to labor" in birth. Perhaps the songwriter intends both meanings, having a play on words with a single word.

154. Although the "mother" is directly mentioned, this reference is similar to the allusions to famous people and events that have appeared already in the Song: Joseph, Tamar, Rahab, Jacob, and Esau have already appeared in the background of certain events. Now Bathsheba, the famous mother of Solomon, appears.

It is no wonder she appears in association with the pain of birth. She had been taken by David the king when her husband was away at war. After she became pregnant, and after David failed to persuade her husband to have sex with her when he was on leave from battle, David arranged the death of her husband. After she mourned, David married her; but the child of their affair died in his first year, and she mourned again. But then she conceived and gave birth to Solomon. So twice she mourned, and then twice she was in labor: with the first child, who died, and then with Solomon, who became king.

On one level, the repetition of "there your mother was in labor with you; there she was in labor" is simply a poetic device for emphasis. But perhaps on the level of allusion, the twofold mention of the pain of labor refers to the pain associated with everything that led to Solomon's birth.

155. The pattern of 8.6 seems to be a short chiastic one: *abb 'a '*, linking "heart" and "fervent love" and then linking "arm" and "strong as death." The love of his heart is as relentless as the grave and as strong and irreversible as death.

156. The word translated "fervent love" is in many translations, particularly older ones, rendered "jealousy." In earlier times "jealousy" could be used in either a positive or negative sense. But since today the negative sense is used almost exclusively, the translation "fervent love" gives a more accurate meaning.

157. The word in the original is Sheol, the place of the dead.

158. This is likely a picture of a row of stones built on top of fortress walls to add to the strength and effectiveness of the wall. A silver stone barrier on top of a fortress wall would not only strengthen but also make more beautiful the fortress. The individual stones on a fortress wall give way to the jewels of a necklace on her neck, which is like fortress tower.

159. The event described here is one more allusion to another famous person in their literature: Ruth, from the land of Moab, who married a man from Israel. Ruth had come to trust in the God of Israel. So when her husband died, she returned to Israel with her mother-in-law, Naomi, instead of remaining in her native land of Moab. In one of the more dramatic and famous statements in their literature, Ruth told Naomi, "Where you go I will go, and where you stay I will stay. Your people will be my people and your God my God. Where you die I will die, and there I will be buried. May the Lord deal with me, be it ever so severely, if anything but death separates you and me" (Ruth 1.16–17 NIV).

When Ruth and Naomi arrived in the land of Israel, they were so poor that Ruth went to pick up leftover grain from the harvest in order to have a modest amount of food to eat. She hoped to find someone who would allow this someone "in whose eyes she found favor." Boaz saw her in his fields and fell in love with her, taking care to provide for her. Twice more Ruth used the phrase "to find favor in one's eyes": in her question to Boaz asking why she had found favor and in her request that she might continue to find favor. This phrase occurs thirty-four times in the Old Testament, three of which are in Ruth.

Just as Shulamith modifies the expression "to swear by God" to "to swear by the gazelles or does of the field," so she modifies the expression "to find grace in someone's eyes" to "to find *shalom* [or fulfillment] in Solomon's eyes." But the use of that phrase still strengthens the allusion to the story of Ruth. Like Ruth, Shulamith was humbly working in the fields when the owner of the fields saw her and fell in love with her, at which time she "found *shalom* in his eyes." Like Boaz, Solomon took steps to properly pursue a marriage. Like Ruth, Shulamith accepted the proposal of the owner, who lifted her to a position of safety and honor.

Perhaps the heritage of Boaz made him compassionate toward women of humble beginnings. His mother was also a foreigner, named Rahab, sometimes referred to as "the harlot"—the woman of questionable character who had nevertheless helped the invading Israelites because she had accepted the God they worshiped. Perhaps Solomon's heritage made him compassionate too. His father had committed adultery with his mother, murdered her husband, and then added her to his harem. Boaz and Solomon knew the pain of difficult beginnings and were compassionate to those in a similar position.

160. The word translated "fulfillment" is *shalom* in the original language. *Shalom* means "peace," "wholeness," or "completion." It suggests the kind of contentment and peace that comes from experiencing the best of the Creator's designs for life. It appears before the name of Solomon in the following lyric and seems clearly a play on his name, as it literally sounds in the original language: Shulamith finds *shalom* in *Shulomoh.*

161. The word for "caretaker" is the same word used when Shulamith recounts her brothers making her "caretaker" of the vineyard (1.6).

162. The phrase "my own vineyard, which belongs to me" is identical to its other occurrence in 1.6.

163. This is the same word for "close friend" that is used only here and at 1.7.

164. The first refrain inviting Solomon to enjoy her breasts when the day comes occurs in 2.17, and Shulamith refers to her breasts as "divided mountains." This occurs at the conclusion of the first two sections. Then, in the central part of the fourth section, Solomon declares his intention to enjoy her breasts throughout the night, and he embellishes her reference to her breasts. They are a "mountain of myrrh" and a "hill of frankincense." The third occurrence of this refrain is the abbreviated form here, and Shulamith has transformed her perception of her breasts to be in accordance with Solomon's perception. They are not simply "divided mountains" but "mountains of spices." Shulamith's request perhaps prompted the advice Solomon gives to all husbands in Proverbs 5.18–19: "Take great joy in the wife of your youth! Let her be your deer of love, your graceful doe. And drink your fill from her breasts of wine so you are always drunk with her love!"

The Elegant Design
of the Song

The Song of Songs displays artistic balance and symmetry in the arrangement of its lyrics. The most common element of the design is a pattern that introduces a series of topics and then reintroduces those topics in reverse order. The literary term for this pattern is *chiasm.*

Sometimes this pattern appears in short sentences, like Solomon's request: "Let me see your form; let me hear your voice; for your voice is pleasing, and your form is lovely" (2.14). The lyric introduces first "form," then "voice," and then in reverse order, "voice, form." It is an *abb ´a ´* sequence.

This pattern can also appear in a series of sentences that make up a paragraph, like Shulamith's account of rising in the night to find Solomon (3.1–4). She is *(a)* separated from him (3.1); *(b)* leaves home to find him (3.2); *(c)* is found by guards (3.3a); *(d)* asks for help (3.3b); *(c ´)* finds Solomon (3.4a); *(b ´)* returns home with him (3.4b); and *(a ´)* is reunited with him (3.4b). This is an *abcdc ´b ´a ´* sequence. It is also an example of the pattern with a central point of emphasis: The *d* is not repeated.

When you compare the corresponding sentences, you see the balance. She begins separated and ends united with him *(aa ´)*. She leaves the house alone but returns with him *(bb ´)*. The guards find her, but she finds Solomon *(cc ´)*. And at the center of the account is an emotional peak: "Have you seen him whom my soul loves?" *(d)*.

The pattern can also govern several units or paragraphs. For example, the lengthy section after the wedding night describing their separation, reconciliation, and love-making displays a balance in the arrangement of its lyrics. She is *(a)* awakened from sleep, alone and reluctant (5.2–8); *(b)* gives tenfold praise (5.9–16); *(c)* aware of his presence in the garden (6.1–3); *(d)* receives his praise in the garden (6.4–9); *(c ´)* recounts her journey to the garden (6.11–12); *(b ´)* receives tenfold praise (7.1–5); *(a ´)* delightfully makes love and, together with him, drifts off to sleep (7.6–9).

When you compare the corresponding sections, you again see the balance. She begins awakened from sleep, alone and reluctant, but concludes making love, then together with Solomon falling asleep *(aa ')*. Her tenfold praise of appreciation for him is met with his tenfold praise of appreciation for her *(bb ')*. She knows his location in the garden and goes to see him there *(cc ')*. At the center of the section is his unchanging love for her *(d)*.

⚜

Frequently, the first series of topics in the pattern is about the same length as the corresponding series introduced in reverse order. But sometimes the lengths are not the same. The subjects are treated more expansively in either the first introduction of them or in the second treatment of them in reverse order. This balance of topics, but not of length, is common in ancient literature.

For example, the night of separation and reunion immediately prior to the wedding is only five verses (3.1–5). And the night of separation and reunion after the wedding is nearly two chapters (5.2 to 7.9). But in the design of the Song, they are balanced with each other, inviting the reader to compare and contrast them.

The songwriter also uses important refrains to create boundaries and order in certain sections. The refrains are of *longing:* "May his left hand be under my head and his right hand embrace me"; and the variations of *patience:* "I want you to promise me...by the gazelles and by the does of the field, not to arouse, not to awaken love until love pleases"; the variations of *unity:* "My beloved is mine, and I am his"; and the variations of the *invitation* to enjoy her breasts: "When the day breathes...be like...a gazelle or a young stag on the divided mountains."

They frame each of the two celebrations of spring love: one preceding the first night of separation and reunion (2.6–16) and the other following the second night of separation and reunion (7.10 to 8.4). In the second celebration, the fourth refrain is not explicitly repeated but is expressed in Solomon's enjoyment of her breasts.

In these spring love celebrations, the songwriter balances *(a)* Shulamith's refrains of longing and patience (2.6–7); *(b)* her beloved's invitation to come *from* her house to enjoy spring (2.8–15); *(c)* the refrains of unity and invitation to enjoy her breasts (2.16–17); and then *(c ')* the enjoyment of her breasts and refrain of unity (7.7–10); *(b ')* her invitation for him to come with her to enjoy spring concluding with the return *to* her house (7.11 to 8.2); and *(a ')* the refrains of longing and patience (transformed to promptness) (8.3–4).

You see the balance when you compare the corresponding sections. During courtship Shulamith longs to make love and admonishes patience to the daughters of Jerusalem, and after marriage still longs to make love and advises promptness to all *(aa ')*. During courtship Solomon invites *her* to come *from her house* to enjoy the spring and disclose herself to him, but after marriage she invites *him* to enjoy the spring, where she will fully disclose herself to him and take him *back into her home (bb').* During courtship, she expresses her unity with him and invitation to enjoy her breasts on their wedding night; then after marriage he enjoys her breasts, and she expresses an even deeper sense of unity with him *(cc').*

The correspondence between the two spring days bordered by the refrains shows that the symmetry is found primarily *between* the two corresponding sections rather than *within* the particular sections themselves.

More specifically, the refrains of longing and patience begin the first spring day section and conclude the second spring day section (2.6–7; 8.3–4). The refrains of unity and invitation reverse this and conclude the first spring day section and begin the second (2.16–17; 7.7–8, 10, 8.14).

In addition, one may observe that the refrain of invitation to enjoy her breasts occurs at the conclusion of the first two major sections (2.17) and at the conclusion of the last two major sections (8.14). Its only other occurrence is centered in the central section of the wedding day and night (4.6). So the symmetry of its usage is clear. It concludes the courtship, is answered in the wedding night section, and concludes the Song.

Similarly, one may observe that the refrain of patience occurs at the conclusion of the first two sections and at the beginning of the last two sections. And its only other occurrence is at the beginning of the wedding day and night. So the symmetry of its usage is clear too. It concludes the courtship, precedes the wedding day, and begins the completion of the Song.

Finally, the refrain of unity appears in its only other occurrence in the lengthy second night of separation and reunion (5.2 to 7.9). The refrain appears just after the second actual night of anxiety (6.2). So the songwriter has artistically placed this refrain just before the first night of anxiety (3.1–4) and just after the second night of anxiety (6.2). Since the other occurrence at 7.10 functions to conclude one section and begin the new one, the songwriter deftly places the refrain of unity before the night of 3.1–4 and after each of the two nights in 5.2 to 7.9. The refrain of unity thus precedes a long night of fear (2.16), follows a second night of fear (6.2), and follows the second lengthy description of a night of love (7.10).

The refrains can apparently function as connectors between major sections, both concluding a preceding section and introducing a new one. So in a grand design of the Song, they could be listed in both the section preceding them and the section following them unless the refrain is functioning as a centerpiece, as in 4.6.

Finally, another important pattern introduces a series of topics and then, unlike chiasm, reintroduces them in the same order. This can occur in short sentences, like "Dark am I, but lovely…like tents darkened, but like the curtains of Solomon" (1.5). And it can be part of larger units, within which chiastic structure functions. For example, in the tenfold praise sections of 5.10–16 and 7.1–5, the units have similar beginnings and endings.

The principles of balance and symmetry appear to govern the literary design of the entire Song. The broad outline of the symmetry I propose displays seven balanced sections:

BRIEFEST OUTLINE OF SYMMETRY OF ENTIRE SONG (1.2 TO 8.14)

A: Beginning of story (1.2–2.7)

   B: Solomon's invitation for Shulamith to enjoy a spring *day*, framed by refrains (2.5–17)

      C: Shulamith's search in the *night* and reunion with Solomon (3.1–5)

         D: Wedding *day* and *night* (3.6 to 5.1)

      C′: Shulamith's reluctance in the *night* but reunion with Solomon (5.2 to 7.9)

   B′: Shulamith's invitation for Solomon to enjoy a spring *day*, framed by refrains (7.10 to 8.4)

A′: Completion of story (8.5–14)

I will show how each of these seven major sections displays symmetry either within itself, in relationship to its counterpart, or both.

The central section is easiest to identify, since it is framed on each side by the *nights* of separation; and then, on each of their sides, by the spring *day* invitations. The content itself also provides borders: the procession and first night, with repeated references to bride and groom, and the emphasis on consummation, identify this section as wedding day and night.

This central section D of wedding day and night is itself arranged symmetrically:

SECTION D: WEDDING DAY AND NIGHT (3.6 TO 5.1)

a: songwriter's own words: scene begins in wilderness emergence (3.6–11)

   b: celebration of the wedding's beginning (3.6–11)

      c: wedding night (4.1 to 5.1); refrain answering invitation to enjoy breasts

   b′: celebration of the wedding's consummation (5.1b)

a′: songwriter's own words: scene concludes in garden paradise banquet (5.1b)

This design draws attention to the songwriter's own words, which appear only here in the entire song. They occur at the beginning and end of the section. Both times the songwriter encourages celebration of love: first urging the joy of the wedding day and then the joy of the wedding night. The centerpiece of the section is the happiness of the couple in the consummation of their marriage.

The sections on each side of the wedding day and night are those that begin in a night of separation and end in reunion. The short account of the experience preceding the wedding night, section C, has been observed:

SECTION C: NIGHT OF SEPARATION PRECEDING WEDDING (3.1–4)

a: Shulamith is awakened, alone and longing for Solomon (3.1)
  b: leaves home to find him (3.2)
    c: is found by guards (3.3)
      d: asks for help (3.3b)
    c′: finds Solomon (3.4)
  b′: returns home with him (3.4b)
a′: is reunited with him through the night (3.4b); transitional refrain of patience (3.5)

The night symmetrically balancing this immediately follows the wedding night. Section C has a broad outline as follows:

SECTION C′: SHORT OUTLINE OF NIGHT OF SEPARATION FOLLOWING WEDDING NIGHT (5.2 TO 7.9)

a: Shulamith is awakened, alone and reluctant (5.2–8)
  b: awakened to give tenfold praise (5.9–16)
    c: aware of Solomon's presence in the garden (6.1–3)
      d: receives his praise in the garden (6.4–9)
    c′: recounts her journey to the garden (6.11–12)
  b′: receives tenfold praise (7.1–5)
a′: delightfully make love, together drift off to sleep (7.6–9)

This short outline invites a comparison with the night of separation preceding the wedding day: both sections begin in sleep and end in reunion, but in between are striking contrasts.

This outline of the second night also reveals a number of important aspects of the section itself. It shows a movement from problem to solution: from being awakened, alone and reluctant, to making love and drifting asleep. It also shows the balance of the tenfold praise: first Shulamith gives praise but then in the later night receives it. Perhaps most importantly, the design of this section places emphasis on the reconciliation scene in the garden, the centerpiece of the section, where Solomon praises Shulamith and they are reunited.

If we expand this short outline, then we can see the continuation of symmetry and balance in greater detail.

235

SECTION C′: EXPANDED OUTLINE OF NIGHT OF SEPARATION FOLLOWING THE WEDDING NIGHT (5.2 TO 7.9)

a: Shulamith is awakened, alone and reluctant (5.2–8)
- she is awakened from sleep
- he desires to see her, but she is reluctant
- she longs to find him
- she is faint from love

b: awakened to give tenfold praise (5.9–16)
- begins section with question by daughters of Jerusalem
- begins praise with twofold "how" (in original language)
- ten parts praised include head, hair, eyes, abdomen, legs
- proceeds from head to toe; concludes with mouth
- images of ivory, towers, Lebanon, lotus flowers, sources of water
- ends praise with summary statement beginning with "this"

c: aware of Solomon's presence in the garden (6.1–3)
- addresses the daughters of Jerusalem
- her beloved went down to his garden

d: receives his praise in the garden: (6.4–10)
- repeats less erotic praise of wedding night
- concludes praise of her body with praise of mouth
- begins and ends praise with imagery of Israel

c′: recounts her journey to the garden (6.11–12)
- addresses the daughters of Jerusalem
- she went down to the garden

b′: receives tenfold praise (7.1–5)
- begins section with question by daughters of Jerusalem
- begins praise with twofold "how" in original language
- ten parts praised include head, hair, eyes, abdomen, legs
- proceeds from toe to head; concludes with mouth (7.9)
- images of ivory, tower, Lebanon, lotus flowers, sources of water
- ends praise with summary statement beginning with "this" (7.7)

a′ delightfully make love, together drift off to sleep (7.6–9)
- love flows through her body
- she is intimate with him
- he passionately desires her, and she passionately responds
- they drift off to sleep

The movement from reluctance and separation to desire and reunion is clear in the contrast of a and a′. The importance of the questions of the daughters of Jerusalem for marking boundaries of subsections is clear in the details of b and b′. Other instructive comparisons arise from the balanced subsections.

The sections featuring the invitations to enjoy spring, B and B´, precede the first night of separation and follow the second night of lovemaking, respectively, each framed by the special refrains of longing and patience on one side and unity and invitation to enjoy her breasts on the other side.

SECTIONS B AND B´: SHORT OUTLINE OF TWO INVITATIONS TO ENJOY SPRING (2.6–17; 7.10 TO 8.4)

a: *refrains* of longing and patience (2.6–7)
   b: his invitation to come enjoy spring, leaving *from* her house (2.8–15)
      c: *refrain* of unity (2.16)
         d: *refrain* of invitation to her *breasts* (2.17)
         d´: *refrain* of invitation to her *breasts* alluded (7.7 8)
      c´: *refrain* of unity (7.10)
   b´: her invitation to come enjoy spring, returning *to* her house (7.11 to 8.2)
a´: *refrains* of longing and patience (8.3–4)

SECTIONS B AND B´: EXPANDED OUTLINE OF INVITATIONS TO ENJOY SPRING (2.6–17; 7.10 TO 8.4)

a: Shulamith's refrains (2.6–7)
- refrain of longing to make love (2.6)
- refrain urging patience (2.7)

b: Shulamith's description of Solomon's invitation (2.8 15)
- he asks her to enjoy spring, leading her *from* her house
- Solomon is "my beloved"
- enjoyment of nature and dove pictures enjoyment of her
- delight in nature and dove foreshadows delight in her

  c: Shulamith's response to Solomon (2.16–17)
- refrain of unity
- refrain of invitation to enjoy her breasts, like a stag on mountains

  c´: Shulamith's response to Solomon (7.10)
- refrain of invitation to enjoy her breasts alluded: "climbing the palm tree" (7.7–8)
- refrain of unity

b´: Shulamith's description of her invitation (7.11 to 8.2)
- asks him to enjoy spring, then brings him *to* her house
- Solomon is "my beloved"
- enjoyment of nature pictures enjoyment of her
- delightful freedom for public kissing foreshadows delightful freedom in private kissing

a´: Shulamith's refrains (8.3–4)
- refrain of longing to make love (8.3)
- refrain urging patience (8.4)

The last two sections, A and A´, are the bookends of the Song. They're similar in design to the two invitations to enjoy spring, B and B´, because the symmetry is primarily between A and A´ rather than within the sections themselves.

SECTIONS A AND A´: A SHORT OUTLINE OF BEGINNING AND COMPLETION OF STORY (1.2 TO 2.7; 8.3–14)

a: Shulamith, Solomon, and the daughters of Jerusalem (1.2–4)

  b: her brothers, their vineyards, and her appearance (1.5–6)

    c: Shulamith's character and beauty (1.7–11)

      d: love's expression (1.12 to 2.5)

        e: refrains of longing and patience conclude section A and begin section B (2.6–7)

        e´: refrains of longing and patience conclude section B´ and begin section A´ (8.3–4)

      d´: love's devotion (8.5–7)

    c´: Shulamith's character and beauty (8.8–9)

  b´: her brothers, their vineyards, and her appearance (8.10–12)

a´: Shulamith, Solomon, and Shulamith's companions (8.13–14)

It is clear that the songwriter has designed these sections to bring artistic symmetry and closure to the Song. First Shulamith, Solomon, and the daughters of Jerusalem are introduced and then they are the last characters mentioned in the Song. The second topics introduced are Shulamith's brothers, their vineyards, and Shulamith's appearance; and these topics are the second to last topics addressed in the Song. Similarly, Shulamith's character and beauty is the third topic and the third to last topic of the Song. Love's delightful expression is then artistically balanced with love's loyal devotion. Lastly, the themes of longing and patience, two qualities of romance thematic to the Song, balance each other in the design.

The comparison and contrast of these correspondences yield helpful insights, particularly when considering the more detailed outline of these sections in the next chart. For example, the linking of the lyrics about her brothers explains how Shulamith met Solomon (1.6 and 8.10–12). Her request to be a seal on Solomon's heart (8.6) is balanced with her declaration that he is a pouch of myrrh on her heart, "between her breasts" (1.12–14). Solomon's gifts of silver during their courtship would be perceived by her to be the rewards for virtuous behavior promised by her brothers but fulfilled by her beloved (1.9–11 and 8.9). Their love awakened under the apple tree suggests falling in love occurred when each gave praise of uniqueness to the other (2.3 and 8.5). Literal riches in a house without love do not compare to the romantic riches in the houses of nature or the house of wine (1.15; 2.4; 8.7). Notice these and other comparisons in the following chart:

SECTION A AND A′: EXPANDED OUTLINE OF BEGINNING AND COMPLETION OF STORY (1.2 TO 2.7; 8.3–14)

a: Shulamith, Solomon, and the daughters of Jerusalem (1.2–4)
- Shulamith longs for Solomon to make love to her (1.2–4)
- her companions, the daughters of Jerusalem, appear (1.4b)

b: her brothers, their vineyards, and her appearance (1.5–6)
- self-appraisal: I am sunburned but lovely (1.5)
- her companions gaze at her because she has worked outside (1.6a)
- her brothers were angry with her (1.6b)
- they made her caretaker of the vineyards (1.6c)
- she is her own vineyard (1.6d)

c: Shulamith's character and beauty (1.7–11)
- unrestricted outside, not promiscuous, seeking Solomon (1.7–8)
  - receives necklaces with silver (1.9–11)
    - he is a locket of perfume between her breasts (1.12–14); transition

d: love's expression (1.12 to 2.5)
- he is a locket of perfume between her breasts (over her heart) (1.12–14)
  - they enjoy the "houses" of nature and the "house of wine" (1.15 to 2.2,4)
    - she delights in him, personified as an apple tree (2.3)
      - she is faint from love (2.5)

e: refrains conclude section A and begin section B (2.6–7)
- refrain of longing to make love (2.6)
- refrain urging patience (2.7)

e′: refrains conclude section B′ and begin section A′ (8.3–4)
- refrain of longing to make love (8.3)
- refrain urging patience (variation) (8.4)

d′: love's devotion (8.5–7)
- she is leaning on her beloved (8.5)
- she awakened his love under the apple tree (8.5)
- all the riches of one's house cannot buy love (8.7)
- she asks to be a precious seal over his heart (8.6)

c′: Shulamith's character and beauty (8.8–9)
- she is young and "has no breasts" (8.8)
- if virtuous, "a wall," she would be rewarded with silver (8.9a)
- if promiscuous, "a door," she would be restricted (8.9b)

b′: her brothers, their vineyards, and her appearance (8.10–12)
- self-appraisal: I was virtuous and beautiful (a "wall," breasts like "towers") (8.10a)
- then Solomon looks at her while she is outside and falls in love (8.10b) *(shalom)*
- she forgives and blesses her brothers (8.12b)
- the vineyards were leased from Solomon (8.11)
- Shulamith gives the vineyard of herself to Solomon (8.12a)

a′: Shulamith, Solomon, and Shulamith's companions (8.13–14)
- Shulamith's companions are with her (8.13)
- Shulamith's longings fulfilled and continued in refrain to enjoy her breasts (8.14)

Outline of the Symmetry of
the Entire Song

Section A: Beginning of Story (1.2 to 2.7)

  a: Shulamith, Solomon and the daughters of Jerusalem (1.2–4)

    b: her brothers, their vineyards, and her appearance (1.5–6)

      c: Shulamith's character and beauty (1.7–11)

        d: love's expression (1.12 to 2.5)

          e: refrains conclude section A and begin section B (2.6–7)

Section B: Invitation to Enjoy Spring Day (2.6–17)

  a: refrains of longing and patience (2.6–7)

    b: his invitation to come enjoy spring, leaving *from* her house (2.8–15)

      c: refrains of unity and invitation to her breasts (2.16–17); transition

Section C: Night of Separation Preceding Wedding (3.1–4)

  a: Shulamith is awakened, alone and longing for Solomon (3.1)

    b: leaves home to find him (3.2)

      c: is found by guards (3.3)

        d: asks for help (3.3b)

      c': finds Solomon (3.4)

    b': returns home with him (3.4b)

  a': is reunited with him through the night (3.4b); transition—*refrain* of patience

Section D: Wedding Day and Night (3.6 to 5.1)

  a: songwriter's own words (3.6–11)

    b: celebration of the wedding's beginning (3.6–11)

      c: wedding night (4.1 to 5.1); refrain answering invitation to enjoy breasts (4.6)

    b': celebration of the wedding's consummation (5.1b)

  a': songwriter's own words (5.1b)

Section C': Night of Separation Following Wedding Night (5.2 to 7.9)

  a: Shulamith is awakened, alone and reluctant (5.2–8)

    b: gives tenfold praise (5.9–16)

      c: aware of Solomon's presence in the garden (6.1–3)

        d: receives his praise in the garden (6.4–9)

      c': recounts her journey to the garden (6.11–12)

    b': receives tenfold praise (7.1–5)

  a': they delightfully make love, together drift off to sleep (7.6–9)

Section B': Invitation to Enjoy Spring Day (7.10 to 8.4)

      c': enjoyment of breasts and refrain of unity (7.7–8, 10); transition

    b': her invitation to come enjoy spring, returning return *to* her house (7.11 to 8.2)

  a': refrains of longing and patience (8.3–4)

Section A': Completion of Story (8.3–14)

          e': refrains conclude section B' and begin section A' (8.3–4)

        d': love's devotion (8.5–7)

      c': Shulamith's character and beauty (8.8–9)

    b' her brothers, their vineyards, and her appearance (8.10–12)

  a' Shulamith, Solomon, and Shulamith's companions (8.13–14); refrain to enjoy breasts

In the chart on the previous page is the symmetry of the entire Song. More details of individual sections are in the previous charts, but the overarching symmetry is particularly clear in this last one.

The patterns of symmetry show, of course, that the songwriter composed a single, unified Song. This may seem too obvious to mention, but some interpreters have suggested that the Song of Songs is not a single song but an anthology of songs, like the book of Proverbs is a collection of various proverbs. But the Song's elegant design shows it to be a single artistic masterpiece.

The design tells us more than that, however. The patterns of symmetry are helpful in identifying central themes of sections, in revealing emphasis, in clarifying meaning, and in comparing and contrasting parallel sections. For example, the blessing of the Great Songwriter at the conclusion of the marriage night at 5.1, "Eat, O darling companions. Drink and be drunk, O beloved ones," is at the peak of the central section and quantitatively also at the very center of the Song's lyrics. The design of the Song underscores the theme of the goodness and beauty of romantic love expressed in 5.1.

The patterns of design are no substitute for paying attention to each individual lyric, since the design arises from their meaning. And a reader must pay careful attention to subtle variations in the meaning of the refrains. Also, the literary design of the Song should not prevent the reader from tracing words or themes through all sections, not just those that correspond in the symmetry of the Song. The parallels in the design simply draw attention to special correspondences and serve to place certain lyrics and sections in a broader context

Perhaps most of all, the elegant symmetry of the Song shows us that the songwriter wished to have a form as elegant as the love he describes within it. The form of the Song is perfectly wed to its content.

Notes to Appendix C

1. David Dorsey discusses this design in the Song and other Old Testament literature, both summarizing the observations of others and offering the design he perceives, in his very helpful and scholarly work *The Literary Structure of the Old Testament*.

2. Dorsey has shown a compelling display of a grand design, and although some interpreters may differ from him in details, his fundamental points are convincing. I agree with most of his analysis, including his division into seven major sections. However, I propose a different symmetry to the opening and closing sections that are the "bookends" of the Song: 1.2 to 2.7 and 8.5–14. I also think it's important to draw more attention to the refrains framing the sections on the enjoyment of spring. And I think we need to give structural significance to the particular refrain that concludes the first two and last two sections and appears in the center of the middle section. I should add that I don't see some of the symmetry he does in the lyrics of the wedding night. It may sound like we differ broadly, but in the context of the overall design, these are relatively minor differences.